Wild Beyond Belief!

Wild Beyond Belief!

Interviews with Exploitation Filmmakers of the 1960s and 1970s

BRIAN ALBRIGHT

McFarland & Company, Inc., Publishers
Jefferson, North Carolina, and London

LIBRARY OF CONGRESS CATALOGUING-IN-PUBLICATION DATA

Albright, Brian, 1973–
Wild beyond belief! : interviews with exploitation filmmakers
of the 1960s and 1970s / Brian Albright.
p.   cm.
Includes index.

ISBN 978-0-7864-3689-7
softcover : 50# alkaline paper ∞

1. Exploitation films—United States—History and criticism.
2. Motion picture producers and directors—United States—Interviews.
I. Title.
PN1995.9.S284A43   2008
791.4302'3'0922—dc22   2008010784

British Library cataloguing data are available

©2008 Brian Albright. All rights reserved

*No part of this book may be reproduced or transmitted in any form
or by any means, electronic or mechanical, including photocopying
or recording, or by any information storage and retrieval system,
without permission in writing from the publisher.*

Front cover: (top) Director Al Adamson (inset) and Russ Tamblyn
in *Satan's Sadists*, 1969 (Independent-International Pictures); (bottom)
Ellen Burstyn from *Pit Stop*, 1969 (photograph courtesy of Jack Hill)
Back cover: Roger Engel (a.k.a. Zandor Vorkov) and
John Bloom in *Dracula vs. Frankenstein*, 1971

Manufactured in the United States of America

*McFarland & Company, Inc., Publishers
Box 611, Jefferson, North Carolina 28640
www.mcfarlandpub.com*

For Adele

ACKNOWLEDGMENTS

Many of these interviews would not have seen the light of day had it not been for my editors: Michael Stein and Jim Wilson at *Filmfax*, Anthony Timpone and Mike Gingold at *Fangoria*, Steven Puchalski at *Shock Cinema*, Joe Kane at *VideoScope*, and J.R. Bookwalter, who published my first articles in *Alternative Cinema*.

The following people gave me leads, information, and guidance, or helped put me in touch with my interviewees: Sam Sherman, John Russo, Joy Wilkerson, Anthony Cardoza, William Grefe, Ted V. Mikels, Bill Rebane, Igo Kantor, Alvin Bubis, Abe Polsky, Tony Crechales, Bruce Kemp (and Rocky), Terry Maher, Don Jones, Michael Levesque, Donna Ramsey, Byrd Holland, Nancy Layton at Crone House Publishing, Robert Dix, Bud Cardos, Gary Kent, Victoria Carroll, Fred Olen Ray, Ewing "Lucky" Brown, Jenifer Bishop and Tom Weaver.

Thanks to Tom Weaver (again), Bill Warren, David J. Skal, Kim Newman, Tim Lucas, David Konow, Michael Weldon, Chris Poggiali, and John Wooley for providing general inspiration and voluminous reference material.

Thanks to Natalie and Eddie at the late, lamented B-Ware Video in Cleveland, and the folks at Video Central in Columbus and Star Time Video in Circleville, Ohio, for enriching my video rental experience. Video Theatre in Parma — you are gone, but not forgotten. Thank you, Fritz the Nite Owl, for hosting Double Chiller Theater, and thanks to my parents for letting me stay up to watch.

Last but not least: thank you, Adele, for putting up with the stacks of DVDs and books, the trips to the library, the late-night phone calls from aging producers, and for sitting through all manner of crappy movies and marrying me anyway.

Abridged versions of some of the interviews in this book originally appeared in the following magazines:
- Al Adamson: "Bikers, Blood Monsters and Black Samurai: A Final Interview with Al Adamson," Filmfax #53, 1995
- John "Bud" Cardos: "This Bud's for You," Filmfax #67, 1998
- Robert Dix: "The Wild Worlds of Robert Dix," Filmfax #108, 2005
- Sid Haig: "Acting on the Edge! Sid (Spider Baby) Haig," VideoScope #26, 1998
- Gary Kent: "Gary Kent: Drive-In Outlaw," VideoScope #63, 2007
- Anthony Lanza: "Put Your (Other) Head on My Shoulder," Shock Cinema #30, 2006

TABLE OF CONTENTS

Acknowledgments vii
Preface 1

Psycho a Go-Go: AL ADAMSON 5
Blood Monster Babe: JENIFER BISHOP 14
Kingdom of the Bikers: JOHN "BUD" CARDOS 30
Wild Wheels: ROBERT DIX 47
Hollywood Hellcat: ROSS HAGEN 59
Big, Bad and Bald: SID HAIG 74
Sounds of Silence: MONTE HELLMAN 87
It's Not Nice to Hate: JACK HILL 102
The Tough Guy: GARY KENT 116
Beyond the Call of Duty: JOYCE KING 134
Put Your (Other) Head on My Shoulder: ANTHONY LANZA . . . 148
Savage Cycles: GARY LITTLEJOHN 159
Axes to Grind: BART PATTON 171
Brain of Blood: SAM SHERMAN 185
The Girl from Thunder Strip: MEGAN TIMOTHY 202
A Thing for Two Heads: JAMES GORDON WHITE 209

Index 223

PREFACE

"We have some good stuff, and we have some crap."— Al Adamson's occasional response when asked about a film's progress by producer Sam Sherman

Sometime in the late 1980s, I first stumbled upon the concept of what it meant for a director to be an "auteur" while I was watching—honest to God, this is a true story—*Blood of Dracula's Castle* (1969), a film that I found in a discount bin at a Hill's department store. I don't think I had even heard the term "auteur" at the time, and I was certainly not impressed by what I saw onscreen—*Blood of Dracula's Castle* isn't a very good movie by any measure. What caught my eye was the film's stunning similarity to two other movies I'd seen on late-night television: *Vampire Men of the Lost Planet* (1970) and *Blood of Ghastly Horror* (1972). The latter I'd actually been tricked into watching twice because it was aired under two different titles, which gave me ample time to analyze its convoluted, cut-and-paste story structure in far greater detail than I might have otherwise. The first time I watched it, I fell asleep midway through; when I awoke, it appeared I was watching *an entirely different movie.*

As it turns out, all three films were the work of Al Adamson, a low-budget director who operated on the fringes of Hollywood for many years making distinctively peculiar films about bikers, vampires and naughty stewardesses. Is he an auteur? Well, as an independent he certainly had a fair degree of authorial control on his pictures, and as with Sam Peckinpah, David Lynch and Woody Allen, there's little chance you'll ever confuse Adamson's films for anyone else's.

In the years that followed, I became acquainted with even more filmmakers that not only shared Adamson's nickel-and-dime ingenuity, but also most of his cast and crew: David L. Hewitt, Gary Kent, Richard Rush, Anthony Cardoza, Joe Solomon, Greydon Clark. I already knew who Roger Corman was, of course, and Corman's films, in turn, led me to the work of Jack Hill, Daniel Haller and Monte Hellman.

This book is a compilation of interviews with those filmmakers that I've conducted over the past twelve years in an attempt to compile an oral history of exploitation films from what is generally considered a revolutionary place and time: the Hollywood of the late 1960s and early 1970s.

During that era, maverick filmmakers like Francis Coppola, Martin Scorsese, Warren Beatty, Jack Nicholson, Sam Peckinpah, and others turned the Hollywood system on its head, initiating a new Golden Age of thoughtful, realistic cinema that was generally referred to as "the New Hollywood."

Alex D'Arcy and Paula Raymond face the dawn in Al Adamson's *Blood of Dracula's Castle* (1969).

It was, as Peter Biskind wrote in the introduction to his book *Easy Riders, Raging Bulls* (1998), "the last time Hollywood produced a body of risky, high-quality work — as opposed to an errant masterpiece — work that was character-, rather than plot-driven, that defied traditional narrative conventions, that challenged the tyranny of technical correctness, that broke the taboos of language and behavior, that dared to end unhappily."

What Biskind and other scholars typically fail to mention is that it was also a time when exploitation filmmakers like Corman, Adamson, Ray Dennis Steckler, Russ Meyer and others marched their ragtag crews of hungry young actors, washed-up oldtimers and Hungarian cameramen into the crumbling backlots of Hollywood, the wilds of Griffith Park, and the dusty trails of the Spahn Ranch to churn out a stream of westerns, biker films, nudie-cuties and horror flicks that helped keep the American theater industry afloat as the major studios teetered on the brink of financial collapse. These films also pushed the boundaries of acceptable onscreen violence and nudity, and reshaped American cinema just as dramatically as their more high-minded counterparts.

This book tells part of the story of that *other* Hollywood. Four years before *Bonnie and Clyde*, Arch Hall's *The Sadist* (1963) had "dared to end unhappily." Could any film have challenged the "tyranny of technical correctness" more than *The Mighty Gorga* (1969), a film in which director David L. Hewitt, clad in half a gorilla suit, wrestles a dinosaur puppet? And if you want to see a film that defies "traditional narrative conventions," I challenge you to watch *Blood of Ghastly Horror* and tell me if *you* can figure out what the heck is going on.

A caveat: Some of the interviews included here are among the earliest I ever conducted, when I was barely old enough to vote. Where possible, I've gone back and re-interviewed the subjects to fill in any gaps, but in some cases, that just wasn't feasible. The Al Adamson interview was the very first one I ever did—and it shows. There are a lot of things I wish I could have asked Al, but he was dead within weeks of our last talk.

Speaking of Al Adamson, you'll notice that many of the people in this book, at one time or another, worked regularly with him. I did not intend this to be a book about Adamson (there's already a good one out there, *Schlock-O-Rama*, by David Konow), but he pops up in about every other chapter, nonetheless.

That's partly because the low-budget filmmaking community during that period was very close-knit. Everyone interviewed here worked with at least one other person in the book on one or more projects. You will hear about certain films over and over again (*The Incredible 2-Headed Transplant, Satan's Sadists, Blood of Dracula's Castle, The Mighty Gorga*) from a variety of perspectives—not just from the directors and the actors, but from the stuntmen, the screenwriters, the producers, and even (in the case of Joyce King) the script supervisor.

Sometimes these accounts dovetail nicely into a coherent narrative; sometimes they contradict each other. That's the way history (and memory) works. It's sort of like *Rashomon* (1951), but with Nazi bikers. Hopefully, you will find it as enlightening as I have.

Psycho a Go-Go

AL ADAMSON

The scene was truly macabre: Exploitation director Al Adamson, found entombed in concrete where his Jacuzzi had once stood, murdered by a contractor who was remodeling Adamson's Indio, California, home. As the details of his death came to light over the summer and fall of 1995, Adamson was suddenly making headlines around the world.

It was, tragically, the most attention Adamson had received in a while, and it came just as the director was planning a comeback of sorts. Long retired from the movie business, Adamson was slowly working his way back into the consciousness of low-budget movie fans. There had been interviews in *Psychotronic* and *Fangoria*, and music journalist David Konow was in the process of researching a book on Adamson. Most significantly, Adamson himself was beginning work on a new film with longtime producer Sam Sherman. I interviewed him in the spring of 1995, when he was poised to re-launch his film career. A few weeks later, he was gone.

You could say exploitation was in his genes. Al Adamson (born Albert Victor Adamson, Jr., in 1929) was the son of silent screen cowboy Denver Dixon (Victor Adamson) and actress Delores Booth. Missouri-born Dixon, a champion rider and roper in New Zealand before he headed to Hollywood, had directed, produced and distributed dozens of low-budget westerns from the late teens into the 1950s, and was one of the most prolific of the self-made indie distributors of the era.

The younger Adamson made his first film with his father in 1958, a western called *Halfway to Hell*, but it wasn't until he connected with Sherman that he truly hit his stride. Together, the two men (and business partner Dan Kennis) produced a string of notoriously cockeyed exploitation films through their Independent-International Pictures banner, beginning with the gruesome biker flick *Satan's Sadists* (1969).

For two decades, Adamson shocked and amused drive-in audiences with his often-chaotic blend of gore, sex, action and humor. He mixed and matched traditional exploitation elements—everything from monsters and hippies to bikers and buxom women—and wrapped them up in Sherman's memorable promotional campaigns.

With the help of his wife Regina Carrol (who often starred in his films) and a disparate crew of technicians and actors that at various times included Bud Cardos, award-winning cinematographer Laszlo Kovacs, director Greydon Clark, Gary Graver, John Carradine, and porn star Georgina Spelvin, Adamson dabbled in almost every genre that crossed the drive-in screen. He made biker films (*Satan's Sadists*, *Angels' Wild Women*), sex comedies (*The Naughty Stewardesses*), nudies (*Lash of Lust*), blaxploitation films (*Black Heat*, *Black Samurai*), westerns (*Five Bloody Graves*, *Jessi's Girls*), and horror films (*Blood of Dracula's Castle*, *Brain of Blood*).

From left: John Bloom, Sam Sherman, Zandor Vorkov (Roger Engel), and Al Adamson on the set of *Dracula vs. Frankenstein* (1971). (Courtesy Independent-International Pictures Corp.)

Some of his films were mind-bending amalgams of all of the above, like *Dracula vs. Frankenstein* (1971), which mixed the titular monsters with hippies and bikers, or *Hell's Bloody Devils* (1970), which tacked even more bikers onto an espionage film about mobsters and neo–Nazis. He and Sherman sometimes re-edited and re-titled existing properties, keeping the films in release on television and in theaters for years. The most convoluted example of this post-production tinkering has to be Adamson's second film, *Echo of Terror* (1965), which was also released as *Psycho a Go-Go*, *The Fiend with the Electronic Brain*, and *Blood of Ghastly Horror*—morphing, over time, into a nearly incomprehensible, Dada-like pastiche of jewel thieves, mad doctors, and zombies.

Adamson stopped directing in the early 1980s after finishing two family films, *Carnival Magic* (1981) and *Lost* (1983). With the decline of the drive-ins, and later his wife's failing health (Regina Carrol died of cancer in 1992), Adamson turned his attention to his real estate business. At the time of his murder, he and Sherman were making a pair of UFO documentaries, and Adamson was looking forward to directing another action film.

When did you decide you wanted to work in film?

AL ADAMSON: Oh God, I guess I've always wanted to work in show business, but I didn't think I had any talent. I tried acting. I tried dancing. I really wanted to be in musicals, but I couldn't sing and couldn't dance. I had good legs because I played basketball. I had good, strong legs, but I couldn't do the turns. I got dizzy. I even went to Louis DaPron, who was Donald O'Connor's teacher. I bounced around doing various things and finally, after I did a little more acting, I found that I was better at giving the orders than taking them!

You did your first film with your father. What year was that?

1958.

What was *Two Tickets to Terror*?

I think that's just another title of *Halfway to Hell*. It was a western.

Were you running a nightclub when you met Sam Sherman?

I had a little place in the valley called The Mutiny. It started out as a beer bar, and we had entertainment on Friday and Saturday nights. We had fix-yourself steak. And it was pretty successful as a beer bar. We even had a lot of stars. Ricky Nelson came in there, and a few others. It was quite a nice "in-crowd" hangout, because we had really great entertainment. Then I got a partner in that brought in a liquor license, and it seemed like we attracted a different crowd. We had fights in there, we had other problems, so we finally decided to give it up and we sold it.

How did you meet Sam Sherman?

He came to California to interview my father for a magazine that he was writing for, and that's when he first met me. He got friendly with my father, and my father started distributing *Halfway to Hell*. He'd go back East and see Sam when he was in the Army. They got to be pretty good friends, and we continued our friendship. When I went back there [New York] trying to sell a couple of films that I'd made, we decided—and my father convinced us—that we had to have a distribution company or we weren't going to be able to make it in this business. If you don't have anywhere to go with the pictures, there's no use makin' films! So that's what we did. We decided that our number one goal was to have a company, and to make films for the company, and then that in turn would make us able to continue.

How many projects did you work on between the time you met Sam and the time you made *Satan's Sadists*?

I would say I probably had about five or six films finished.

Were all of those distributed?

Russ Tamblyn in *Satan's Sadists* (1969), the film that launched Independent-International Pictures. (Courtesy Independent-International Pictures Corp.)

Every one of my films was distributed. Not one that wasn't.

Where was *Blood of Dracula's Castle* [1969] shot?

That was shot in a castle in Lancaster, California. It's outside of Los Angeles about a half an hour.

What were Paula Raymond and Alex D'Arcy like to work with on that film?

Both of them were very cooperative. Alex was a little nervous, but Paula was a sweetheart. I used her in a picture after that [*Five Bloody Graves*, 1969]. Rex Carlton was my partner on that, and he had done a few pictures. *The Brain that Wouldn't Die* [1962] was one of his, and he had been around the business a little while. He had some contacts and some friends, but I don't remember how those people [Raymond and D'Arcy] came into the film. I wanted Carradine to do Dracula, and they wanted D'Arcy. I said, "I want Carradine to at least do the butler," and I got him in.

Where did the idea for *Satan's Sadists* come from?

Me. It was out of pressure. I was supposed to do a picture in Spain, and it was a co-production deal with ABC. I had a contract with ABC here, and they gave me a letter of credit for $200,000, and I was getting the other $200,000 for a $400,000 budget. That was a lot in those days. I had Robert Taylor, George Montgomery and Robert Lansing all signed to go do the film [*Last of the Comancheros*, a.k.a. *The Unavenged*]. When I got over to Spain, the other people couldn't come up with their end of the money. I sat there for awhile and tried to put it together with other people, and finally abandoned it and came back to New York. I was broke. That was back in 1968. So Dan Kennis told Sam and me that if I could write a story they liked, they would give me the money to go back to California to make it. So I went back to a little ten-dollar-a-night hotel room — a dive, since that's all the money I had — and I wrote *Satan's Sadists* in one night. A completely detailed, 20-page treatment, and I turned it in the next day. They liked it, and the day after that I was on a plane back here, and the rest is history. That was the start of our company.

What was Russ Tamblyn like?

He was great, as long as I gave him a little freedom. He liked to have freedom to ad-lib and improvise. That's why he didn't last in the majors later because it got to the point that that's all he wanted to do. He didn't want to have somebody say, "You've got to say it this way." He wanted to be able to create, and I gave him the opportunity to create.

Were you the one that brought up the idea of using older stars?

No, that was Sam's idea. Carradine was the first one that I used. It seemed like most of the ones we picked were not being used in Hollywood anymore, because they had been drinkers or whatever. We brought back Carradine, we brought back Scott Brady, we brought back Broderick Crawford. All of these people had not been working. But it seemed like once they worked in our pictures, their careers started all over again. It was amazing.

Where did you get the idea for *Five Bloody Graves*?

Five Bloody Graves was brought to me by Robert Dix, Richard Dix's son, and he brought that to me just after we finished *Blood of Dracula's Castle*. They'd been trying to put it together for a few years. They had a whole company, and they were ready to go. Well, of course, I said, "If I become involved, I want to direct it." So that was the compromise: they got rid of the director they had, he became the assistant director, and I became the director. I put in some money, and I put in some raw stock that I had from the other film. We went up to Utah, and that was my idea because we'd shot *Halfway to Hell* up there. It's some of the most beautiful scenery in the world. [Vilmos] Zsigmond shot most of it, but he had to leave with one week to go, so we used another cameraman for the last week.

Tell me how *The Blood Seekers* became *Dracula vs. Frankenstein*.

It didn't work as *The Blood Seekers*. You know how pictures sometimes just don't work? We weren't happy with it, and we wanted to try different things. We added this to it, and we added that to it, and changed the story around a little bit. And that's how it finally became *Dracula vs. Frankenstein*.

Adamson (right) poses with Kent Taylor on the set of *Angels' Wild Women* (1972). (Courtesy Independent-International Pictures Corp.)

What was Lon Chaney, Jr., like?

Great. He was a nice man, no problems at all with Chaney. I don't think I had any problems with any of the older actors. The only ones I had trouble with were the young know-it-alls. They thought they were stars because they were working on a picture.

Was Chaney's character mute because of his health?

Chaney was all right until we did *The Female Bunch* [1969]. That's when he was dying, and he knew it. When we finished *Female Bunch* we did a little commercial, and it never got out. It's a shame it didn't get out. He was telling the world, "Don't smoke. Look what it's done to me. It's killed me." He smoked all his life, and that was what killed him. He knew it, and he died just shortly after that. That was his last picture.

I read that Chaney requested to do his own fight scene with Anthony Eisley rather than be doubled.

To tell you the truth I don't remember — we changed the picture so many times! Eisley was the big hero in the original picture, and then his character got killed. I'm not sure that Eisley was even there when we did that. Eisley was not happy with the picture because we had changed so much of it, but of course we didn't do it to hurt him. We just did it to try and save the picture.

What was Eisley like on the set?

He was fine; I never had a problem with Eisley. He was very cooperative, a very classy man. I've never really heard the interviews where he's knocked the picture, but according to Sam he has at times. We know that he mainly did it because he saw the picture afterwards and it wasn't the same picture he shot.

What about J. Carrol Naish?

Naish was another very nice man to work with, but he had a problem with his teeth. When he would talk his false teeth would chatter. So we had problems with the soundtrack. Other than that he was a pro. Unfortunately he was crippled at the time. Again, it was his last picture.

Is it true that *The Female Bunch* was shot at or near the Spahn Ranch?

Not true. We shot *The Female Bunch* in Utah. When I was finished, I had a problem with the producer on it. He wasn't happy with it, and I was having to rewrite the script every night to save the thing. I gave him a pretty good picture, but I don't think I gave him as much sex as he wanted. So he went back and shot some stuff with Cardos, and they added some sex scenes in the picture. Now they might have shot that at Spahn Ranch, I don't know.

Tell me about some of the members of your "stock company," like Robert Dix and Bud Cardos.

Well, Dix was a hard worker and a good actor. I haven't heard from him in a lot of years. The last time I saw him was in Palm Springs. He came through and said he was doing some sort of promotion thing for a Marilyn Monroe look-alike, and that was the last I saw of him. I hired him as an actor on *Blood of Dracula's Castle*; he was a friend of Cardos, who came on as production manager. The thing I liked about those guys was that they would act in front of the camera, they would work behind the camera, they could do everything. Cardos would do stunts, and Dix would do stunts, and they would choreograph stunts for other people. Having those people around in those days was a real plus.

You also worked with Tommy Kirk on *Blood of Ghastly Horror*.

It's funny, I just ran into a guy that knew him when he was a Mouseketeer, so we've been talking about Tommy Kirk a lot. Sam [Sherman] ran into him recently, and Tommy said if we could use him in the next picture he'd love to work.

What do you remember about the two stewardess movies you made?

Both of them were Sam's ideas. The first one [*The Naughty Stewardesses*] was more of a drama with a lot of sex in it. *Blazing Stewardesses* (1975) was more of a fun picture, with the Ritz Brothers, and Don "Red" Barry, Yvonne DeCarlo and Bob Livingston.

How did performers like Livingston and DeCarlo adjust to being in a sex comedy?

I think Bob Livingston just accepted it for what it was and did the best he could with it. It was a little more for Yvonne DeCarlo, but she's done a whole lot worse than that since then. But I think she was just a little nervous.

What about *Girls For Rent* [a.k.a. *I Spit on Your Corpse!*, 1974]?

Somehow we got into some story about some drug rings and smuggling from Mexico. And then we tied it in with what we thought would be more theatrical. We made a good little chase picture out of it. Georgina Spelvin was not my favorite person to work with, but the picture worked.

Bill Bonner clobbers an unidentified stuntman in *The Female Bunch* (1969). Al Cole, the evil head in *The Incredible 2-Headed Transplant* (1971), is behind the bar.

You had an interesting cast in *Death Dimension* [1978], with Aldo Ray, George Lazenby and Harold "Odd Job" Sakata.

I made that for Harry Hope [who had sold several IIP pictures to Asia]. He miscast the picture, in my opinion. He should have used Bob Minor, who was a pretty successful stunt coordinator, in Odd Job's role, and Odd Job [Sakata] should have done his role. Odd Job was just handed too much dialogue. There wasn't anything wrong with him, but he just had never been given that kind of a thing. Lazenby, I guess, was having trouble getting work and he did a good job. Aldo's always good. I used Aldo in several movies. Every time I get those pros in a picture, we have a better picture. But *Death Dimension* came out a lot better than I thought it would. I thought it was a good picture.

You also worked with Jim Kelly in *Black Samurai* (1977).

Jim Kelly was all right. He had a big ego. I've used a lot of black actors. I used Tim Brown [*The Dynamite Brothers*, 1974], and Fred Williamson [*Hammer*, 1972]. I used Kelly in two pictures. *Black Samurai* was a spoof on a super black hero. He caught me at a time when I wanted to work, and I said, "Okay, how much do you want to spend?" I just got a copy of it recently.

What was your relationship with Hemisphere Pictures?

We made *Brain of Blood* [1971] for them. Grant Williams was in that, and Vicki Volante, my wife, Kent Taylor, Reed Hadley. We also had Zandor Vorkov in it. I wasn't happy with some of the makeup in the picture, but other than that it came out all right.

People seem to have the idea that you spent a lot of time reassembling other pictures.

We've had so many titles on some of our films. We're businessmen, and if a title doesn't work we don't let it destroy our lives. We might change the title, we might add some additional footage, we might try to make the picture better. Sometimes we don't make it better! I think that must be where people get that idea, because there were very few pictures that we did that with. There were a couple of pictures like *Lucifer's Women* [released, with additional footage, as *Doctor Dracula* in 1981], where the guy was in trouble and we tried to help him. Believe me, it's easier to go out from the beginning and make a film than it is to try to fix one. We happened to be very good at it, so I guess that's where we got the reputation. We did some great jobs, especially on *Uncle Tom's Cabin* [1976]. I think that was the best thing we ever did.

Many of your storylines were pastiches. Was that strictly a commercial consideration?

I think there were certain elements that we always tried to get in. What we did was try to make a film about what was happening at the time, either in the news or in the films. If we saw a successful trend, we'd make a similar picture. *Satan's Sadists* was in that category, but *Satan's* became a classic. Some of the other biker pictures we did didn't do that well.

The last two films you did were "family films," *Carnival Magic* and *Lost*. Was it hard to switch gears?

Ninety percent of our pictures were "R." On these last two films I was hired strictly as director, and I made the best film that I could out of what we had to work with. I wrote *Lost* originally, but I had nothing to do with the writing on *Carnival Magic*. When I finally saw *Carnival Magic* I was pleasantly surprised. I thought it worked. I wish I had the rights to it right now.

Why did you leave filmmaking?

I could see the writing on the wall when the drive-ins started going out. We weren't sure where we were gonna go, and I had a family to take care of. So I bought a business up in Utah, and I dabbled in real estate. And most of it was what made me some money. With the budgets on our pictures, I didn't get rich!

The film you're working on now is a documentary. Are we going to be seeing any more action movies from you?

I hope so. That's what I want to make. I've got two storylines that I'm ready to go on. One is a little more a comedy-action-romance film. It's called *Gold Fever*. I've got one that's strictly all action, *Lethal Justice*. We're trying to work out a co-production with Australia, and perhaps one with Italy.

Do you think a lot of the criticism leveled at your films is unduly harsh?

Few films ever come out that everybody likes. That's number one. Number two, it's always easier to knock the smaller guy. Number three, I would put my films against any director in the film industry today and defy them to do a better film for the money. We had to work with what we had, and our budgets were minuscule compared to the pictures that come out today. If you go to the movies today, you see an awful lot of really bad films. They might be mounted well, and they might have great explosions, but the pictures are bad. They're not even entertaining, and they cost $20 million or $30 million to make. We never made a picture that cost $20 million, and we never made a picture as bad as that.

And your films have outlasted a lot of more expensive ones.

We tried to make an entertaining film. I must have had at least twenty interviews in the last two years from people who were either fans of mine or whatever. They must have liked our films. They're not out there just to do an article. I've got fan clubs all over the world, and for my kind of little crap pictures, that's something special.

Of all the films you've made, which are your favorites?

I think that out of my 32 films there are probably five or six that are really good. *Satan's Sadists, Jessi's Girls* [1975]. *Death Dimension* is one. *Girls for Rent* is one. All of those I would put up against anybody's films. *Bad Girls* [1994] came out last year with some big stars in it, and that picture was made for I think $15 million or $18 million. I made *Jessi's Girls* for $65,000, everybody paid, all SAG, shot part in California and part in Utah, and that picture is a better picture at $65,000. I defy anyone to see the two pictures and not think so. *Bad Girls* was a direct rip-off of my picture.

How would you sum up your film career?

I think we tried to make an entertaining picture within our limits. In other words, if the script calls for 50 Indians and we can only afford five, we do it with five. But at least we did the pictures and got them out. And there's not too many people around who can say they directed 32 films. Now I'm back again and I'm gonna be making another 10 or 20 before I retire.

Blood Monster Babe

JENIFER BISHOP

Al Adamson populated his films with so many competing plot elements—bikers, monsters, naked women, Col. Harlan Sanders—that actors sometimes got lost in the shuffle. Jenifer Bishop, however, was difficult to miss. The raven-haired actress was a key player in Adamson's early stock company, and one of the few women other than Mrs. Adamson (Regina Carrol) who regularly scored starring roles in his offbeat films.

Bishop's debut in the Adamson oeuvre was as the scantily clad cavegirl in *Horror of the Blood Monsters* (shot in 1965, released in 1970), providing the link between new footage of a group of space explorers, and existing footage of Filipino actors battling bug-eyed monsters from the film *Tagani* (1965). As Barbara Bishop, she was menaced by Alex D'Arcy's lisping Count in *Blood of Dracula's Castle* (1969); decked out in riding boots and a bad attitude, she menaced Russ Tamblyn in *The Female Bunch* (1969).

But her work with Adamson is only part of the story. A California native (born in 1941), Bishop won a scholarship to Desilu Studios in the early 1960s, then scored her first film role in Boris Sagal's *Dime With a Halo* (1963). She spent two years in New York studying with the legendary Lee Strasberg before returning to Hollywood, where her career took a peculiar turn after a chance meeting between her then-boyfriend Bruce Powers (who appeared in *Horror of the Blood Monsters* and sang the theme for *The Female Bunch*) and then-aspiring director Adamson.

Bishop remained active on television during this period, appearing on *Mission: Impossible*, *Cannon*, *Barnaby Jones*, *Starsky & Hutch*, and other shows, as well as the Shelley Winters film *The Mad Room*, and Dan Rowan and Dick Martin's *The Maltese Bippy* (both 1969). Based on her work in the Rowan and Martin film, Bishop was cast in the pilot episode of *Hee Haw*, and appeared as one of the original Hee Haw Honeys for two seasons.

Her Adamson films alone would guarantee her cult status, but Bishop also appeared in two films for producer Anthony Cardoza (*Bigfoot*, 1970, and *Outlaw Riders*, 1971), and three more for Florida schlock mogul William Grefé (*The Godmothers*, 1973, *Impulse*, 1974, and *Mako: The Jaws of Death*, 1976, her final film before retiring from the screen).

Where did you grow up?

JENIFER BISHOP: I grew up in Camarillo, where I am right now. I came back here to take care of my mom after my dad passed away. She had Alzheimer's, and she's since passed away. I have a 16-year-old son that I adopted. He loved it here, and I thought, "Why shouldn't he?" It was a wonderful place to grow up. So we stayed here. Kids don't like change too much, so I thought maybe I should just stick to what works. He's a very good student, a straight-A student, and that's a good thing in this day and age.

I was in the first graduating class of Camarillo High School. I was the first queen Camarillo ever had. When you become a large duck in a small pond, it's kind of interesting at the time when you're a kid. I went two years at Ventura College. From there, I won a scholarship to Desilu Studios in Hollywood from my wonderful drama teacher named Dr. Wilkenson. I studied with Anthony Barr, who was then the vice-president of ABC. I was at Desilu Studios

Actress Jenifer Bishop in a posed publicity shot taken in the early 1970s.

studying method acting for two years. Then I wound up in a movie called *Dime With a Halo*. It's a wonderful, darling little movie about the five-and-ten at Caliente or whatever it's called. It starred BarBara Luna, and a wonderful character actor that I can't even remember right now. I played a Mexican stripper! I had a good scene in it. He put in a very good scene in the dressing room where three of us girls were in there with BarBara, and we were all deciding how we were going to help this kid.

Boris Sagal directed that.

Yes he did. A very good director, I might add.

The cast I've got listed was BarBara Luna, Roger Mobley and Jay Adler.

Roger Mobley. Oh my gosh! Was he in it? You know I'm 64 now, Brian. Some of the electrolytes have burned out!

You aren't listed online in the credits.

I was going through my identity crisis then. I don't know what my name was then. It might have been Barbara, it might have been Joa-Marie. It was always Bishop, though.

What was your given name?

Oh, don't ask that! My father's name was Albert, and my name was Alberta because I was first born. After enough peaches, and enough Canada, I decided maybe when I got a career I'd change it. My middle name was Joa-Marie. I took my grandmother's name, and my mother's name was Maria. I just combined my grandmother's name and my mom's name and became Joa-Marie Bishop. I don't even remember what the name was I used. But I always kept Bishop, because that's where it all started, I guess.

It would have been LaVeck, but my grandfather had it changed. Wouldn't that have been wonderful? Joa-Marie LaVeck — my God, it sounds like a bubble dancer!

What got you interested in performing?

I started out in school plays. When I moved back here, we had a wonderful get-together, all of us girls that went to school. One of them, her name was Smith, and her mother, Mrs. Smith, was my eighth grade English teacher. She said, "Why couldn't you have been more like Alberta? She knew what she wanted to be when she was in the fifth grade!" I guess I had aspirations early, early on!

That was fifth grade. I wanted a ticket out of Camarillo, and I got one, because after I did my stint at Desilu and had my little five minutes of film in my hand, I headed for New York and studied with [Lee] Strasberg at Carnegie Hall. I did that for two years.

I'm not so sure if that was the right move, because Kim Darby was in my same acting class at Desilu, and she went on to become quite famous, and I ran off to New York to do stage and study with Strasberg. I don't know whether that was a good move in retrospect or not, but it was something I had to do.

I did a couple of Off Broadway shows. I modeled during the day, I was a Playboy bunny at night, and I studied with Strasberg. That was about '63 or '64. I came back here in 1965. I remember my brother got out of the service and I came home from New York.

I left here with a one-way ticket and 500 bucks in my pocket. Does that tell you how eager I was to get out of town? And when you're young, there's no stopping. It's all go. You can only do it once in your life.

What was it like working with Strasberg?

It was devastating! It was something I hadn't encountered. I spent some of the classes with Paula and some of them with Lee. I wouldn't have chosen to do it again if I had the choice. I finally ended up with Mira Rostova, and her claim to fame was Montgomery Clift. I found her far more palatable to my kind of acting, what I wanted to do. First of all, he was bigger than life, and he was a little tiny man. He was very strict. I remember one time on stage he said, "Why don't you try reading the phone book? Maybe you can get more emotion going out of that." I'd just studied method for two years. I thought, "Oh my God, I'm going to die. I won't make it through this class." But I did study with him, and I liked Paula, his wife. It was an interesting time. I was working all night at the Playboy Club, then going to classes during the day. As I said, you can only do it when you're young.

I'll tell you how young I was, and the year it was. Sammy Davis was at the Copacabana, which was right behind us at the Playboy Club. He couldn't get in the front door then. He was the headliner, and he had to go around to the side entrance where the help went. That was the year it was. So it was long ago.

How'd you get into writing?

I have a degree in journalism. While I was in college, I started interviewing people who made low-budget exploitation films.

You know why I ended up in so many of those films? I always had in my contract that I wouldn't do nudity because I—well, you know what I looked like. I didn't have a lot of choices. Either they wanted me to take my clothes off, or I opted to do horror films and different kinds of movies so I wouldn't have to do that.

It wasn't in my make-up. It worked out well because, in retrospect, if I had done that, I wouldn't have probably been able to adopt my son. I got him from St. Anne's here in Los Angeles, and that was one of the first questions they asked. They check you out when you're adopting a child. Wow, they really check you out! If I had opted for that, it might have been a different road I'd have to have taken. So it did work out fine.

I had to do it my way. And thank God I did because I've got this beautiful 16-year-old boy that I'm rearing, and he's the apple of my eye. And that was one of the first things they asked me: 'What kind of movies did you do?'

When you came back to California, did you start working again immediately?

You know what happened? My boyfriend at the time, a singer, was on a plane with a man named Al Adamson who was going to do a movie called *Vampire Men of the Lost Planet* [a.k.a. *Horror of the Blood Monsters*]. I don't know if that's on the list or not. It's a real lulu. It's like a combination of about three movies that they put together.

It had several different titles.

Al always did ten different titles. Always. He covered his tracks every which way he could. He was an interesting man. He grew up very poorly. His father was a bit player, and he also was in the newspaper business. Al delivered newspapers for years and years, and he had these aspirations. And they came to fruition. He stuck it out until he was able to direct. He didn't push his women into doing things that they didn't want to do. He was honorable, I guess. When I think of the way he died, it's devastating.

I interviewed him right before he died.

When I read that, and then I saw that documentary they did on him, my heart just sank. What a way to end up. It was more bizarre than any of the pictures he'd ever done.

Nice man. I hope you got that from the interview. He was a sweetheart of a man. We did movies where we traveled in the backseat of a station wagon to get to location in zero-degree weather in Utah and all these places that we went to, and he was just a kind-hearted, good man. He really was.

I have to ask: After studying with Strasberg, how did you prepare for your cavegirl role in *Horror of the Blood Monsters*?

[*Laughs*] You don't want to ask that! You *don't* want to ask that. I haven't got a logical answer. I think I was on remote control!

Do you remember the rest of the cast? Most of your scenes were with Joey Benson.

No, I don't remember, I'm sorry. He was a nice guy, though, Joe was. And the blonde in the picture, that was my boyfriend, and he sang. His name was Bruce Powers. (He just passed away about two months ago. He came to see me and he was dying of cancer.) That's how I met Al. From there I went on to do two or three other movies with him.

The next one would have been *Blood of Dracula's Castle*. You spent a lot of time at Marineland in that film.

Oh yeah [*laughs*]! They've been edited and re-edited. I've got copies of some of them. That

Bishop with director Al Adamson circa 1965. (Courtesy Independent-International Pictures Corp.)

one I do have a copy of, and it's a kick in the head. You know I can't even get my son to look at these? He says, "Mom, you get killed in every one of the movies you ever did. I don't want to watch that." It shows up at Halloween.

John Carradine was just a dear heart. What a wonderful, nice man. It was funny because come six o'clock, that was cocktail hour. He was absolutely not to be seen after six. You know he had a photographic memory? He never blew a scene. He'd look at the script and he'd just do it. He had a lot of stage training. Delightful man.

In fact, there was a birthday party on the set, and in walked David and Keith. I didn't know David was as old as he was, because he was older than I am. But Keith, it was his birthday, and he was just a kid. I have a tape of them singing "Happy Birthday" to him. It's cute. I don't know what possessed me to even keep it, but I had it on an old cassette and threw it in a drawer somewhere, and there it was.

Do you remember much about your co-star, Gene O. Shane?

Very nice man. I don't ever remember seeing him in anything else.

He did a few other films, and even played Jesus in one movie.

He was good-looking, and Jesus—that would have been good casting. I just don't remember that much after that.

I later did a lot of stage work, and I traveled with Forrest Tucker for seven years and directed. We worked with a repertory company that had a lot of good people in it: Morey Amsterdam and Lana Turner, "No-No" Nanette Fabray, Pat O'Brien. Really good people. Tuck and I, we did two plays together, *George the Gentleman* and *Hanky Panky*. I directed and starred in it with him. Seven years we went out off and on, because that's when I was trying to get pregnant and do my thing, which didn't work out real well. My poor husband—I was dragging him in from everywhere.

There was another girl in the Dracula film who worked with Al a lot, Vicki Volante. Did you know her?

I saw her at my uncle's funeral two months ago. I'm the one that got her that role. Her father was my grandmother's doctor, so they were friends of the family for a long, long time. My aunt called me one day and said, "Vicki would like to be in the movies. Could you possibly introduce her to somebody?" I said okay, and P.S., she ended up starring in my part for the next three movies that he did. It was really interesting. Now, I won't even go into why, because I don't have to.

According to Bob Dix and Sam Sherman, Al was interested in her romantically.

That's right. That did have a whole lot to do with it. Bob Dix, he was nice. He had that father of his that was quite famous in westerns. In fact, I think that's one of the reasons he and Al became friends, because Al's father had done westerns. Sherman ... I must have met him, but I don't ever remember. I think at one time Dimension—wasn't that the name of the company?

Al did films for Independent-International and Dalia during that period, and Dimension came later.

Oh, Dalia. I always thought, "What happened to the last company?" but it wasn't any of my business! But Al was better in business than any part of it. He just was a survivor, and he just had tenacity that wouldn't quit, which is what it takes. And to start out with really not a lot of credit to your name and to build up and do as many films, whether low-budget or not. Some of those films were done for, I think, $50,000. I know what my salaries were, and how we got there. Needless to say, there wasn't a makeup trailer. We didn't even know what one was. There wasn't a wardrobe because that was non-existent. He really pulled himself up by the bootstraps and just did what he had to do.

That was filmed in an actual castle in the desert.

Interesting castle. This was the story: The man had built it for his wife, who was wheelchair-bound. I can't remember if he died before it was completed, or she died before it was completed. It had an interesting past to it. It was great. I loved it.

Carradine did an interesting thing on that movie to me. They wanted a natural reaction, so in one of the scenes where I was down in the cellar, I'm backing up into a coffin before I turn around and open it. When I opened it, he was lying inside and smoking a cigarette. The bastard scared the hell out of me! It blew me right out of the frame, I screamed so loud. That's what they wanted, this natural reaction. I screamed so loud, and jumped so high, that I went right out of frame. Kind of a funny thing. But he loved doing those little practical jokes every once in a while, and so did Al. Like the mice were white when we rehearsed the scene down in the basement. When we shot it, all of a sudden they were these ugly-looking black things, and we had the cheese between our toes so they would nibble nicely.

Jenifer Bishop (credited as Barbara Bishop) and Gene O. Shane confront the monstrous Mango (Ray Young) in *Blood of Dracula's Castle* (1969).

I think your next film with Al was *The Female Bunch*.

Oh yes, that was my starring role.

That was a tough character.

Tough. True. Dykey tough. I don't know. We were smuggling drugs from Mexico. Who was the producer?

Mardi Rustam?

No, not Mardi. The Israeli guy. I ended up suing him, because of a nude scene. They faked a nude scene and put it in the movie. If you look at it closely, they panned another person's body, and then the pan showed my face. I took 'em to court with a lawyer from Desilu Studios, and I won. I got it stopped in the United States. The judge didn't understand why I had done the movie to begin with. I don't know what script he had, but there wasn't any problem winning it, because I ain't had that kind of a breast my whole life [*laughs*]! Never. Those would have cost me a fortune!

Rafael Nussbaum was the other producer. The first time I met him, I remember he pulled a bottle of vodka out of his attaché case. He must have made a fortune on that movie. He said he was going to make me a big star. I've heard *that* before.

It wasn't allowed to show in theaters for a long time. That was what I won. That was the settlement. That cost me quite a bit of money, too. I couldn't find Al. He was in New York and I couldn't find him to be at the trial and verify what had happened. Russ Tamblyn didn't want to get involved, because at the time he was into other things. Russ didn't want to press charges or do anything, or stand up, and I couldn't find Al, so I went to court on my own. But I did get it knocked out of the United States. And then they released in it in Europe. I guess the scene was back in it. I have a copy of it, and it isn't in mine, but then I don't know what they did after that. But Al said to me, "Why didn't you contact me?" This was the kind of guy he was. I didn't know where to get a-hold of him. "Well, you could have called!" He was with Sherman in New York.

Do remember much about Al's wife, Regina Carroll?

I liked Gina. She was a good dancer. They came to visit me. I had a condo in Palm Springs. That's when Al first started buying houses. He had purchased a house — an old silent star lived there, Harold Lloyd. He had purchased the house and he was remodeling it, and I invited them over for dinner one night. First I invited Gina over, and we had a little girl chat kind of a thing, and she swam in the pool. And you know Al. She said, "He gets me so angry. He won't turn on the air until July." I said, "Oh my God, you've got to be dying. July in Palm Springs!" She was in the pool and said, "This feels so good." She was very nice. And very friendly. She didn't die any good death, either.

She was sick for a long time.

She was into chemo when they came over for dinner. She had a white turban on, I remember, and I didn't know what was going on until she told me she'd lost all her hair. And that was sad, because you know what? He didn't have insurance on her. Did you know that?

I don't think they were married yet at that time.

I think they were. Well, maybe they said they were. I don't know. You know, sometimes when I answer questions, what I'm saying is what I know. I'm not sure whether they were married or not. I know they were living together, which they did for a long time.

Was part of *The Female Bunch* shot at the Spahn Ranch?

Yes. And do you know, every time I rode over I kept thinking about that — that was where that guy had been buried, that was killed there. The stuntman. They never found his body.

You mean Shorty Shea.

It was somewhere on Spahn Ranch, they figured. Every time I rode that horse, I thought to myself, "Oh my god, I'm probably riding right over his body!"

Did you get along with Lon Chaney and Russ Tamblyn?

Lon Chaney was a dear man. He was dying, which we didn't know. He'd talk like this [in a raspy voice], "Hello, Ms. Grace." I mean, you had to figure something was wrong. But he never complained. He was a very nice man. I thought he was a very fine actor.

There was one scene where I had to — the stunt girl had started hemorrhaging. I guess she was pregnant and started hemorrhaging, so I ended up doing a lot of my own stunts in that movie. They weren't any great shakes, but they were stunts and I fancied myself to be an equestrienne. I'd been riding my whole life. There was a male horse on the other side of this ravine. They put me on this darling old pony, and she took off to go meet the guy down the hill, and I went flying over this ravine — about six or seven feet across—flying over it. When I landed, I didn't land exactly great. The horse went one way, and I went another, and apparently Chaney was looking at me from the cabin where we stayed. It was like five degrees below zero, it was so cold. He said to me the next day before we started shooting, "Was that you I saw down there on the ground? The horse went one way and you went the other!" I said, "You saw that?" He said, "What happened? You told me you could ride." And it was funny because I told him what they had done. He said, "Oh well, that was an interesting way to get you across that ravine!"

At the time it was very funny because I thought to myself, "Son of a bitch!" I never knew what they were doing. But Al would do anything. He wired me once — was that the movie? He wired me once on this movie where Bud Cardos was the stunt man. Do you know about him? He's a nice man, too. But he had a terrible accident, didn't he? Did he have an accident and he was paralyzed?

No, that was Bill Bonner.

Oh, that was Bill! Isn't that strange? When I heard the story I thought it was Bud. It was Bill Bonner. That's right, it *was* Bill Bonner. That was an awful thing that happened to him.

But anyway, he blew me up! I'm looking up on the hill and I'm watching — I think it was Cardos — he's got this thing in his hands, and he's ready to plunge down on this dynamite or whatever the hell it was, and I thought to myself, what a wonderful thing that I had a padded bra on, because it blew me to smithereens. And if I hadn't had any padding on, I'd have been burned. You know what? When he did some of these things it used to crack me up because I'd say, "You can't even use it. You blew me right out of the shot!" That was the second time. Gosh darn it. It was funny. It wasn't so funny — it scared me to death, but Al was very good at those things. How is Bill Bonner?

Greydon Clark told that Bill Bonner checked himself out of the hospital after that accident, and nobody's seen him since.

Really? I'll be darned. He was an awfully nice man.

He did a few films for Greydon.

He wouldn't give me a job, Greydon. He didn't like me, I guess.

I think his wife got most of the good roles in his films.

I think so, too [*laughs*]. That's okay. That's cool. It should be that way. I wouldn't expect anything else if I had a husband in the movies. If he didn't do that, we wouldn't be married, right?

Did you do any television during that period?

A lot of it. *Cannon, Barnaby Jones, Gilligan's Island, Starsky and Hutch, Mission: Impossible, Mannix,* the Jonathan Winters TV special, *Banyon* (1971), which was a movie of the week.

How did you get the *Hee Haw* gig?

Time-Life bought *Hee Haw*. I did the first two years on the show.

So how did you wind up on the show?

In 1969 I did *Hee Haw*, I did the original pilot, and I did *Hee Haw* for two years after that. What happened was, I met this man called Bill Davis [one of the directors] on an interview, and he said he was going to do a pilot. He said he'd seen me in a movie — was it the movie at MGM called *The Maltese Bippy*? Somewhere around there, that time frame. It was 1969 that I did the pilot.

You would have just done *The Maltese Bippy* then.

That's when I met him then. He and his wife. He said he was going down to Nashville to do this new show. It was the answer to *Laugh-In*. Oh, it had to be that, because Rowan and Martin were in *The Maltese Bippy*. It was really an interesting film. It was shot in sequence. I had met Everett Freeman long before at a cocktail party or something, and he said, "Oh, I'm going to do a movie with [director] Norman Panama," and yabba dabba doo. And I'm talking about *way* before the movie came out. Anyhow, I got the role in that. It was shot in sequence because Rowan and Martin had never done films before — or since! They were wonderful. I was in the beginning, middle and the end, so I made a bundle just on that one film. That bill! Once you start work, they've got to carry you through. That was a good thing.

I did a lot of commercials, too. Maybe about fifteen of them in between. I can't remember. It's been too long ago. I get residuals for, you know, like 25 cents. A dollar ninety. Sometimes I don't even cash the check. I wonder why they even send it. It costs more for postage than the residuals!

So I met Bill, and he said he was doing this [*Hee Haw*] pilot, and Frank Peppiatt and John Aylesworth were the producers on it, whom I didn't know, never met. So we shot here in Griffith Park and a couple of other locations. Craziness. Just madness. In an outhouse, in a Whistler's Mother outfit, in a werewolf mask. I thought, "What the hell kind of a show is this?" Anyway, next thing I know they got picked up. I said, "You've got to be kidding." I might have said that out loud. They had already cast the two girls, Jeannine Riley and Gunilla Hutton from *Petticoat Junction*, but Gunilla couldn't start work right away, and they wanted somebody else to take over. I think she had a baby or was pregnant or something. So he said to me, "Do you want to go down to Nashville and shoot this?" So that's how I got on the show. It was a far cry from anything else I'd ever done before. You know, I am now getting paid because Time-Life bought *Hee Haw*, and I did the first two years on the show, 35 years ago!

Did you enjoy *Hee Haw*?

I can tell you an interesting story. I climbed out of the plane with my dog and my luggage and everything, and it was late getting in, and this guy picked me up in a limousine. I said, "Oh, thank you, here are my bags," and he carried my bags to the car. It was some kind of a car, maybe not a limo. So I got back to the hotel, which was King of the Road — that's when Roger Miller was real popular. I gave the guy a couple of bucks, and I thanked him for bringing me to the hotel. He just stood there, so I tipped him whatever I had on me. So the next morning I started work and I saw this same guy. I went over to my friend Brigit Jensen — she ended up being one of the co-directors or co-producers on *All in the Family*, but she was a secretary there — and she said, "Do you know who you gave money too? John Aylesworth, the producer of the show!" He didn't have his hand out, but I couldn't figure out what he was waiting for, so I gave him money! I thought she'd die. It was very funny.

Anyway that's my claim to fame. The people were fabulous on the show. They were wonderful people, and I loved meeting all of them. And they were all on the show, from Johnny Cash to Dolly Parton, to you name it. Every single one of them. They were really nice people, interesting people. If you started talking to them, usually you found out that last year they were married to somebody else's wife. I don't know how the kids ever figured out who their real mom and dad were. There was a lot of swapping around.

But it wasn't my cup of tea. I felt like a misfit putting on pigtails and jumping up in cornfields. But you know what? My husband tells me right now I'm really a star in Oklahoma! I'm known as the cornfield girl. Thirty-five years ago. If they could only see me now in my gray hair! Nobody thinks you get any older when you're in this business.

What were Rowan and Martin like?

Very much to themselves. Dan Rowan, he was amicable. The other one — I think they were really kind of concerned a lot about doing their roles on there. I expected them to be kind of funny and like Rowan and Martin, but they weren't anything like that on the set. There was a wonderful man there that I became friends with, Fritz Weaver. And also Mildred Natwick was in it, and she was darling. Julie Newmar was very nice. She ate a lot of health food, a lot of birdseed. She has that *fabulous* body.

You were also in *The Mad Room*, directed by Bernard Girard.

With Shelley Winters and Stella Stevens. Oh, there's another television show I did. I had done a show called *The Virginian*. The director was Barney Girard [who also directed *The Mad Room*]. At that time I was helping Bing Russell take his kid down to the studios because he was only ten. His name was Kurt Russell. We did a *Virginian* together.*

He was so cute. He fell madly in love with me for about five minutes. I said, "One day you're going to marry a lady that looks just like your mom." And Goldie Hawn could double for his mom. Nice kid, nice family. I had done a play here with his father, Bing Russell, and that's how I met the family, and my family knew their family. They lived in Thousand Oaks then. He just recently died, Bing Russell. He was doing Clem in *Bonanza* then, I think. And that was right before Kurt landed *The Travels of Jaimie McPheeters*, which put him in the Disney world.

You did a couple of films with Bill Bonner for producer Anthony Cardoza.

Oh, Tony Cardoza, the little darling! I've got an album cover here, *Outlaw Riders*, and I was

---

*This was most likely the episode "A Father for Toby," which aired in November 1964, or "The Brothers," from September 1965.

Bishop in *The Mad Room* (1969), in which she co-starred with Shelley Winters and Stella Stevens.

the guest star with Lindsey Crosby and Rafael Campos, who ended up being my manager for five minutes. What a crazy guy he was.

How did you wind up in those two films?
I don't know. I don't think I can trace that for you. I had to meet him somewhere. I think I went on an interview. Oh yeah, because at the time — boy, are you stirring up a lot of memories! — at the time, Sonny West was Elvis' bodyguard, and Judy Jordan (a beautiful girl), they were going together. I met her — I'd been over to Elvis' house a couple of times, because when I went to Desilu Studios I hung out with Cissy Wellman for awhile, and she was [director] Bill Wellman's daughter. I'd been over to Elvis' house, and I'm trying to think if that's where I met Judy. It's kind of fuzzy. We had some mutual friends, I guess.

Anyway, we all went on an interview together for this movie. Then Tony asked me if I wanted to put money into it. I said, "No, I don't want to put money in your movie." I guess he thought I was rich, I don't know. I said I wanted a job. So he said, "Okay, you can guest star in it with Lindsey and Rafael." Then I met a girl named Alesha [Alesha Lee, a.k.a Aleshia Brevard], I don't know what happened to her. I was in contact with her for years. Anyway, she ended up in *The Female Bunch*, the redhead. Do you know anything about her?

Not really.
She was interesting. A transvestite. I don't know if anybody knew, but I became friends with

her. She took good care of me. She was very nice. She said, "Oh, mama won't let anything happen to you." And I was about as green as green can be. She was a Vegas showgirl, beautiful, beautiful girl, and I don't know what happened to her. She had this gorgeous alabaster skin. She went to New York, she got married, and then all of a sudden I didn't hear from her. I knew her for ten years after that movie.

How did Rafael Campos wind up being your manager?

I don't remember exactly, except that he thought I'd be an ideal person to manage. He didn't do anything for me that I remember, except I went to a couple of parties. Oh, I don't want to get into it. He had problems of his own at the time. It wasn't anything. I sound like such a prude. I wasn't. Drugs and that just scare me. I still carry that to this day with my son. Man, it's a frightening thing, how many lives were ruined with that. You know at one time Rafael was married to the black blues singer Dinah Washington. He did a lot of interesting things. I wonder sometimes if he knew who he was.

You and Bill Bonner also had parts in the *Bigfoot* movie Cardoza did.

Yes [*laughs*]! At least I didn't wear an outfit, but Alesha did. That's where I first met Alesha Lee. That's where I met Judy Jordan and Sonny West. He was a bodyguard then to Elvis. Sonny and Red West. Crazies.

I was trying to get in touch with Anthony Cardoza through his ex-wife, Joy Wilkerson, but he seemed reluctant to talk.

He married her?

They were married until the late 1970s.

You're kidding! Joy Wilkerson. That's amazing. Tony was nice. I used to take a lot of those films, and hopefully they were stepping stones to get to bigger places.

He's reluctant to talk to you? Probably because no one ever got a friggin' dime out of him! I did so many movies like that. I really did. I didn't get any money. I didn't get residuals for *Mako: The Jaws of Death*. We haven't even gotten to Grefé yet! Richard Jaeckel used to call me all the time and say, "Jenifer, if anybody can get some money, you can." I said, "Really? I've got news for you. Not a dime!"

Before we get to Grefé, you did one more film for Al, *Jessi's Girls* [1975].

I could have played any role I wanted in that. I could have had the lead if I'd have taken my clothes off. But that was Sondra Currie. I used to wait tables at Mickey Finn's with Sondra Currie.

Were there any more harrowing stunts in that one?

Well, I did all my own. I mean, it was more horses. I loved horses. There was a nice guy in that movie, I don't know whatever happened to him, Geoffrey Land. He and Al were friends for years, they played basketball together. I saw him years later in West Hollywood. I guess he was divorced from his wife.

He's another guy who worked for Al and then vanished.

Yeah, he was into something else. He was a Vegas card dealer. I don't know how he got to Al, but I mean, he was a dealer in Vegas.

He could have known him through Regina. She worked in Vegas.

I don't think so, though. I have a feeling he knew Geoffrey Land way before Gina. I didn't even know how he met Gina.

He met her at her father's coffee shop while he was getting ready to make *Satan's Sadists* [1969].

Oh, that's one I missed. That's a shame [*laughs*]! Well, remember at the time I first met Al, he had a girlfriend who was a singer, and he was managing her. I don't remember her name, but he was madly in love with her. But I think she dumped him.

We'd go a few years, and I never read for him after the first time, because he knew what I could do. Every once in a while I'd read about something he was doing and I'd call him up and say, "Al, I need some work." It was kind of like that.

How did you wind up working for Grefé?

Socrates Ballis [who appeared in Grefé's *The Hooked Generation*, 1968] was my fiancé, and he was going to do a movie. (He died, too, of an aneurysm.) He was the producer on that. He was my fiancé, and I had a writer named Tony Crechales who was writing a script for me [*Impulse*]. Isn't it interesting how this all fits together? I gave the script to Socrates, and Socrates gave it to Bill, and that's how that happened. Then he came out, asked me if I wanted to do another film with him, and that was *Mako: The Jaws of Death*.

I can't remember how I met Socrates. It might have been through Cardos. They're all Greeks, you know. When I was with Socrates, he was friendly with John Cassavetes, who ended up shooting a couple of movies—the one with Ben Gazzara [*Husbands*, 1970]—in my apartment at the time. That was Ben Gazzara and Peter Falk and that whole gang. Talk about resilient! His wife Gena Rowlands waited so long before she really got a chance to do what she did best, and she had to wait until he died. I think I met all of them through Phedon Papamichael.

He was the art director on *The Female Bunch*.

He made this beautiful black and white photo of me. His son's in the business. I saw his name on a poster not too long ago.

***Impulse* has quite a reputation, mostly because of Shatner's weird performance.**

Clarify what you're saying.

He threw himself into more than you'd expect on such a low-budget picture.

Do you remember that time? That timeframe?

He wasn't working much.

He wasn't working at all, but do you remember who he was married to? Marcy Lafferty, Perry Lafferty's daughter. Darling girl. Very nice. She was into health foods. It was an interesting combination.*

He and the little girl really stood out in that film.

Thanks! What happened to me?

---

*Impulse was filmed in 1972 as Want a Ride, Little Girl?, *then re-titled and re-released. In a later interview, Shatner said of this film: "I've forgotten why I was in it. I probably needed the money. It was a very bad time for me. I hope they burn it."*

Well, it's a given that you did a good job.

[*Laughs*] He *was* way over the top. The one that I fell madly in love with was Harold Sakata. We became very good friends. He took me dancing at the Roosevelt when he came out to California. We remained friends for a long time after that picture. Sweet man, dear man. Wonderful dancer.

I guess as a wrestler he probably would have been pretty graceful.

I don't know. He was just this big pussycat. You look at him and you think, "Oh my lord!"

Marcy Lafferty and Shatner were both in films that Bud Cardos directed.

I know, the one with the tarantulas [*Kingdom of the Spiders*, 1977]. I knew that because Bud called me about that one, but I couldn't handle the spiders. Grefé did another one with snakes [*Stanley*, 1972], but I didn't want anything to do with that, either. I did do another film for him, *The Godmothers* [1973] with Mickey Rooney, but I don't think that was released.

What do you remember about *Mako*, other than the lack of residuals?

It was *hot*. It was *sultry*. And I worked with one of the all-time pros ever. Richard Jaeckel was a doll. Just a wonderful guy to work with. Just a wonderful man. He and I were in the same motel. I'll tell you a funny story. One night I heard *thump, thump, thump, thump* against the wall. I thought, "Wow, he's really getting it on. I wonder who he found?" The next morning when he came out of the motel, we had an early call. I said, "Richard, you were very active last night. I'm surprised you're still up." He said, "What are you talking about?" I said, "I don't know. The walls are thin." He said, "Oh, I was doing my hand presses up against the wall!" *Thump, thump, thump.* I said, "I was picturing you having the best time of your life." He said, "I'm married to an Italian just like you, and I've been married to her for years. Do you think I would even go there?"

Ruth Roman was a kick in the head. Ruth thought that I looked like a young Ruth Roman. She took special interest in me. She taught me how to get close-ups, which Grefé did not care about. And she looked after my wardrobe. She was really quite like a mother hen to me. You remember her in *Champion* [1949]? That's when she said I looked like her. And she was gorgeous in *Champion*, so it was a nice compliment.

The other film that Tony Crechales wrote that you were in was *House of Terror* (1975).

I loved it. That was a good one. That was interesting. That was with Jacquelyn Hyde, who hated me, and Arell Blanton.

Irenee Byatt was in it, too.

Oh yes, she was a funny one. She played the wicked lady who ran the house. Then there was the guy from New York, I don't know where he came from, but he was a New York actor, nice-looking fellow.

Why did you like it so much?

It was very low-budget, but Sergei Goncharoff just took an interest in it, and he was just a different kind of a director than the others. When you do a lot of low-budget films, there's not a lot of attention paid to directing. It's mostly paid to how quickly they can get the job done, and how little money they can spend. I think he just took a little more caution. I also made some money on it!

Was *Mako* your last film credit?

Yeah, probably. Just stop me before the porno started, that's all I can say. You know that there's a porno star with my name—have you seen her listings? I didn't know this until a friend of mine ran Jenifer with one n, Jennifer with two n's. And why does she have my name? How is she allowed to do that?

I don't think they follow SAG rules in the porno industry....

Oh, is that what happened! I thought, "Oh my God!" when I heard the credits. I went to Al Adamson. I thought, "That bastard, if he did this...." [*laughs*], because he had a hundred different titles.

I went on the road for about seven years on stage. Off and on. That's when I was going through trying to get pregnant and the rest of the jazz, which worked out the way God wanted. You know, there's a master plan out there. I ended up adopting an absolutely wonderful boy. Had a girl first, but Mom changed her mind, so I got a boy because God said, "Hey, she's too strong, too vital, too crazy. Give her a boy!"

Do people ever recognize you from your films, and say, "Hey, aren't you the woman from *Blood of Dracula's Castle*?"

They do. I hear things like, "Last time I saw you, you were screaming your lungs out!"

So your son has no interest in these movies?

[*Laughs*] He bought me one of them when we were in Albertson's or something. He said "Mom, is that you?" It was *Blood of Dracula's Castle*. Al—twenty ways to skin a cat, and he knew all of them.

Kingdom of the Bikers

JOHN "BUD" CARDOS

There are plenty of low-budget filmmakers who are better known than John "Bud" Cardos, but few have been as prolific. It's not much of an exaggeration to say that, were you able to wander onto the set of any random exploitation film during the 1960s and 1970s, you had at least a fifty-fifty chance of bumping into this busy jack-of-all-trades.

Scan the credits of any number of 1960s films, and you'll find Cardos in the oddball western *Run Home Slow* (1965), the Bobby Darin-Sandra Dee film *If a Man Answers* (1962), and Arch Hall's *Deadwood '76* (1965). Look again, and he's popping up to punch Jack Nicholson in the face in *Hell's Angels on Wheels* and *Psych-Out* (1968), acting as a bumbling policeman in *Nightmare in Wax* (1969), then directing second unit for Sam Peckinpah on *The Wild Bunch* (1969), and production managing *The Incredible 2-Headed Transplant* (1971). In between, he wrangled birds for Alfred Hitchcock, scouted locations for Dick Clark, and chased Charles Manson off a movie set for Al Adamson.

Born in 1929 in St. Louis, Cardos moved to California with his family when he was four years old. He was born into the industry: His father and uncle managed Grauman's Egyptian and Chinese theaters, and he's related to the famous Skourases of 20th Century–Fox. From a young age, Cardos literally worked almost every job in the movie business, starting out as a child actor at Hal Roach Studios. He became a rodeo rider during his teen years, and eventually parlayed his riding skills into regular gigs on TV shows like *Sergeant Preston of the Yukon*, *Wagon Train*, and *Bonanza*.

After paying his dues behind the scenes, Cardos made his directorial debut with *The Red, White and Black* (a.k.a. *Soul Soldier*, 1970), a black-cast western starring Robert DoQui and Cesar Romero, followed by *Drag Racer* (1971) with Jeremy Slate.

After the well-received *Kingdom of the Spiders* (1977), Cardos made a series of horror and science fiction films, including *The Dark* (1979) and *Mutant* (1984) for Ed Montoro's Film Ventures International (FVI), and *The Day Time Ended* (1980) for Charles Band. He also continued working on other directors' productions, including Bob Clark's *Dead of Night* (1974) and Michael Winner's *Won Ton Ton, the Dog Who Saved Hollywood* (1976).

After a handful of African-lensed films in the late 1980s—*Skeleton Coast* (1987), *Act of Piracy* (1988) and *Outlaw of Gor* (1989)—Cardos moved back into production. He continues to work in television, commercials and film, and has recently begun appearing at fan conventions alongside frequent collaborators Robert Dix, Greydon Clark and Gary Kent.

Did you act during your teenage years?

JOHN CARDOS: Through your teen years in those days, there weren't that many parts in

John "Bud" Cardos directs Lincoln Kilpatrick in *Soul Soldier* (a.k.a. *The Red, White and Black*, 1970). (Photograph by Hedy Dietz/Courtesy Gary Kent)

motion pictures; not like today with so many kid parts in television. So I didn't do a whole bunch again until I started riding rodeos when I was sixteen or seventeen, right in there.

I lived up in Big Bear Lake. My dad bought a place in 1941, and I'd go up there for the summers and stay. I worked in the different stables up there, so I started working on Roy Rogers pictures and Gene Autry pictures, 'cause they made 'em all up there. They'd rent horses from us and I'd work as a wrangler.

In the 1950s, when the independent motion pictures started, if you could deliver lines and do small parts (and still do all your own stunts), then they eliminated a lot of the stuntmen. Up until then, I don't care if the guy was a bit part, they'd have to bring a stunt guy in to ride a horse for him, and bring a stunt guy in to make a little fall or something. In the independents they couldn't afford to do that. That was when a lot of westerns were being made on television. I started acting then, and I did, my God, all of the television shows: *The Monroes, Wagon Train, Maverick, Overland Trail, 26 Men, Judge Roy Bean, High Chapparal, Bonanza.*

I'd also do parts in the pictures at the same time. That's how I met Al [Adamson]. When Al started out, we were making them on a shoestring. I did a lot of behind-the-camera stuff, but I'd come in as a production manager, a stunt man, as an actor. You'd wear four or five hats at the same time!

Oh, another picture I did back [then] was *The Birds* [1963] for Alfred Hitchcock. At that time I was collecting a lot of the birds for the picture. I was working as a bird wrangler with one of the biggest men in town at the time, James Dannaldson. He did all the big monster stuff, the big lizards for *One Million B.C.* [1940] and all those kind of things. The signposts on the corner of the streets, those are usually hollow and those English Sparrows would nest in there. Every night I would go around with a sack, throw the sack over one end, poke it with a stick and they'd fly into that sack. I'd be doing this at three o'clock in the morning, when there was nobody around.

One night this police car followed me. I could see he was following me with his lights off, you know. So this guy got out and he said, "I don't know what you're doing. I haven't seen you break any laws yet, but would you mind telling me...." I explained to him what I was catching them for, and he laughed his ass off. I found out later that this cop was also a writer for *The Daily News,* so before long they had a big article in the news.

I remember we made *Blood of Dracula's Castle* [1969] for something like $60,000, and that had John Carradine, Alex D'Arcy, Paula Raymond — it had some good people in it. I was in all those pictures that Al made in one part or another. I did *Hell's Angels on Wheels* and a lot of those big motorcycle pictures, too, because I rode motorcycles and horses. It worked out pretty good in those days. Kept busy as hell all the time.

When did you first start doing stunts?

I started driving teams and runaway buckboards and stuff way back at Big Bear Lake in the late 1940s, before I went into the service.

Did someone train you?

I worked at a stable. Nobody trained me. I was a cowboy back in those days, too. I was working at a horse stable. They furnished all the horses and livestock for all the westerns. We had the buckboards and stuff, so I knew how to drive and harness those horses, because I was doing it for the hayrides. When you'd rent out the buckboard or something, the driver went with it.

I think *Sergeant Preston of the Yukon* was probably my first one. That really goes back a ways! I did a couple of jumps or falls off those snow cliffs. Here again, it was because of the livestock and horses. I did that, and figured I could do a lot of the other stuff. I got some contacts also in the late 1940s, because I belonged to a couple of those rodeo clubs up and down the river bend here, out in the Glendale area. They had a whole bunch of stables, and each one of the stables had their own little rodeo group, so we used to have contests about every other Sunday. Some of the stunt guys used to hang out down along the river bottoms there. They saw me and said I should be doing some of this stuff, too.

Then, to top it off, one of the most famous stuntmen back in those days actually didn't teach me things, but he told me a lot of things. That was Buster Wiles. Buster was one of the top ten back in the days of [Yakima] Canutt. He was Errol Flynn's double all his life. I met him when I was 18. He used to come in my dad's restaurant. He had a restaurant in the L.A. area. A lot of the movie people used to come in there.

What kind of restaurant was it?

It was called Cardos Club Café, and he specialized in prime ribs and stuff. It was a cafeteria during lunchtime, and then a regular restaurant in the evening and morning. He'd go through at least seven full prime ribs a day. People would line up down the street.

Did you sustain many injuries when you did stunt work?

I was very lucky. I didn't get any serious ones at all. Broken finger, something like that. I had broke my wrist one time, but that was after a full day of shooting. I fell off this horse about ten times at a dead run and spinning and all. I came home and was soaking in the tub, having a drink, and I stood up and fell and broke my wrist [*laughs*]! Of course I never told anybody back in those days. I said I did it out there while I was working. I wasn't going to tell them I fell in the bathtub!

I got burned a couple of times, singed the hair on the back of my head a couple of times, a few bruises. Nothing really serious. Now it's serious; back then it wasn't. Now I've had two shoulders replaced, and I've got a knee to be replaced pretty soon. I heal pretty quick. I was driving three days after I got out of the hospital, and riding my horses a week later. But you still have to take care of things. You can't just abuse yourself. I did that while I was young, which is why I'm replacing all these parts now.

What do you remember about *Blood of Dracula's Castle*?

I was doing production work at the time. I remember the office, it was a little dumpy office at Hollywood Stages. Who told me about Al, I don't remember. You always get something off of another picture, and somebody told me about it and I went over to see him. We sat down and talked and hit it off pretty good.

Tell me about the production.

Well, Carradine and D'Arcy were professional actors. We'd get everyone from Lon Chaney and Broderick Crawford, all of those Academy Award actors, over-the-hill guys. There's a castle out here in Lancaster, California. In those days I had an airplane — I still do — so I used to fly out every day and run the film back and forth. We shot a lot of the exteriors and part of the interiors out there. Then we came in town and shot on a sound stage where Al's office was then.

Al was a great guy. He let most of the people do what they wanted to do. He was a promoter. He could find the few bucks it took to make the picture. Almost everybody had a free hand to do what they wanted to do, as long as it played in the realm he was looking at. I can't say anything bad about Al; he was a dynamite guy, he really was.

Laszlo Kovacs was on *Blood of Dracula's Castle*, too.

Leslie and Willie! In those days, most of the time Willy Zsigmond was the D.P. and Leslie was gaffer. In fact, on that particular show that was the way it was. They did *Five Bloody Graves* also. Al really gave them a start, because they'd just come over from Hungary. Now they've gotten Academy Awards!

Al and Sam eventually lost control of *Blood of Dracula's Castle*.

That I don't know about. That's in their political end of it, which I never got involved in. Once I was through with the show and tied up all the ends, I was gone. I was either working somewhere else, or I was getting ready to do another show.

***Blood of Dracula's Castle* ran as a double-feature with *Nightmare in Wax*, which you also acted in.**

That was not an Al Adamson picture. I worked for the other guy quite a bit, too. Cohen, Marty Cohen. We did one with him called *Rebel Rousers* [1970], and one other one. With the Dick

Clark Company, I did *Psych-Out, The Savage Seven* and *Killers Three* [all 1968], and I did a television special with him called *The Werewolf of Woodstock* [1974]. In fact, I did the wolfman in that. You remember Tige Andrews? Well, he was supposed to be the guy that turned into the wolfman. Every time he turned into the wolfman, I was the wolfman. He wasn't physically capable of doing all the things, athletically and stuff. This wasn't just a wolfman that turned by the moon. It was different. That was done after my son was born. I can remember because my son was born in '68, so I can remember the pictures by whether they're before my son or after my son!

My son did his first picture with me, that girl picture that I did with Al. It's called *The Female Bunch* [1969]. On the one-sheets, that's me being drug by the horse, wrapped in barbed wire. I played that role in that one. That was with Jenifer Bishop, Russ Tamblyn, and Lon Chaney, Jr. Al and I directed that for Dalia Productions.

You acted and you were production manager on *Nightmare in Wax.*

Back then, you usually got hired for more than one job. I had a pretty good record back in those days helping small companies out. I had a pretty good reputation with bailing people out. It got to the point that SAG would call me sometimes when they had a picture that was in trouble. If they put me on, then they'd let their actors work.

How did you get involved with the two films we were just talking about?

Well, Al Adamson, I'd been working with him. Rex Carlton knew Al, and they worked together. That was it. They were going to make a picture and I always worked with Al, so I was on the picture.

What was Rex like?

Rex was a real quiet, nice guy. He was a decent writer, I guess. I don't know how else to explain him. He wasn't on the set every day or anything. He came and went. I think he was also probably one of the associate producers.

What about Martin Cohen?

Marty was fine. He was a pretty good guy. I don't remember a whole lot about the ones we did, but he was always there, he always paid his bills with us and everything. That was the important thing back in those days, was to make sure your paycheck cashed.

As production manager on these films, what were some of the things you had to do?

Promote as much as you can. If you needed some dressing for a set or something, you'd go out and promote the darn stuff, get it for free. You need a bus, you go out and get it for free. You need Coca-Colas, you get 'em for free. Anything you could put together for free was saving you money. I got pretty cocky after I'd done a few of 'em, and I'd go in and say, "If I don't save the money each week, then you don't have to pay me." But that was in my young days [*laughs*].

In *Nightmare in Wax*, you played a policeman with Scott Brady. Did you know him well?

Oh, he was another good friend of mine from way back. He, Jim Davis and I went back quite a ways. Scott was great. He was a superstar at one time, back in the ['40s and '50s]. He had some big starring role pictures. And here again we had Scott Brady and—

Cameron Mitchell.

Yeah, Cameron Mitchell. Hell, I was a friend of Cameron's up until the time he died just a few years ago. But he put on so much weight in his last few years I couldn't believe it. I did some pictures down in South Africa and met him down there, and I couldn't believe it was the same guy.

Scott and I and Jim Davis, we were all very good friends. I met Scott and Jim both in the 1960s. In fact, that was when Jim was on his downhill run before he hit *Dallas*. He was really hurting. When we went to do *Five Bloody Graves*, I said, "Hey, I know Jim a little bit. Why don't I go talk to him and Scott?" They both wanted to do it. After that I think we did *Nightmare in Wax*, then Jim did something else with Al. He did the pilot for *Dallas* before he did *The Day Time Ended*, because he talked about it a little bit. He said he didn't think it would go because it was a contemporary western, but it sure took off for him.

In most of the movies you worked on, you would usually act. Did you enjoy that?

I really did. *Nightmare* I did a lot more acting than in *Blood of Dracula's Castle*. In *Blood* I was just a guard and got hit over the head. In *Satan's Sadists* I was one of the co-stars. *Five Bloody Graves*, I played two roles in that. I did a lot of acting, not just for Al.

You and Scott were pretty funny in *Nightmare in Wax*.

Well, it was just my deadpan and whatever. Scott was the one; I was just like the second banana. He was the one who did all the reactions, and I didn't understand any of it, you know. We had fun doing it.

How long would it usually take to film these low-budget films?

Eight to ten days. Two weeks on a western, something like that. Not much longer than that. To tell you the truth, we did 'em in that length of time and still did 'em under what they're making them now. You go to work now for a TV show or something, and they walk in with a twelve-hour day, transportation walks in with fourteen hours. That's their daily hours. We didn't work that many hours! We didn't have all the toys they have to waste our time, either.

There was one title I wanted to ask about from the mid–1960s, but I don't think the film was ever made: *Devil Wolf of Shadow Mountain*.

Yeah, I remember that. I remember the script very well. It had a wolf on it. No, I don't believe it did get made. I don't even remember whose it was.

I think you, Gary Kent and Bob Dietz were trying to pull it together.

Oh, that's the one about the werewolf in the western.

Do you remember how you first met Gary Kent and Bob Dietz, and the rest of that crew?

Gary Kent and I probably go back to about the same time that Bob Dietz did. I was on a picture called *Run Home Slow* [1965] with Tim Sullivan [a.k.a. Ted Brenner], who was the producer-director on that.

How did that film come together?

Mercedes McCambridge was in that, too. Tim Sullivan — I don't know if he got me. I can't remember. He got a-hold of me through somebody else, and I just don't know how. He was talking to me about doing the hunchback in that picture, then some guy came up with money, and that's where the part went [*laughs*]! So I did a lesser part, and I did all the stunt work and gaffing, and I did work as the unit production manager on it. But how it actually started, I don't remember except Tim Sullivan called me. I went out to his place and he started putting it together. And on that picture is where I met Bob Dietz, and Hedy [Dietz], and I met Gary Kent on that picture, also.

In *Five Bloody Graves*, you had a dual role as Indian brothers.

I doubled Jim Davis in that, and I did all my own stunts, naturally. It was a fun movie to do. It was a good picture. Bob Dietz and Hedy, his wife, were on that, and you want to talk about cameramen — we had Laszlo Kovacs and Vilmos Zsigmond.

Were you able to recognize their talent while you were doing those low-budget films?

Hard to say back in those days. We went out and knocked out the pictures with a bunch of different cameramen. These were two guys that came over from Hungary or wherever, from behind the Iron Curtain. We just all worked together. Nobody knew who was going to take a leap and a bound, including when Jack Nicholson was working with us. You didn't stop to think about those things in those days. You didn't stop to say, "Well, this guy's really got talent," or something. We probably didn't know talent! I mean, seriously, you look at some of those pictures and they're horrifying! I look at some of the ones I did with Al and say, "Holy cow, I ought to buy all those copies up so nobody can see what I did!"

Cardos poses with good friend Jim Davis for Al Adamson's *Five Bloody Graves* (1970). (Photograph by Hedy Dietz/Courtesy Gary Kent)

What's funny is, you can see some flashes of really good work here and there. Even in *Blood of Dracula's Castle*, which is pretty stagy, there's a great scene where the camera is following Bob Dix down this creek in a pretty good hand-held shot.

We did quite a bit of hand-held that way. I can remember shoving Kovacs down Hollywood Boulevard in a shopping cart to make a dolly shot. We improvised in those days. We couldn't afford to rent those big items. And a crane shot? I remember one time we took a two-by-twelve and put it across a log, and built it up a little bit, and put the camera and him on one side, a bunch of us got on the other side and pushed down on it. We did all those things! Oh God, yes. You didn't have the money for all that fancy stuff.

I enjoyed doing the picture. I enjoyed working in Utah. There is some pretty good action in it. If you've seen it, you know the cabin burning down and all the horses running around. Hell, I built that cabin with two or three guys in one day. There's a story about that, too. I was riding that Appaloosa, as the Indian chief. That horse was really a dynamite horse, a powerful horse. I just had a war bridle on him, just a little rope around his lower jaw. I didn't have a bit in his mouth or anything. On that particular scene where we burned everything down, I had to lead my charge in there with all my Indians and run around the house. At first I came in there at a dead run, and that horse went right on through all the camera people and all the people that weren't being seen, and he jumped up in the grip truck. There I was up inside this grip truck on that damn horse [*laughs*]! He knocked over reflectors and everything. So, take two! Everybody scattered, and all I could think was, "Don't fall off this son of a bitch!" It was pretty hard to get me off a horse. I always said, if they had hair on 'em, I could ride 'em. But that wasn't always true [*laughs*]. You just think you can. There's an old cowboy saying: "Never a cowboy couldn't be throwed, never a horse couldn't be rode." It works both ways.

What do you remember about *Satan's Sadists* [1969]?

Well, let's see, that was Kent Taylor. I remember it was way out in the middle of the desert, up on some pass, out of Palm Springs. It was really a pretty nice area to work in. Here again it was Russ Tamblyn and Gary Graver, who worked with Al a lot. In fact, he went out and did a couple of cheapies himself. It was a fun little picture to make, one of those motorcycle things. I played the half-breed with the Mohawk haircut. I always went for these weird things! You know, with all of Al's pictures, none of them were easy. We all went out there and busted our asses and ate baloney sandwiches sometimes. It wasn't like today. I mean, if we wanted the camera up on the top of a hill, we had to drag it up there. We didn't have all the equipment and all the putt-putts they do now. I go on these shows nowadays and I just shake my head. They get cranes out there at the drop of a hat; they get big lights.

Kent Taylor was great to work with, and having worked with Russ before — we did three pictures, I think, with Russ. We did *The Female Bunch*, we did *Satan's Sadists*, and I think we did one more.

***Dracula vs. Frankenstein* (1971).**

Yeah, there we go. Okay. It's hard to say what went on, because I can't remember all the funny things that happened that you would have remembered at the time. It's been a while since I even discussed these things.

Al Adamson told me that he shot *The Female Bunch* in Utah. Did you shoot some scenes at Spahn Ranch?

Actually, on that particular picture Al was hired as a director, Raphael Nussbaum was a producer. We did shoot most of it in Utah, but we went back to Spahn Ranch after we shot in Utah to do some pick-up shots we missed. In fact, I knew George Spahn, having worked with him at that ranch every once in a while, even when we were doing some of the early TV stuff. Also at a place called Corriganville, that was just over the hill from George's ranch. It was a funny thing because when I first went to the ranch to talk to George about shooting there, the Charles Manson gang *was* there, but I didn't know who the hell they were. It was just a bunch of these young girls running around, and heck, in those days I was chasing every skirt anyhow! I thought, "Hey, this is gonna be pretty nice working here!" But I kind of thought to myself a couple of times, "There's old George in his house there, and all these young girls." It just wasn't like old George, you know? And he was almost blind, anyhow.

We went there and scouted the location. I talked to the old gal that was the wrangler there, tough old broad. She was the one who ran the place because he was blind. I remember going there and seeing all these kids there. So I said, "I'll go see old George." I knocked on the door, and some of these teenage girls let me in, and George was there with a half-dozen girls all around him. It was hard to even talk to him. I could tell he didn't want to talk too much. They just kind of followed him all the time. I got him outside and went on a little walk. He didn't tell me anything bad about anything. I said, "George, what are you doing with all these young girls?" He said, "What the hell! I'm an old man, I need some help." But he did not say anything, because I think he was scared, you know.

We had a dune buggy, and we knocked off the mufflers. I took it down and talked to Charles Manson, and he put the mufflers back on. Then later on, the next day or so, I ran him off the set because he was making too much noise. I met him up close!

What went through your mind when you heard about the murders?

We thought we were lucky. One of the guys that was with him and disappeared, his name was Tex and he was a cowboy. I did a picture very shortly after that one, my first. It was called *The Red, White, and Black*, down in Texas, and I took Tex with me as a wrangler. And I didn't know he was running! He was down there with me for a month or so, and then he just disappeared after he left me. [Author's note: This may have been Spahn ranch hand Juan Flynn, who went into hiding prior to testifying at the Manson trial.]

How did you get involved in *The Incredible 2-Headed Transplant*?

Yeah, Bruce Dern. John Bloom. The little guy that played the other head [Al Cole] is a chiropractor! He got out of the business a long time ago. John Bloom passed away. I used him a couple of times after that. I used him on *The Dark*.

How did they get Al Cole up there on John Bloom's back? Some of the shots came off pretty well.

Actually, his head was just resting on top of his shoulder. You got the closeups all right, but when they start to move we had a phony head that sat on John's shoulder. I thought it looked really realistic. When we needed Al to be up there talking, it was always standing still or sitting still.

The producer was John Lawrence.

There we go. AIP, John Lawrence. How I got involved in that? I don't know. They called me to probably do the UPM [unit production manager] work. I was pretty well known throughout all the independent motion pictures. I went from one to another. Sometimes I was gone away from home. I'd only be home a month or two out of the year. It was just word-of-mouth stuff. So it's very difficult to think on a picture like that. I knew Anthony [Lanza] as an editor.

Were you able to make a good living working on independent productions?

As much as they paid in those days. I was making more money; if I was getting $250 a week, the normal wage was about fifty bucks. I usually got at least $250 a week, as I remember. About '63 I joined SAG. In fact, when we were doing *Five Bloody Graves*, Phil Dizen, who at that time was one of the agents, they traveled all the way up to Utah. That was when I joined. I've been in ever since. SAG was something like three and a quarter a week or something.

How did you first get involved with Dick Clark?

The first picture I met Dick on was *The Flower Children* [*Psych-Out*]. He was one of the producers on that. I just met him on that. Then we finished that and went to *The Savage Seven*. Now I had a lot of background as a UPM and doing stunts, and Dick didn't know a whole bunch about me. He and I were sitting at the bar one time in Searchlight, Nevada, where we shot *Savage Seven*. We were all sitting at the bar and just talking. *Daniel Boone* or something came on TV, and there I was in a co-star role. He said, "I didn't know you did all that stuff."

I told him, "Can I talk to you flat out?" He said, "Sure." I said, "You're getting fucked!" That's what I told him [*laughs*]. I told him this stuff can be done cheaper this way and that way. You don't have to have all this kind of crap. You can make this picture for AIP and make it work. Dick had a three-picture deal with them. The third was *Killers Three*.

When we got through with that film, a week didn't go by before he called me into his office. He said, "I've got a picture we're gonna do called *Killers Three*. I want you to go down to the Carolinas and find me the location. AIP just did *Three in the Attic* [1968] in Chapel Hill, so the UPM on that show suggested that's where you'd go."

I had my own plane at the time. I flew there with my assistant, and I called my other buddy from South Carolina. I went to Chapel Hill, I called Dick and said, 'This town won't work for you." He said, "Well, find me something."

So we went on the road. We picked up a couple of the people that had worked on *Three in the Attic*, and they must have thought I was completely nuts. We didn't stop for nothing. If you wanted to eat, grab a can of sardines and some crackers 'cause we're on the road, baby! We're here to do a job, not to sit around! We finally found a little town called Ramseur, North Carolina. One street, they had an old supermarket from the 1940s, which was just perfect, and it was empty. It had all the other features that we needed.

So I went to the bank, and here I was kind of grungy, no shave for three or four days, my sunglasses hanging in my pocket. I went in the bank after I talked to Dick, and I said, "I'm here for Dick Clark Productions, and I want to open a bank account. I only have a little bit of petty cash. I'll open it for fifty bucks and have him send you some money." He said, "*Sure* you will." They wouldn't open the account for fifty, so I said, "I'll have Dick wire you a few bucks tomorrow." And the next morning, they wired me $50,000 cash to that bank. And the banker was a pilot, he had a nice piece of ground, a little grass airstrip. Long story short, we became very good friends. And we laughed about that. He said, "You looked like you were gonna hold up my bank! I had the guard standing by. You didn't have a shower for three days, and you come in here saying you want to open an account for fifty dollars?"

That started the ball rolling. Now that was an all-union show, and I was not in the union as a UPM or second unit director. I was just SAG. I was doing all this stuff under the table. I bought the entire town, every store in the town signed a paper, and I got it signed by the mayor, and I paid $200 [*laughs*]! When all the IA people came and all the union people came,

I showed 'em I had everything, the permits, blah, blah, blah. Dick just laughed at all these union people, because he didn't care much for them anyhow.

I'll tell you one thing, a lot of people say Dick is a hard guy, but he's a beautiful man. I still see him quite a bit. I was with him a couple of weeks ago. I came on Memorial Day weekend on *Killers Three*. Dick had me doing certain things, and the UPM always had me doing things. Elliot Siegel was his name. We were having lunch one day, and Elliot said, "Bud, after you get done eating I'd like you to do something." And Dick said, "Well, I've already got something for him to do, so can you get somebody else?" I didn't know what Dick had in mind. I had my plane there, and sometimes I had to fly some papers down to one of his TV stations or something. I did all kinds of stuff.

After lunch he said, "I want you to hop in your plane and go up to Greensboro." He put his American Express gold card in my hand. He said, "This is Memorial weekend. I don't want to see you for four days. You've got a reservation on Continental. Hop in your plane, get up there, and I'll see you in four days." He gave me his gold card, and a first-class ticket to go back and see my wife and kids. He said, "If I don't see you've spent some money, I'm gonna kick you in the ass. Take your family out, take your wife out, do whatever you want to do." So that's Dick to me. I could tell you a hundred tales like that.

The other film you did in the Carolinas was *The Road Hustlers* [1968]. What was it like working in the South in that period?

It was great. Especially on that one, I don't know where Larry [Jackson] got all the pull, but

From left: An unidentified actor, Cardos and Bill McKinney prepare to chase down some moonshiners in *The Road Hustlers* (1968).

we had a big ranch house right on a lake for most of us, and then we had a hotel downtown for a lot of them. Andy [Devine] wanted to stay at the ranch, Jim [Davis] wanted to stay at the ranch. They all wanted to stay at the ranch! You'd get up in the morning and have all kinds of good breakfast, and the people in town had to go to a restaurant. Weekends and stuff we had boats, water skiing, all kinds of stuff going on. It was really great. Then we had the private lake to work on when Bob Dix had the boat, and the dynamite was going off. I wrecked seven cars on that.

The director, Larry Jackson, got blown up in the boat sequence.

That's right, and the script supervisor. That's because they *weren't paying attention*. See, it took me eight hours to rig dynamite underneath all the water. I was doing that myself and setting off my own explosions. I was being towed behind on water skis and those explosions had to go off at the right time to blow up the back of my skis. They went out there — I wasn't even with them — and ran right over the top of one. Blew the boat in half.

Do you remember *Las Vegas Strangler* [1968]?

Oh my God, how far back are you going with me? That was Bob Dix and me. Holy cow. Oliver Drake was the director. The producer was Runaway Gannaway, Al Gannaway. I was the UPM on the damn thing and did a part, also. I used to have to go beat on Al's door to get a few hundred dollars to do anything. It was like going into a speakeasy to try to get money. Oh, it was terrible! "Al, they're taking our cameras! I've got to have some money!" It was like that all through the whole damn show [*laughs*].

In the late 1960s, you did second unit on *The Wild Bunch*. How did you get that assignment?

You know, I don't know. Well, it was probably Bo Hopkins. That was one of his first pictures. I don't remember. Bo and Sam Peckinpah are pretty good buddies.

It was just like *Won Ton Ton*. That was Michael Winner. Now, I knew nothing about Michael Winner, but the dog handler knew me very well, and they needed second-unit directing with all these dogs and stuff. So that's how I got in on that one. That's the way I got in on a lot of the stuff, because I knew the action or special effects people or whatever.

On the Peckinpah film, what did you shoot?

I shot some of the stuff in the big battle at the end, where a lot of the machine guns were going off. I shot some of the stuff, after they left the town, and there were a few scenes he wanted shot of the guys shooting and falling off the building. I did a few of those kinds of things. I was not on it very long. Maybe a week.

How did you meet Igo Kantor?

I did a picture called *The Red, White and Black*. I had post-production at another place, and there was a whole story how I got the picture in the first place, but the head editor was dragging his feet all the time. Finally, I just got upset and packed up everything. I knew about Synchrofilm, so I just went down there and took all my stuff down there, and set up to have the rest of the post done there. The next thing I know he had me working as a UPM on a picture called *Jud* [1971]. I designed and did all the big car chases, which got a write-up that said it was just as good, or a low-budget version of *Bullitt* [1968]. I got a lot of good publicity off that one for the car chases.

Tell me about making that first film, *The Red, White and Black*.

Well, I was getting to be known pretty good as a production manager that could bail out a picture. In those days, if a picture folded, the Screen Actors Guild didn't get their money.

Phil Dizen called me and said, "Bud, I've got a picture here, and they shot this and that and they owe me money." He was trying to help them because the producer knew nothing about motion pictures. A couple of writers wrote something, and got this attorney to put up a lot of money. So the attorney was in already about $300,000, and Phil was trying to help out so he could keep his actors working. He introduced me to the guy, his name was Stuart Hirschman, and here again he's been a close friend of mine ever since then. So they flew me back to Kansas, that's where his offices were, and I spent three full days looking at footage, all shot in 16mm, and all shitty. I mean, it was a shame. The western wardrobe, I don't know where they got it. They had zippers, the girls were wearing tights with capris, shit that was just unreal. So bad! So I told him, "You haven't got anything here that you can even use." And he said, "Oh my God, I've got $300,000 in this!"

I took the script to the writers and told them what I thought. They re-wrote some stuff, and I took it and made a budget on it. It was about $750,000. I told him that we'd just start over. We had Cesar Romero and Barbara Hale in it, and it did quite well except that he gave it to the wrong guy to distribute! [The film was distributed by Joe Solomon's FanFare Films.] He was supposed to have a big premiere on Hollywood Boulevard and everything. Isabel Sanford was in it, Lincoln Kilpatrick was in it, Robert DoQui. Anyhow, he opened it here and had a fight with the distributor. To make a long story short, the distributor put it out in Canada and overseas, and never gave the guy a nickel! He finally got bailed out and everything, but he had to go through a lot of lawsuits.

Do you know what ever happened to *The Drag Racer*?

I have a copy, but I don't have any idea. Robert Glenn was the producer, and everything just went to him. I don't know what happened to it. It had a pretty good cast, and it was a story about drag racing. It went out and made a few bucks here and there. You know the picture *The Sons of Katie Elder* [1965]? The guy that plays the deputy sheriff? He was in it, also, Mark Slade. And Jeremy Slate and Deborah Walley. Those were the three main characters. That had to be in the mid-seventies, because *Soul Soldiers* was in '70 or '71. Then I did *Kingdom of the Spiders* [1977]. That was a picture we shot down in Sedona, Arizona. Beautiful country. We had William Shatner, Woody Strode, Sammy Davis's wife, Altovise Davis. Good actors. We used something like 5,000 spiders in the picture.

I saw another credit for you for a film called *Billy Black*, which might not have been filmed. Frank Saletri was the producer.

Do you know who Frank Saletri was? He was an attorney. That's all he was. He wanted to make pictures. Frank was an attorney for a lot of us years and years ago. He bought Bela Lugosi's house up there in the Hollywood Hills, and Bela Lugosi's house was just like Bela Lugosi in real life [*laughs*]. He had a spiral staircase going to the lower part of the house, with this giant fireplace and all these gargoyles around it. I mean, a crazy house. But no, I didn't work on the picture [*laughs*].

How did you like working with the tarantulas on *Kingdom of the Spiders*?

I enjoyed it. I did some action work in that picture, where the plane crashes into the building, and I got a lot of comments on that. I also got a lot of comments on the scene where the water tower fell on top of the sheriff's car at the end of the picture. In fact, Dick Clark had a TV show called *Live Wednesday*. He would bring people out and have them re-enact certain things that were outstanding in several movies or something. So he had me come and I rebuilt the entire tower there at NBC.

The spiders didn't bother me because I was around that kind of stuff all the time anyhow. The way we were casting was funny. Juliet Mills came in and wanted to do that role, see. And also Bo Svenson. Bill Shatner had just kind of fallen out. It was before he came back and did a lot of big stuff again. So I had two spiders in this little aquarium on my desk, big large tarantulas. When they'd come in and we'd start talking and stuff, I'd take one out and just hand it to 'em! Not too many of 'em grabbed it. Tiffany Bolling was fantastic. She wasn't afraid of 'em at all. She'd pick 'em up and play with them.

What's funny with Bill Shatner, I'd done a picture with him called *A Whale of a Tale* [1977] before that. I was the production manager, did a lot of stunt work, underwater second-unit directing. He turned down this *Kingdom of the Spiders* script. I talked to the producer, and I said I'd go over to Bill's house and talk to him. So I went over there and we sat down. I was drinking some wine and eating some cheese, and I went through the stuff I had in my head about how I wanted to direct it. He called them and said he'd do the picture.

We had a lot of spooky people in the town [*laughs*]. They've probably still got some Mexican tarantulas running around in that area somewhere. In that plane sequence, where the spiders are crawling over the pilot while he's in the air, we had about 200 spiders working around that airplane. They had to take all the paneling off the outside. There were spiders all the way back down the fuselage and everywhere! We were always losing spiders. They were all over the place.

Cardos as Firewater in the Al Adamson film *Satan's Sadists* (1969). (Courtesy Independent-International Pictures Corp.)

Then you did *The Day Time Ended.*

With Charles Band, Jim Davis, Chris Mitchum. And here again I had Bill Shatner's wife in that. That was a fiasco in itself, because Charles Band in those days was almost even worse than Al Adamson when it came to bucks. We went out to Lancaster and picked a location, and they built a house out there. One of the problems was—and I couldn't get it over to him—he had his guys doing everything. The trouble was, they weren't prop-makers. They built this barn like it was gonna stay there for a hundred years. Instead of using false fronts, they would actually use timber and two-by-twelves and everything. It was just unreal, and really cost me a lot of time.

I remember going out there and nothing was ready. I had the whole crew and everybody coming out. So we just had to shoot some of the desert traveling shots. That wasn't one of my happier pictures. In one scene they're in the vortex itself, and

Jim Davis is supposedly walking through this graveyard of all this stuff. I had spent a lot of time locating different things like hulls of ships. I had the Condor Squadron that was gonna fly in out there and have all these World War II airplanes out there. I had really built it up so it would be something dynamic, and the only thing I got was that one shell of a plane. The Condor Squadron actually flew out there and landed on this dry lake. I was getting ready to put them in position and they said they were supposed to get a check. The guys never showed up with the money, so they flew away. It was just things like that that were a constant threat to the picture every time. So anyhow, that was *The Day Time Ended*. It was called *Vortex* at the beginning.

You did two films for VCI, Ed Montoro's company, *The Dark* and *Mutant*. On both of those you started out as a production manager, and then took over as director.

The Dark was supposed to be directed by Tobe Hooper. Tobe was not in the Guild at the time, so I even signed to get him in the Guild. But if you notice it's co-produced with Dick Clark. Dick wanted me to direct it. Ed Montoro wanted to use Tobe Hooper because of *Texas Chain Saw Massacre* [1974]. *Chain Saw Massacre* took Tobe two years to make. He went out and shot on weekends. That's good, that's fine. But anyhow, he got his first feature, and he didn't know what to do. It buried him. In three days he was a week behind.

Dick said, "Well, if Bud isn't going to direct it, he'll be there as our line producer." Ed said fine, because Ed knew my work. He just thought that Tobe Hooper would be a good director for that. Dick came to me and Ed and asked, "Can you take this over for us?" I was pretty prepared because I knew the script. I didn't get the prep I wanted, but I knew everything that was happening. But as the director, I like to pick a lot of my own locations.

Good cast in it: Cathy Lee Crosby, Richard Jaeckel, Keenan Wynn, William Devane. We did that right here in town. It was a thriller picture. It wasn't anything spectacular. Originally the way it was, this guy was not some monster from outer space. He was a kid that grew up with a family and he was insane, but not a violent insane. He was just big, and they kept him locked up in a room.

Did you know Ed Montoro very well?

Yes. I went out with he and his wife to dinner, with Igo and everything.

He eventually disappeared.

Yep. Took the money and went to Mexico. Might still be there. It was his money; he didn't steal it from anybody!

As I understand, *Mutant* had a fairly substantial budget for a VCI film at that time.

I don't know what the budget was, because there again I took it over in about three or four days. But that was a harder one for me to take over because the kid that started it had never done a picture before, and I was married to some locations that really sucked, as far as I was concerned. You go in and see the inside of a veterinarian office, it's about six or eight feet. You can't shoot there because you don't have room to put your camera equipment in there.

Here again, Igo put me on that thing to make sure that I was there in case something happened. And sure enough, after about three days Ed Montoro came with his hat in his hand and said, "Bud, I've got to ask you again to take this over." I said, "Ed, I've got at least three days to really run around and do my homework to see what I want to do." I didn't have enough prep time. I really had to change my head around and look at locations. When I direct a picture, I usually take five or six weeks, and I make schematics of every scene I shoot, where the camera is, what it's gonna do, basic lenses and the whole thing. When I don't have all this, it's really tough to just go out and shoot it off the cuff.

You worked a lot in Canada and Africa during the 1970s and 1980s.

I did a lot of second-unit stuff over the years. I did five pictures in Canada. I did *Breaking Point* [1976]. Bob Clark directed it. Also, I did a picture called *Find the Lady* [1976] up there with Mickey Rooney. *It Seemed Like a Good Idea at the Time* [1975] was a John Candy picture. *Find the Lady* was almost a sequel to it. John Candy played a dumb cop in the first one, and they liked it so much they made him a major character in *Find the Lady*. Then I did a thing called *A Day in the Country* with Ernest Borgnine, and the title may have been changed to *A Sunday in the Country* [*Vengeance Is Mine*, 1976]. He was a farmer and these three outlaws come to his place. One of them was Michael J. Pollard. Then I did a picture with New World called *Angels of Mercy* [1974, a.k.a. *Candy Stripe Nurses*]. That's a Corman picture.

I got sent to South Africa for Cannon and did a picture called *Outlaw of Gor*, with Jack Palance. He was really the only one in there. They had a couple of Playboy Bunnies, Rebecca Ferrati. Then I went right back for Cannon and did another picture called *Coast of Skeletons* [a.k.a. *Skeleton Coast*]. The Coast of Skeletons is on the west side of Africa. I had a good cast on that one. That picture I liked very well, but they wouldn't give me the right post-production on it, and I think they had a lot of bad cuts. That little picture there could have been a good picture except for the editing. I got a copy of it and it just made me sick the first time I saw it.

Then I went back down and did a picture called *Act of Piracy* with Gary Busey for Warner Brothers. It was Gary Busey, Belinda Bauer, Ray Sharkey. It was Ray's last picture. That came out to be a pretty nice picture. I made a lot of residuals on that one.

Then a couple of years ago I did *Legends of the West* [1992], and I got nominated for outstanding western TV pilot, 1992, and got entered into the National Cowboy Hall of Fame for it. That was Jack Palance in the first one, and then Jack Palance and Brooke Shields. I did two episodes on that.

What do you think low-budget filmmakers have to do today to keep making films?

You realize how many pictures are being made in this town every day? I'm talking about under a million dollars. I could name a half-dozen different companies. Ninety percent of this stuff goes to tape, so the independent motion picture guy, anything he makes he can sell. Roger Corman's knocking out twenty some pictures a year. Friend of mine's a driver coordinator for him. God, he's got so many lined up you can't believe. And that's his subsidiary company that just makes these shitty little cheap pictures. They get anybody to make 'em. They get a director that's just went to college or something. They don't pay any money. His drivers get like a hundred dollars a day for eighteen hours or something. You can go anywhere in this town and see five or six movies being made at one time, all independents.

When we made a picture, even back to the Al Adamson days, when we got through shooting, we were through. If we went back for any pick-up shots, it might have been a couple of inserts or something like that. These people think nothing of busting their asses fourteen hours a day, six days a week. They get out there and do all this work, and then a month later they'll shoot a week or two on pick-up shots. That ain't pick-up shots when you go out for two weeks! Every single one of my features that I've done, I've done twelve total, I've always come in on time and on budget.

What do you think about the movies you and Al made being rediscovered as cult films?

Anybody that's a movie buff has got to go back. I think that a lot of the new guys coming out of these schools should know about a lot of this stuff. Have you ever read a book called *The African Queen*? It's a small book written by Katharine Hepburn. This book tells it like it is, with the big stars out there dragging the *Queen* out of the mud, the big stars hanging their wardrobe off of a tree and changing. You work on these little pictures now and everybody becomes a star. You've got to have a room for this, a room for that. When me and Al were doing those pictures, hell, even Jim Davis and everyone was running around out there in their underwear trying to get their clothes on! And Jim was a pretty big actor back then. So was Scott.

They [today's indie moviemakers] are trying to be like the majors, and they'll say, "We gotta do this cheap, cheap, cheap," and see how much money they waste by ordering cranes every day, or getting lights that cost $1,000 a night. It's unreal. People like Leslie and Willie, they know how to light. We don't need all that shit to light something, you know? They get too many new toys.

Wild Wheels

ROBERT DIX

During his two decades in front of the camera, actor Robert Dix saw the best and worst of Hollywood in a long — and occasionally strange — journey that led him from rubbing elbows with Glenn Ford and Doris Day at MGM, to almost getting arrested (dressed as a Nazi biker, no less) while working for exploitation director Al Adamson.

Exploitation fans are familiar with Dix through his roles in films like *Satan's Sadists* (1969) and *Horror of the Blood Monsters* (1970), but he has an A-list acting pedigree. His father, Richard Dix (nee Ernest Brimmer), was one of the few leading actors who successfully made the transition from silents to talkies, appearing in such popular films as the Oscar-winning *Cimarron* (1931) and *The Whistler* series in the 1940s.

Born in 1935, Robert Dix had a front-row seat for Hollywood's golden age. The younger Dix's entry into the entertainment business was far from easy, though. His father died young (age 56) in 1949, followed by his twin brother Richard in a logging accident in 1953. At odds with his mother's second husband (Walter Van de Kamp), teenage Robert struck out on his own, eventually joining a theater group in upstate New York.

But Hollywood beckoned. In the early 1950s, Dix was put under contract at MGM, where he appeared in a succession of comedies and musicals before landing a plum supporting role in the sci-fi classic *Forbidden Planet* (1956).

With the end of the contract system, Dix's career took a number of twists and turns. He found parts in everything from westerns like Sam Fuller's *Forty Guns* (1957) to Richard Cunha's schlocky *Frankenstein's Daughter* (1958), then appeared almost exclusively in exploitation films.

Working both in front of and behind the camera, Dix appeared in a number of horror movies, biker films and violent westerns, working with Adamson, Arch Hall, Larry Jackson, actor Scott Brady, and longtime friend John "Bud" Cardos.

Although he had his father's leading-man looks (the resemblance is especially eerie in Hall's *Deadwood '76*, 1965), Dix was cast in a succession of oddball character parts — a homicidal maniac in *Las Vegas Strangler* (1968), a vicious biker in *Hell's Bloody Devils* (1970), an Indian warrior in *The Red, White and Black* (1970), and even a Mexican fisherman in *The Rebel Rousers* (1970). He also worked steadily on TV westerns like *Gunsmoke* and *Rawhide*.

Dix's last screen appearance was a bit part in *Live and Let Die* (1973), a role that came to him through Roger Moore, a friend from his MGM days. Since then, Dix's résumé has grown even more eclectic — he managed an office building for his family at one point, and even hosted a religious-themed public access program in Milwaukee.

Was *Forbidden Planet* your largest role at MGM?

ROBERT DIX: At the time it was the largest. In those days, under the studio system, contract players were put into one- or two-liners, and you worked your way up to supporting roles, then finally feature roles and so forth. At that point in my young career, it was the most exposure I'd had, yes.

Do you remember much about the director, Fred Wilcox?

Yes, I remember Mr. Wilcox. As a matter of fact, one of the reasons I remember him is that he suddenly didn't show up for work for about two or three days in a row. Somebody else stepped in and took over the directing of the movie. To my knowledge, he didn't return, although he got full screen credit as director.

What was your impression of Robby the Robot?

The guy that was inside the robot, Frankie Darro, was a rather small man, so he could sit inside Robby the Robot. I think he was a jockey at one time. Anyway, he was inside that thing and I remember the poor guy was just sweating like a stuck pig, because it was hot in there. He was moving the arms and legs and all that stuff. Robby the Robot wound up being the big star out of that movie.

It had a great ensemble cast, nonetheless.

Jim Drury, who later became The Virginian, he and I were pretty tight friends for a long time, then we got separated in the ways of Hollywood. But there were a lot of people on that who went on to do some real nice things and had extensive careers. Earl Holliman, the cook, went on to do *Police Woman* with Angie Dickinson. Jack Kelly, he ended up over at Warner Brothers working on *Maverick*. And, of course, Leslie Nielsen—I saw him not too long ago. He was grand marshal of the Great Circus Parade in Milwaukee. I was back there visiting my son, and here comes Leslie walking toward me. I said, "Hi, commander, how are you?" It stopped him in his tracks! I hadn't seen him in 50 years, but we remembered each other and had a nice visit. He's a funny guy.

What year did your contract end with MGM?

That was from 1954 to 1956 that I was under contract to MGM. At that time, Dore Schary was head of the studio, and he just eliminated the whole contract actor idea, which I personally thought was most helpful to the young actors, because you had a little job security, and you were learning your craft. I think the other studios did it about the same time, too. So I was then a freelance actor finding out that life is either chicken or feathers!

Around that time you did the Sam Fuller film, *Forty Guns*.

That's correct. As a matter of fact, Sam was the one that helped me break the rumors around Hollywood that I was still under contract to MGM. I was having trouble getting interviews, because everyone just assumed I was still with MGM studios. So it was that role, Chico in *Forty Guns*, that got me out there in the community and active as an actor again.

Both Sam Fuller and Barbara Stanwyck had very strong personalities. How did they get along on the set?

Well, they got along famously. Missy (Barbara's nickname; she insisted everybody called her that) was such a trooper. I was a fan of her work anyway as a young actor, and I was very

Robert Dix and Dovie Beams in Ken Osborne's *Wild Wheels* (1969). Beams would later gain notoriety as the mistress of Philippine dictator Ferdinand Marcos.

Dix (fourth from left) prepares to be reprimanded by Warren Stevens (at left) and Leslie Nielsen (first from left) in *Forbidden Planet* (1956).

impressed with her professionalism. Sam and Missy got along just fine. They were friendly, and she was most cooperative. She did a lot of her own stunts. She was quite a horsewoman, you know. It was a fun shoot. We did most of it on the back lot of 20th Century–Fox

Barry Sullivan and Gene Barry were both co-stars in it. Originally the story, as written by Sam Fuller, was about Wyatt Earp and his two brothers, but the TV series [*The Life and Legend of Wyatt Earp*] with Hugh O'Brian was coming out about that time, and there was some kind of glitch with the legal department at 20th Century–Fox, so they changed the characters' names from Earp to Bonnell, a fictitious name that Sam Fuller came up with.

There's a scene where my older brother, Barry Sullivan, is such a deadly shot that when Johnny Ericson uses Barbara Stanwyck as a body shield in a gunfight on the main street of the western town, Sullivan shoots Barbara in a non-lethal place. She drops, and then he proceeds to shoot Johnny in one arm, then the next, then a knee and another knee, and then finishes him off as he walks by. He tells me, "Chico, get her to the doctor, she'll be all right." Well, I go out to pick her up, and unbeknownst to me I was standing on her skirt! I go to pick her up, and it was one of my best belly flops, but I managed to get her laid back down on the ground before I crashed.

During that period when you were doing a lot of work for Fox, you also wound up in *Frankenstein's Daughter*.

I don't remember how I heard about that interview. I never really had a very active agent [*laughs*]. I got most of my jobs myself, and I don't remember who told me that this movie was casting, but I went and interviewed, and got the part of the detective in it. I know that the character I played was Mr. Dillon, and with *Gunsmoke* being so popular at the time, everyone was running around yelling "*Mister Deeeelllon*" on the set. But that's one of those movies I did to help pay the mortgage.

You did another Western, *Young Jesse James* [1960], during that time as well.

I played Frank James, and I've lost track as to what's happened with that movie. It was in black and white and, except for the stuff they show on Turner Classic Movies, most stuff on TV is in color now. But I remember playing the role because I researched the whole James family, and at the time discovered that every living member of the James family worked for a bank! I guess if you can't beat 'em, join 'em.

I enjoyed playing Frank James in that role. That was related to the *Forty Guns* breakthrough, because I began doing quite a few things for 20th, and its subsidiaries Regal Films and Associated Producers Inc., both of which Bob Lippert headed up.

Later in the 1960s, you did *Deadwood '76*, where you were first credited with a number of people you worked with quite a bit later — John "Bud" Cardos, soundman Bob Dietz and cameraman Vilmos Zsigmond.

We were kind of like an extended family that worked in the independent field. The best memory I have of *Deadwood '76* was playing Wild Bill Hickok. I was able to go to Western Costume Company in Hollywood and get the same outfit my dad wore when he played Wild Bill in a movie called *Badlands of Dakota* [1941]. The same coat and vest, everything except the pants. My legs were a little longer, but everything else fit okay. It was a fun thing to do — not a great movie by any stretch of the imagination, but it was a fun role to play because of the family history involved there.

Liz Renay was also in that, and relatively fresh out of prison at the time.

Yes. Last year I was at a horror film gathering at the Roosevelt Hotel in Hollywood, and Liz was there. Bud Cardos and I went to say hello to the folks, and there was Liz sitting there like she was still an ingénue, you know. What can I say? She was a very attractive lady who had trouble reading a line.

One of the other early movies you did with Bud Cardos and the others was Al Adamson's *Blood of Dracula's Castle* [1969]. In that film you worked with John Carradine who had, coincidentally, also played Frank James.

Blood of Dracula's Castle was the first time I ever worked with John Carradine, and it was such a pleasure to work with that old pro. He was such a nice man, really. We got along famously, and after that we did three or four other movies together, and he was just a real sweetheart of a man. I really enjoyed his company. He could sit and recite Shakespeare until you wanted him to quit, you know. You'd say, "Okay, John, that's enough!"

He could make even the most ridiculous lines sound very serious.

Oh yeah, and he had a photographic memory. There was one scene we did in *Cain's Cutthroats* [1971], with Scott Brady and John Carradine and myself. We had shot day for day, and then had to go right out and shoot night for night. It was probably one or two o'clock in the morning, and at this point Mr. Carradine, to stay awake or for whatever reason, had been sipping on brandy. Everybody was a little concerned about him getting out of his chair and remembering his lines. When it came time to call, "Mr. Carradine on the set please," he stood up, hit his mark, and did about two pages of dialogue without missing a beat. Then he sat back down and was just as drunk as he was before he got up.

That was a pretty intense movie.

It was. At this point in my life I will say that movies like that, as far as my own personal belief system is concerned—I watched that with my daughter, who was a young girl at the time, and of course I'm looking at a movie through different eyes than an audience. I looked over at my daughter, and her eyes were like half dollars. I suddenly realized that there's a responsibility involved with this business, as far as affecting people. It was about that point that I started segueing from being in front of the camera and active as an actor. Frankly, a lot of the stories and screenplays submitted then, and a lot of the stuff that's in theaters and video stores today, I wouldn't do as an actor. It's just gone to the belt buckle or below. I'm not a prude, but on the other hand, I do feel that there's a responsibility Hollywood has to the world that, in my opinion, we're not fulfilling correctly.

For the budget, that film had some impressive special effects.

We had a guy called Black Powder Harry [Woolman], that was his name. He had an old '58 Cadillac loaded with black powder. You didn't want to go down the freeway next to that guy! He'd ask, "Do you want a little boom or a big boom?" Harry was an excellent special effects guy, and we had some good makeup people to take care of the blood makeup and things like that. It was fun working with the independents, because you had to be inventive all the time. You didn't have a hundred-and-some odd people on a crew doing things for you.

Speaking of moving behind the camera, you were also assistant director on that film.

In the independent field I worked as a soundman, a first [assistant director]; I even worked as a grip at times. You keep life and limb together as best you can; no use having false pride about it. I worked behind the camera if I didn't have a job in front of it. I found in my case, once you start being involved with independent companies, I didn't — except for one other part — ever get called back into the majors to do anything. It's like you're a maverick or something.

Why do you think that is?

I don't know. I think it's, for lack of a better term, a little class-consciousness. In those days, you were either an actor with the major studios or networks, or you were out there with the independents, moonlighting with a crew or working with a skeleton crew. I don't think it has the sting it had back then, since there are so many independents now that are making product. In my case, after I became involved in doing some of these independent movies, I didn't get a call back until my friend Roger Moore asked me to do a little vignette thing in *Live and Let Die*. Other than that, I did not work for a major studio again. It was always independents. Some of the product wasn't so bad, and some of it was stuff I like to forget.

Rex Carlton, who wrote *Blood of Dracula's Castle*, also wrote the script for what became *Hell's Bloody Devils*. You were in the biker footage that was added later.

I believe so, but frankly, I don't remember working on a movie called *Hell's Bloody Devils* [*laughs*]! And Adamson and Sam Sherman were famous for that. They'd lift sequences from one movie and put it on another, and release it under another name.

For example, *Five Bloody Graves* [1970] was originally shot as *The Lonely Man*. I wrote the screenplay, but I was not terribly pleased with what wound up on the screen. Al fell in love with one of the lead actresses, and he was terribly distracted during the whole thing. It was based on a gunfighter, Ben Thompson. He was a lethal gunfighter that people didn't know much about in the old west. He had been in love with his first cousin back in Manhattan, and she ran off with somebody else and got married. Ben came west and had a death wish, basically. He was fearless. So I based this story on the gunfighter Ben Thompson. We went up to Fruita, Utah, and shot the movie. Ziggy [Vilmos Zsigmond] shot it. I think that was his fist major feature that he did, and he went on to win all kinds of awards.

We had the nucleus of a good little western. I saw it not so long ago, and of course having written the screenplay and seeing what's on the screen was like two different movies.

You both wrote and helped get that film financed. What was involved in raising money for a film like that during that period?

Well, I didn't know it at the time, but Al was totally flat as a fritter. He didn't have any money. I put in good faith money to get the ball rolling — I put five thousand bucks in the bank. Somehow, Al matched it. He got it from some source, and that was the start of our production account. As we went along, Al and Sam gathered the additional funds necessary for production. It was Al who had scouted out that Fruita, Utah, location. It was really beautiful country, and it made a great background for the story. Oftentimes the background was much better than the story [*laughs*].

From the inception of the idea through distribution to the world market is a giant thing that not many people, certainly not many actors, have experienced. I have, because I've been in the independent field. I've been out there selling movies, touring with people from American International Pictures, opening at theaters. I've had that experience on the marketing end of it. Frankly, the theater owners are just looking for product now. Can you imagine how many movies have to be out there to fill these multiplex theaters now on a weekly basis, if they're going to turn one over every week? It's just a monumental job.

Getting back to *Hell's Bloody Devils*, Sam Sherman said that during the credits sequence, the California Highway Patrol was actually arresting one of the bikers.

Yeah. I was the one that got arrested! What happened was, we used these bikers [The Hessians] out of Ventura, California, and I guess there were 20 or 25 of these guys on their Harleys, flying colors and doing all of that stuff. We were parked, stopped and waiting for the camera to be set up at kind of a rest stop area. The cops came around, about five or six of 'em in cars—just boom, came in on us—and this guy came up to me, walked by me, handed me a gun, and said, "Here, take this." So I put it in this jacket, and as I walked by the hood of this truck, I put it on the truck and then I went over and stood by my motorcycle.

Well, the cops were checking things, and giving tickets because the bikes weren't far enough off the ground and all this other stuff. I saw this cop walk over and pick up my jacket and start searching it—oops, here comes the gun! "Whose jacket is this?" I said, "It's my jacket." He asked, "Is this your gun?" I said, "No." Well, they handcuffed me and put me in the back of the police car. I've got all my ID there and everything, and we had permits to be shooting there, but these guys didn't know that. So I'm locked up in the back of the police car, and Gary Graver, the cameraman, is shooting this whole sequence of them busting me. I was in the back seat of this police car, and this cop was calling into the station saying he got this bad guy named Bob Dix who's with this gang of motorcyclists. Then I heard, I guess, the commander on the radio saying, "You stupid son of a—let Mr. Dix out of the back of the car!"

It was probably difficult to be taken seriously when you were dressed like a Nazi biker.

Yeah, right. One of the guys said, "You ought to be ashamed of yourself." I was 35 years old or so at the time. "What's a man like you doing out here with these guys?" I tried to tell him—I mean there were reflectors all around, camera equipment—we're making a movie! *Sure you are....*

What was Adamson doing all that time?

He was talking to some of the cops, trying to explain to them that we were not what we looked like. I don't even think Al knew what was going on until it was over. But Gary was smart enough to turn a camera on. The whole thing was photographed and used as a prologue to the movie.

Do you remember much about your frequent Adamson co-stars, Vicki Volante and Bambi Allen?

Al Adamson was just in love with Vicki. As a matter of fact, sometimes it would influence his life to the point that he'd forget to shoot a scene or a pick-up shot. I don't know what happened to Vicki. I think she got married and had babies or something, because all of a sudden she disappeared. I worked in several things with her for Al Adamson and for MovieTech, with [Ewing] "Lucky" Brown.

Bambi, I remember her as a little sweetheart. She ended up going with my attorney for a while after that movie was over. We had a really kind of rough rape scene in the front of it. One of the things I remember very specifically about Bambi was silicon breasts. You'd bounce off those things. You could stick a glass of water on there and not spill a drop!

You also were in Adamson's *Satan's Sadists*. Had you known co-star Russ Tamblyn from MGM?

Yes, I'd know Russ as an acquaintance. We weren't close buddies or anything. As a matter of fact, for that movie, I took my personal car and I picked up Russ from his residence up in

Topanga Canyon and drove him and others out to location in Indio, California.

What do you remember about the shoot?

Well, the first thing that comes to mind is we went to location in Indio, and my wife insisted on bringing our cat. She left the window open a little bit, and the cat jumped out the window and chased lizards across the desert. We never found him again. That's the first thing I remember, because she was hysterical over that. The other thing is that a lot of the guys on that movie, particularly Bud Cardos and I, had worked on a lot of different things together. Bud and I to this day are really close friends. Kent Taylor was in that. Kent was an old drinking buddy of my dad's, and he had a lot of wonderful stories to share. We were out in the middle of nowhere most of the time. We worked up off that Patton Memorial that's up on the summit of I-10, before you descend into the valley toward the Colorado River. That was a very interesting location because Patton trained all of his tank commanders up there in that desert country.

Dix as he appeared in Al Adamson's *Satan's Sadists* (1969). (Courtesy Independent-International Pictures Corp.)

All of the biker characters were oddly accessorized — Bud Cardos had a mohawk wig, you wore an eyepatch and a Panama hat, and Greydon Clark had a hearing aid.

Yeah [*laughs*]. I pretty much invented that stuff myself. I think Greydon Clark did, too. I don't think that was in the script. I think we just kind of evolved our characters and tried to make them a little different from the other guys. A funny side story on that is that my son was in a sports bar in Milwaukee with some of his buddies, and they were running these old movies all the time on the television. All of a sudden he looked up, and there I was with a rattlesnake wrapped around my neck. He said, "Hey, there's my dad!"

It was a typical Adamson shoot. We were on a shoestring and nobody made a lot of money, but I think, considering, it turned out pretty well.

Your family had a ranch, so you knew your way around a horse. Did you also ride motorcycles off screen?

Yeah, I had my first motorcycle as a young guy, late teens or early twenties, so I knew how to handle an iron horse. I guess there were seven or eight of those motorcycle movies where I was riding Harleys and stuff. I didn't have any problems, but there were some New York actors who had lied about being able to ride a motorcycle. They would show up on the set and they'd have to go to school for a while, you know. When you're leading a bunch of these guys down a highway, it can get a little nerve-wracking if the guy next to you is wobbling around.

You worked alongside some actual motorcycle gangs on several of them.

One of those was called *Wild Wheels* [1969] — dune buggies and motorcycles up in Pismo Beach, California. That was the main location. We had the "one-percenters" out of Ventura. At the time, the motorcycle people said there's only one percent of motorcyclists that are bad, so of course these guys called themselves the one-percenters. The director, Ken Osborne, said, "Okay you guys in the background, we want some fighting going on back there." We had some foreground scene going on, so Kenny called "Action," and these guys really started a fight. He forgot to tell them to fake it! They were knocking each other down and punching each other. Kenny was hollering, "Whoa, cut, cut, cut!"

Casey Kasem was in that, too.

God love him, I know this is not out of school — Casey wears a rug, a hairpiece. There was a scene, again during this conflict within the motorcycle club itself, they were having an argument, and this guy threw Casey in this lake. I'll never forget. The first thing that came up was his hair. Then Casey came up. I think he was more upset about losing his hair than about being soaking wet on a cold morning.

You were also in Bud Cardos' first film as a director, *The Red, White and Black* [a.k.a *Soul Soldier*].

Which also went under the name of *Buffalo Soldiers*. I played Walking Horse, the Indian. I played several Indians throughout my career, mostly for Andy McLaglen on *Gunsmoke*. My most memorable moment from that movie was when I showed up the first day of shooting. My horse that I was supposed to ride was in a corral by itself. All the other horses were in another corral. I said, "Why is that horse by itself?" The wrangler said, "Oh, I don't know, he's just not as friendly as the other horses." I asked if the horse was gun-shy. "You won't have any problem," he said. So I went to the prop department and got a 44/40 and loaded it with full blanks, and a Winchester, loaded it, and I walked out there and this horse was tied to a post in the middle of this corral. I fired that thing off behind my back, and that horse must have jumped four feet in the air. I was supposed to ride him with a war bridle on, no saddle, firing a rifle on his back. So I survived the shoot, but I had some hairy moments.

What was it like working with Cardos on his first directing job?

Of course, Bud and I are very close. To me he's one of the best action directors in Hollywood. The opening sequence where the guy comes out of the window, and all the action stuff you see in there, was staged by Bud. I was real happy for him that he had this breakthrough from being second-unit director to getting full screen credit. I still think Bud, though he's getting up there in his years now, is very much perky and inventive and creative when it comes to action stuff. I was happy for him he got that break.

***The Road Hustlers* [1968] was shot in South Carolina. Did you interact much with the locals?**

First thing that comes to mind about that picture: We had these black Fords. They were moonshine cars. We were billeted at a ranch maybe eight or ten miles from the location of the lake we were working at. One morning, I took off first, heading for location, and a local redneck cop got on my tail. There were no plates on this thing, and I was dressed in a moonshiner's outfit — overalls — and this cop put on his sirens, pulled me over, came up alongside the car with his gun out pointing it at me. Of course, I got out of the car, I had got my hands in the

Singer Sue Raney serenades Robert Dix in *The Road Hustlers* (1968), a moonshine comedy-action film made in South Carolina.

air. I was telling him, "We're here making a movie." *Sure you are.* About this time, the guy playing my brother, Bruce Yarnell, he went driving by in exactly the same kind of '58 Ford. He went driving by and flipped me the bone, and kept going. Behind him a few minutes later comes Andy Devine *in exactly the same car.* He stops. Now the cop is completely confused. Andy Devine says, "Will you please let Mr. Dix go? He has to go to work!"

It was a fun movie to make. Jim Davis was a sweetheart of a guy.

How did you first meet him?

The first time I met Jim was when we were doing the western in Utah. He got cast along with Scott Brady in one of the parts. We were all isolated up there in Fruita, which is the end of God's country. There was one gas station up there and a barracks type of place, and a cafeteria, and that was it. So we all became like extended family, Jim, John Carradine, Scott Brady, Paula Raymond, myself, my future wife Tara Ashton was there. Jim and Scott and myself did a couple of movies after that. We were friends. I really enjoyed working with him.

According to *The Road Hustlers* pressbook, the scene where the boat explodes was actually an accident.

That's true. Larry Jackson, the director, was driving that boat, and I guess it was missed timing on behalf of the special effects guy, but he blew it up right under Larry's butt. It blew him straight up in the air and really severely injured his back. I remember he was on the mend last time I saw Larry, but it could have killed him.

What was South Carolina in the 1960s like for a bunch of guys from California?

It was an experience [*laughs*], with the good ol' boys, "Bubba" and all those guys. One of the first things that happened when we checked into the ranch house where some of the actors were billeted — the crew was in a motel in town — this guy came up with some moonshine ("guaranteed not to be over 90 days old"), 180 proof or something like that. I had to sample it with some fruit juice, and about two sips of that was all I could handle. But Scott Brady was a heavy drinker, and when I went to the airport and brought him back to the ranch, I said, "Now, these guys are going to offer you this moonshine, and it's 180 proof, Scott. Don't go drinking it like you drink your bourbon." Well, big ol' ex–Marine Scott, he said, "Give me some of that." He took half a glass of that and half a glass of juice. He drank about three of those and fell like a redwood tree. I woke him up the next morning and said, "See, I told you so."

Were a lot of these films non-union?

We were all moonlighting. If I had gotten caught, as a member of SAG at the time, they could have fined me five hundred bucks and suspended me six months from working in Hollywood.

We were making a movie called *Las Vegas Strangler* [1968] for Ollie Drake. I helped him put the deal together, and we went up there and shot this thing. I played the Vegas strangler. One day the DP comes running through the set saying, "Bob, get out of here. The union guys are here." They put me in a room with one of those Vegas models. She was bare-ass naked, and they gave me a little body sponge and some makeup, so I was putting makeup on this gal when the guys came through. "Hey, here's our body makeup guy."

Was it difficult to make a living that way?

Well, you got paid sometimes a little above SAG minimum when you're playing one of the lead roles. I'll tell you, with Al Adamson it was like working for your money twice. Without exception, every movie I did with him, I'd have to go chase the accountant or whoever and get them to cut checks for the crew and for the cast. It was like pulling teeth to get your wages. But Al always managed to pull it off. He'd be a day late and a dollar short, but he'd end up getting the funds from some source. That part of it was never fun.

You recently made your very first convention appearance at the Memphis Film Festival. Did you enjoy it?

Very much so. In fact, I was pleasantly surprised that there are so many people interested in our movies. It's all ancient history to me, though I'm still somewhat active in the business, but very much in the background. Of course, never having been to one of these things before, I didn't know you were supposed to bring eight-by-ten glossies and sign them for folks. So I get there, and they've got this stack of pictures of me when I was 18 years old at MGM. I'll be 70 the 8th of May, so there's quite a difference.

Your last screen appearance was in *Live and Let Die*. What did you do after you stopped acting?

Because of my dad, we had a 42-office building in Palm Desert, California, and I became the manager of the building for the family. That's one of the jobs I did going from last to first. For a while there I traveled throughout North America helping set up twelve-step programs with the Baha'i faith. There were people suffering with substance abuse issues who were, let's say, going to Alcoholics Anonymous, but it was like wearing two hats or living two lives. They were not telling their Baha'i community that they were in recovery, and they weren't telling the recovery group that they were Baha'is. I formed, with others, the Baha'is in Recovery fellowship. I traveled to local spiritual assemblies all over North America in a motor home and would set up these practice meetings, and show them how the twelve-step sharing works — no cross talk, and pass the eagle feather, that kind of thing, and I'd teach people how to share. So that took about two or three years out of my life as I set it up, the whole itinerary, and then I traveled from San Diego to Vancouver, then across Canada to Toronto, down through Niagara Falls all the way to Homestead, Florida, and back to my residence at that time in Bisbee, Arizona. So that took up a lot of my time, and I have been very active in the Baha'i community nationally and locally. It's a process that I enjoy sharing with others, if they're interested. Baha'is don't have any clergy, and every Baha'i man or woman is a teacher according to his or her capacity or knowledge of the writings themselves.

Many of the people who worked on those films in the 1960s, like Jack Nicholson [in *The Rebel Rousers*], became part of the "Hollywood New Wave." At the time, were you at all cognizant that there was this change going on in the industry?

I would say there was a very distinct understanding of the difference between the majors and the independents. Within the independents and the lower budget movies made by Roger Corman and other people, it became apparent that talent like Jack Nicholson and Bruce Dern — and many others that came out of those XYZ movies that went on to have very successful careers — wouldn't have had a start or a leg up if it hadn't been for the independents.

Just keeping life and limb together in Hollywood, as I said before, it's either chicken or feathers. You're out there, and ninety percent of the time you're working to get your next job. It's much different than the average conception of making movies in Hollywood. The job security aspect of it is practically nil.

I used to tell young actors and actresses, when they'd ask me, "Do you think I should be an actor?" — even if they were a talented young person, I'd say, "No. If you have to ask me, you're not confident enough to get out there and get in this mix." It's a tough life. It's been glamorized terribly, but it can be fun. When you get around creative people, they're always interesting. You don't find many dull people in the movie business. They may be a little nuts, but they're interesting.

Hollywood Hellcat

ROSS HAGEN

Younger audiences may know him only for his appearances in Fred Olen Ray's ultra-cheap schlock films, or for being mercilessly lampooned on *Mystery Science Theater*, but there's much more to Ross Hagen than his acting résumé would imply. In four decades as an independent actor, director, producer and writer, Hagen has weathered the ups and downs of the film industry during a prolific and diverse career.

Hagen (born Leland Lilly in 1938) was raised in Arizona and Oregon, and originally headed to Hollywood on a lark after working as a stand-in on *Route 66*. Hagen quickly found work on popular TV westerns like *The Virginian* and *The Wild Wild West*, as well as a regular role on *Daktari* as Bart Jason during the 1968-69 season. A smirking, square-jawed tough guy in the mold of Steve McQueen and Jeremy Slate, Hagen made his film debut in Robert Slatzer's *The Hellcats* (1967), which he followed with leading roles in *The Mini-Skirt Mob* (1968, with Slate) and *The Devil's 8* (1969).

Not content to be just another grizzled face, he produced *The Sidehackers* with Gus Trikonis in 1969, and launched a productive career behind the camera in the 1970s, usually working alongside his wife, actress-producer Claire Polan (who died in 2003).

Hagen produced *Pushing Up Daisies* (1973), *Wonder Women* (1973), *Bad Charleston Charlie* (1973), *Supercock* (1975) and *Night Creature* (1978), frequently casting himself alongside friends like Christopher George, Eric Lidberg, Hoke Howell and *Flower Drum Song* star Nancy Kwan. He made his directorial debut on the Rosey Grier-John Saxon film *The Glove* (1979), and since then has directed another half-dozen films.

When I spoke to Hagen, he was just putting the finishing touches on his latest directing project, the noirish *Murder on the Yellow Brick Road* (2005), which he also appears in, along with Kwan, Charles Dierkop, and P.J. Soles.

You were born in Arizona. Did you grow up there?

ROSS HAGEN: Williams, Arizona, the gateway to the Grand Canyon. I spent until the third grade there. My dad worked on the railroad there, the Santa Fe. The town kind of died when they stopped running the train into the Grand Canyon. Williamson had a rebirth because they reopened the train, and now it's the gateway to the Grand Canyon. You know that you've made it when they've got a Starbucks in your hometown of 50 people.

When did you move to California? Did you go there specifically to act?

About 1962 or 1963. I worked for the forestry department in Oregon and it was a vacation time. There was an old series called *Route 66*. They were shooting over in Astoria. I was on

Ross Hagen (at left) appeared in a number of biker films, including Al Adamson's *Angels' Wild Women* (1972). (Courtesy Independent-International Pictures Corp.)

vacation, and everybody said they were looking for stand-ins for *Route 66*. I went there and they said, "Oh, you'd be great to stand in for Marty Milner," one of the leads in the show with George Maharis.

I went down and stood around. I watched these guys working 18-hour days, laughing and having a hell of a good time. I thought, "What a fun business!" I mean, they get to travel around and do all this stuff. So I stayed with them, and then I got to know everybody and they gave me a letter of introduction to come to Hollywood and Columbia Pictures. They said, "You shouldn't be in Oregon; you're so nuts you should be in California." I guess all the morons and idiots end up in California! It's one way of getting everybody out of the other states. You know how everybody thinks everybody in California is nuts, right?

They're all *imported* nuts.

It's one big insane asylum! Hollywood is one of the greatest towns in the world. Where else can you have a nightmare, come to town and tell somebody about your nightmare, and sell it? It's an unbelievable town. It's amazing. The weirdest shit in the world — let's make a movie about that! Great!

Then you went to live in Hollywood after that?

I was on vacation after that, and I said, "Well, hell, I'll go down there." I went by my folks' house and said I was going to Hollywood to see what's going on down there.

So I came down and literally a couple of months later I made a record — the A side was called "Spooky Movies" and the B side was "The Big Masher." I had my first job on *General Hospital*. Got it right away. And then of course being from a hillbilly family, the first time they see you on TV, Granny Puss called up and said, "Hon, now that you're a millionaire and a TV star, can you get me some teeth?" I said, "Granny, I'd love to get you some teeth, but it costs more to join a union than I made on my first job!"

Who did you make the record with?

A guy named Buddy Hill? I'd have to look on the record. Remember when the Big Bopper and all those guys got killed? It was at that time. I have this very deep voice, and I can do all that stuff. So they said, "Oh man, you should do a record." So I did it and I lived off it for about a year. I don't know if you've ever seen what it's like to be a teenage idol for fifteen seconds of fame. You walk out on this stage and people are screaming. They screamed like a bunch of vampires. The hours are horrible. It wasn't the kind of lifestyle that I liked. I like to get up early and listen to the birds. So I kind of let the music thing drift away. I wasn't that interested in pursuing a career.

What name did you use on the record?

Lee Lilly.

How did you pick your stage name?

I don't know, it just popped into my head. We had an act up in Oregon called The Gunman. We used to draw guns on each other when quick-draw was really in. We went around and put on quick-draw shows. At that time I just picked that name. It kind of stuck.

So you first jobs were on television.

I did a lot of TV. Quinn Martin, I did a ton of shows for him. TV was a lot of fun at that time. *Gunsmoke* was still on. I got in at the end, and I got to work with Barbara Stanwyck, Walter Brennan. I got in with a lot of solid, pro actors that really helped me a lot. But when you first come to Hollywood, they've got a very interesting thing here. You have to have an agent to get a film, and you have to have a film to get an agent. I thought that sounded kind of dumb. The first film I did, we went out and made it on our own. It was Wally Campo, at the Actor's Theater, and Peter Sorel. I organized the whole thing. We went out and actually shot a film on weekends. It took us almost a year. Instead of lying around watching television, we actually made a movie called *Mark of the Gun*. That was our film. We showed it to agents and it got us started.

Did that get released?

Mark of the Gun is sitting in my vault right now. We made it in black and white. Laszlo Kovacs and Vilmos Zsigmond were the cameramen on it. They had just escaped from the Hungarian revolution, and they had a bag full of film and they were running around saying, "We're cameramen, we're cameramen." You sound like dishwashers! You don't sound like cameramen to us! That was our team, Laszlo Kovacs, Willie Zsigmond, Peter Sorel. We had a ball and it got us all started.

Who directed it?

Wally Campo, our acting coach. In fact, he hadn't seen the film in all these years, and I just got a copy of it. It's been sitting in the lab all these years. The negative was lost for years. It's beautiful. We just got it back, and we're enjoying looking at it. It's like your first child. You meet it again. You know at that age, everybody thinks they're brilliant? You're not [*laughs*]! We were legends in our own minds.

Was *Hellcats* the first released film you appeared in?

I loved *The Hellcats*. We had 16mm short-end film. Tony Cardoza, Bob Slatzer — he was married to Marilyn Monroe for a while. We all kind of got together. Tony is a great guy, Bob, all of them were just fun guys. We went out and made this little film on 16mm short ends, and we took it over to Crown International, and we sold the film. We thought we really knew how to make movies!

How did you get hooked up with Cardoza and Slatzer?

Well, they all knew me from my television work, so they came to me and wanted me to be in the film. It thought it would be fun. That was the time we were all making these bike films, like *Easy Rider* and *Born Losers*.

That had Tony Lorea, Tony Huston, Eric Lidberg, Ray Cantrell. A lot of those guys did other films with you.

Tony Lorea, I met him when we did *Mark of the Gun*. He's a great character actor and we used him in a lot of films. We used him in *Sidehackers*, in *Supercock*. He did a great job in *Supercock*. Eric Lidberg was also at the acting school, so a lot of us tied up when we were in the acting class. We just kind of stuck together. Eric became kind of the production manager and an actor, and everybody did multiple jobs, as we had to. Mike Pataki, he was in it. Diane McBain — we did a film called *Mini-Skirt Mob* for AIP, that's where Diane and I met. I said, "We'll make another movie," so we made *Sidehackers*.

You had incredibly tight pants in *Hellcats*.

You know what Tom Jones calls those pants? There are the pants that you eat and sit in, and then there's the "fuck you" pants, the ones that you can't sit or eat in. It's hard being a movie star [*laughs*]! Can you imagine setting yourself up to be a movie star? What a stupid thing to do. Look at Tom Cruise. He's 44 now and they're saying, "We think he's too old. His last film only opened with $48 million. He's a loser." That's why we call it Hollyweird.

You and Gus Trikonis did *Sidehackers* next. How did you get financing?

Jon Hall. Gus, Jon and I met on a thing called *The Wonderful World of Stunts*. Jon had this anamorphic lens, and we shot this damn thing, it was cute as hell. We went in the water with it. It was just a goofy thing. Then Jon said, "I've got all this camera equipment — why don't you guys write a script?" We'd done *Hellcats*. I went over to Crown and told them I wanted to make this movie. They said, "What's the movie, kid?" It's about sidecars. "It sounds good to me."

I said, "Well, I've learned the film business, and this time I want a percentage. I don't want to just be paid off." He said, "My God, you really know the business!" We took 75–25, 75 for us, 25 for them. Sounds like a good deal, huh? Wrong! The 75 is called producer's net. Eddie Murphy calls it monkey points. We took 75 percent of monkey points, and they ended up with 25 percent of the gross. It took us years to get our money back. He said, "One day you'll learn the film business!"

That was Red Jacobs at Crown?

Yeah, Red. The best. He was our guru.

Ross Hagen goes undercover to stop drug-dealing bikers in *The Hellcats* (1967). Here he shares his motorcycle with actress Dee Duffy.

Did you get to know him well?

Yeah. Mark and Marilyn [Tenser] are still around. They still have Crown. We're still very good friends. He taught us the business.

He'd been around forever.

A showman. There are very few of the real show guys left. They've become almost corporations with no head. Like sponges, you can't find the real head. Red, he was the head. "I make my movies, I'm the head." In other words, we only deal with people who can't be fired. They can't fire me and they can't fire Red. If you go into a corporation, some of my friends have gotten into development hell here. Making a film for Paramount, it goes around and around and never gets made. Ninety percent of them never get made.

I read online that Roger Patterson, the man who made the famous Bigfoot film, stayed with you for awhile.

Yeah. I actually did a recording for Roger. He came down, and a friend of mine, Jerry Merritt,* had a band that we knew in Oregon. Roger was living with them up in Washington. He came down there scared out of his wits. He said, "I saw this fucking thing." What is it? He

---

Jerry Merritt was a legendary rockabilly singer-guitarist whose band, The Crowns, played the Pacific Northwest for many years. He was a close friend of Roger Patterson, and composed music that was used in Patterson's Bigfoot film.

said, "I don't know, but look." Very straight, honest guy. Incapable of doing the special effects that would have required. The sophistication wasn't even there. You could have been the top guy in Hollywood, and if you don't believe me, look at *Planet of the Apes* [1968]. You can tell they were guys in ape costumes. So Roger came down and stayed with us for about two weeks. We had all of his stuff there, the footprints and everything. He was trying to convince people that he really saw something. Well, it's like those guys that have seen an alien. Everyone kind of goes, "What?" Now it's become kind of like a legend, this footage. But he was a very nice guy. Very down home.

Sidehackers **was the first film you produced. How did that experience go for you?**

It's very interesting, because the producer gets all the shit together. When you produce something like that, you take on a responsibility for the whole team. It's kind of strange. But I think you always need a point man, the one who's not afraid to be rejected. If you're afraid of being rejected, get out of town. I think that, as producer, I had a lot of fun on the film. Gus and I went through hundreds of rewrites. We had this little apartment in Hollywood, that was our office. Oh God, it was fun [*laughs*].

When I talked to Gus Trikonis, he described you as a wild guy, but didn't share any details.

Gus and I, we've known each other for a long time. Each person has to take their own route in Hollywood. He's a fabulous painter. I've still got two or three of his paintings hanging around here. He painted one of me once. He gave it to me and said, "This is you." It's a guy sitting with a dog in the middle of a field with his head back.

You also turned up in an Elvis film, ***Speedway*** **[1968], during that era. It was directed by Norman Taurog.**

Norman, yeah. Elvis and Sonny and Red [West] all became good friends on the set, because we're all hillbillies. We could speak each other's language. We didn't speak Hollywood. People would ask him, "What's it like being Elvis? What the hell is it?"

The Wests were in the Slatzer films, too.

Yeah, he was in *Hellcats*. Red turned into a hell of an actor. Good boys.

Mini-Skirt Mob **was a western-themed biker film for AIP.**

They just wanted me, based on my work. They wanted me to do the roles.

You were paired off against Jeremy Slate.

Right, and Harry Dean Stanton. Did you see Harry's new show, *Big Love*? He's hysterical in it. Another friend of mine, Bruce Dern, is on it.

Did you ride motorcycles?

No. I always had a stuntman. I could roll into the shot and get off. That was it. Jeremy was a good bike rider. He liked it. I never found any fun in it. Just rolling into the shot and getting off, doing the acting. I let the stuntmen do all the work in between.

Any memories of Maury Dexter or Burt Topper?

Maury is very, very efficient. Probably one of the most efficient directors I've ever seen in my life. He had it planned down to the minute detail. He was very, very quick, very efficient.

Burt Topper was a lovey, huggy kind of guy that you just like to be around. It was very easy to be around Burt. We used to tease the hell out of him. John Milius wrote the script for *Devil's 8*. John came up, we were all sitting around a fireplace at Lake Arrowhead where we shot it. "Hey, what do you guys think of my script?" he asks. We all took 'em and threw 'em in the fireplace [*laughs*]! I mean, we'd do that shit to each other.

At that point, were you already thinking about doing more writing and directing?

It's so hard to put a film together because you need so many elements. It's one of my favorite sayings, "Effort gives value to man." In other words, without effort, we don't appreciate anything. It's the effort, and that's what I like more than anything, the challenge of doing something almost impossible — of making a movie. I remember when I was doing *Bonanza*, we opened *Sidehackers* in L.A. at like 150 theaters. Dan Blocker came up to me — I was guest starring on *Bonanza* at the same time the film opened in Hollywood. He said, "Is that you? How in the hell did you make a movie?" I said, "One shot at a time, Dan." [*Laughs*] The making of a movie is very similar to war. You really have to plan.

Did you have any influences as an actor or director?

No. The one thing that you fight your whole life as an actor is to get rid of that word "actor." You've got to get to where you're just you. It takes a long time. You've got to get through all the bullshit, the phony acting, the phony looks, the phony smiles, all that phony crap. It takes years to get through that. It's almost like you have to tear yourself apart to find the real actor within yourself. I never patterned myself after anybody. It's who I was.

One of the last biker films you did during that period was Al Adamson's *Angels' Wild Women* [1972]. How did you meet him?

We had our offices together. Al had all this stock footage left over from about seven films he'd done [*laughs*]. This is true. He said, "What if I mix all this stock footage and we can do a little film?" Hell, let's try it and see what happens. We were experimenting, you know what I mean? We weren't afraid to experiment. I think that's what the independents give you, the ability to experiment.

We went out with Al's films, we shot with the Manson family. We didn't know they were the Manson family then. They were there, I mean with the things in their hair and kids running around with snot running out of their noses, Hell's Angels running all over the place. At one point they thought I should be their leader, because I was playing this tough guy.

How much of that film was shot at Spahn Ranch?

All the exteriors. All the exteriors were shot at the Spahn Ranch. The interiors were shot on a soundstage, and then we were out on the desert running around doing the biker stuff. One time we had a shot where a bike went through a windshield, and I was supposed to be driving the car back. All of a sudden the cops come running around and stopped us. "What the hell is going on?" We're making a movie! Who else would run around with a bike stuck through the front of a truck [*laughs*]?

Al seemed to have a lot of problems with the cops busting up his movie sets.

You go along with whatever is happening. You can't make rules on how you make it. Can you imagine somebody standing behind Picasso telling him to put more purple on a painting? When you're making a film like Al did, he petted his dog and kind of let everybody else do their thing. Gary Graver did most of the work. You just let it happen. What are you going to do today? Let's see what happens.

His father-in-law, Regina's dad, owned the little restaurant that we all used to eat in. We'd all go into Barney's place. That was kind of our hangout. Barney would furnish the food on the set. Then we all just went and had fun. We never knew what the hell it was going to look like. What kind of movie is this? An Al movie. Perfect. We don't judge anybody else's work.

He was a nice guy.

That was sad, it really was. He would have made a movie about his own death. Have you talked to Sam Sherman?

Quite a bit.

Sam's great. We had a memorial for Al here a few years ago. It's funny because all these damn stupid movies we've done have been more popular than the big ones. I think what it is, it was the birth of film, it was the birth of new people trying to start and do good things. I mean, you take a guy like Spielberg. He's facing his own fame now. You know, when you suddenly have to have that hundred zillion dollar box office weekend, the pressure is horrible. He'd be better off taking a half-million bucks and making a personal film on weekends, just to get back to the core of what it's all about. Like some actors need to go back to the stage. I hated the stage; I couldn't stand it. Doing the same shit every day? But a lot of guys love it.

Tell me about *Pushing Up Daisies*.

Ivan Nagy was the top photographer in town. Ivan and his girlfriend and Nancy Kwan, we all got to meet each other. He goes, "How do you make a goddamn movie, man?" He saw *Sidehackers*, and said, "Jesus, that's great. How do you do that?" I said, "Let's make a movie." Out of that came *Pushing Up Daisies*. We filmed that on weekends, and we put it together, and that's how we did it. I produced it, Ivan was directing, and we all just kind of got together. We called in all of our friends and relatives and made the film.

How did you know Christopher George?

Chris George and I had been friends for years. We did *Devil's 8* together. He was from New York. He came out and we all got along. Chris and I were like brothers for years until he passed away. I used him in *Bad Charleston Charlie* [1973], I used him in *Pushing Up Daisies*. We just did whatever the hell we wanted.

Wonder Women **[1973] was the first thing you did in the Philippines.**

That was my first film that I actually took all the way through without a break. The rest of my pictures had been made on weekends. We weren't sure if we could actually push on all the way through without a break. We figured we could pull it off, because we got the equipment rental on a Friday, but we actually got to keep it until Sunday. We got three days of shooting for a one-day price. That's why we did 'em on weekends.

When *Wonder Women* came along, this friend of mine wrote a book called *Midnight Cowboy*, Leo Herlihy, and he had given me the rights to his next book as a film. I took it to all the studios, great story, the guy's coming off *Midnight Cowboy*, for Christ's sake, and everyone said it was too depressing. Nobody wanted to do it.

So I got really pissed, and I was sitting around and I came up with the worst idea I could think of, *The Wild Women of Cannibal Island*. I called Don Gottlieb at General Film, and I said, "I have a great idea for you guys. I'll pitch you this one: A plane full of models crashes on an unknown island, and it's like the *Lord of the Flies* with chicks running around, and

Hagen takes a shot on the jaw from Christopher George in *The Devil's 8* (1969), directed by Burt Topper.

they're *wild*." They said, "We love it! Let's do it." Three days later, Bob O'Neill was on his way to the Philippines with a script that was started by Lou Whitehill. Bob and I met for the first time on location in the Philippines [*laughs*]. He was rewriting it with cement falling on him. We had no idea where the hell we were. We landed in a foreign country two and a half weeks later. What a trip [*laughs*]!

Were you just in the Philippines for two weeks?

Then we started filming, and we there two or three months until we finished the film.

You survived, obviously.

We survived because we had fun. The only time I ever do a film is because it looks like it's gonna be fun. If it looks like it's gonna be a pain in the ass, I don't do it. In fact, I don't do anything unless I love doing it. If I go into something and I don't know if I want to do this, that's a bad attitude to take to anything. I always try to have the right attitude.

You took Gus back to the Philippines to do *Supercock*.

Yep.

Which is a great concept.

It was so much fun, because we were laughing our asses off. Being stupid like I was, I never realized that even though there's not a dirty word in the film — it's a complete PG-rated film, 'cause we don't do those other kind of movies. We came back and I said, "Hey, it's *Supercock*." Well, I got my ass really nailed, because we opened the film in Louisville, Kentucky, and the *Louisville Times* wouldn't take the ad. I booked a plane and I flew into Louisville. I walked into their offices and I said, "I hope you guys don't have your dicks confused with a chicken. Look what it is. Look it up in the dictionary." They finally gave in and put it in the paper.

    The review came out and said this was the most pornographic film we've ever seen, good for locker room trash only. There wasn't a cuss word in it. The cockfighters, when they get together, they talk about how they feed their cocks. My cock's name was Friendly and Nancy Kwan stole my cock. I ran around the whole movie looking for my lost cock. They beat it. They exercise their cocks. They throw it against the wall. They rub it [*laughs*]. So we never had to do anything except choose real dialogue from the actual cockfighters. Then we just added dialogue. "What do you feed your cock? I feed mine only organic corn. I exercise him a lot, especially late at night." The film is hysterical. Gus and I had a lot of fun making that film. He did a hell of a job directing that.

Did you distribute it yourself?

Yes. I wanted to see what distribution was like.

What was it like?

It was fun. You wonder how a dollar goes from a person's hand into the box office and gets back to the filmmaker. Lots of people are picking away at the dollar before it gets back to you. I had to learn that so I would understand the distribution business. I purposely released the film myself because I could. We had a ball doing it.

Were you able to successfully navigate the whole system and make some money?

Yeah. You get through it.

Was *The Glove* [1979] the first film you directed?

Yeah.

Did that project start with you?

I owned the script. Bill Silberkleit was the exec on it. Bill and I met through Don Gottlieb at

General Film. We had *The Glove* and we liked the concept. We kept running around looking for a director. I wasn't interested in directing at all. That never entered my mind. We interviewed these different guys, and one day Bill looked at me and said, "Ross, you tell the story, you're a good cameraman. You direct the son of a bitch."

It ended up with me directing, and Gary Graver was our cameraman, who saved my ass. I didn't know what I was doing. I had no idea. I didn't even know how to turn a camera. So without Gary Graver I couldn't have got through it. About three weeks in, he finally was teaching me how to set shots and look through the camera. Eventually I started getting it. Imagine being lucky enough to be trained on set. Then I started getting it, and since then I've still been getting it [*laughs*].

What did you think of *The Glove* when it was finished?

I hated the music. I thought that the acting was good. All of the actors, Mike [Pataki] and Rosie and John. In fact, it's still one of John's favorite films.

I always liked it.

It was fun because that was a true thing. That glove was invented in the prison system to keep these guys in line, instead of billy clubs and stuff like that. It was a fun film. It did very well.

What was *Jane* [1982]?

Jane was going to be a film with a guy named Ken Hartford. He was kind of like a foreign distributor–type guy. Video was just coming in strong then, and we have a lot of videos in our film library, so we were negotiating because it was just coming in and everyone was going around buying video like they are DVD today. We met Ken and he said he wanted to do a film called *Jane*. So we played around with the script, and got some artwork done on it, and then it kind of just all collapsed. Sometimes that happens. It collapsed into nothing. Ken thought he was Tarzan and he was showing some of the girls how you are supposed to swing from a vine. The idiot crawled up in a tree and swung from a vine, and he fell down. We had to take him to the emergency room. He squashed himself on the cement [*laughs*].

You then worked with Robert O'Neill a few times, including on the *Angel* films.

Bob did *Angel* [1984], he and Joe [Cala] did that first one. That really hit nice for New World. Then they came along and made another one. Bob and I had been making films together. He was in *The Glove*. Any time I do a film I try to put Bob in. We flip back and forth. The *Angel* franchise became very good. Then Bob went over to Universal and did something there called *Code of Vengeance* [1985]. We were there for about a year at Universal developing movies. We had fun.

At what point did you meet Fred Olen Ray?

Fred and I met at Ken Hartford's. He was going to do some special effects. Fred's into making good monster stuff. We were going to do something and I had an idea for a science fiction film where somebody ends up flat as a pancake. We tried to figure out how to do that. Then Fred and I just became friends, and over the years we did a lot of films together.

He makes more films faster than just about anybody else.

You know what's funny, Fred is one of the few guys in the world where if he says that you're gonna be off the set at eight o'clock, you're finished. He doesn't believe in all that other stuff. He keeps the actors really on their toes because you never know what he's gonna do next. He might just shoot 10 pages. "Just stand there and say the lines." He makes films differently than anybody I ever met. We had a lot of fun with those films. God, we did so many, I can't even remember how many.

What that does for you, and a lot of people don't realize this, is you keep practicing your craft. If you want to be a good tennis player, you practice. You've got to practice acting in front of a camera. So all of a sudden, these are times to experiment, to have fun, stretch yourself and see how far you can go. The other night somebody called me and said they just saw that film with Jan Michael Vincent, *Alienator* [1989]. We did the special effects on that. Fred and I were smoking cigars, and would actually blow cigar smoke under the crashed spaceship. That was the special effect! It was a kid's toy [*laughs*].

When we did the film where I played a cowboy—*Armed Response* [1986]? No. It was *Commando Squad* [1987]. Russ Tamblyn wasn't used to the way Fred shot. Fred doesn't like to take a lot of time messing around. We're having our rehearsal, and we're sitting around eating donuts, and I said, "You better put your donut away, 'cause Fred's gonna be shooting." The next thing you know, action! Russ is like, "What's going on?"

Russ did quite a few films with Al Adamson, too.

You know our little girl is doing really good, Amber [Tamblyn]. She's in New York doing a film now. Her first film was with me.

That was *Rebellious* [1995], directed by Nancy Kwan's son.

Bernie Pock. It's a very kind of a poetic film. The guy's going through a spiritual journey in Spain. Amber and Bernie and I, and Nancy, all worked in the movie. Fred actually just got it out.

By the time you started working with Fred Olen Ray, you'd been making independent films for a few decades. How had the business changed during that period, in terms of finding financing and getting the films released?

I always believed that if you wanted to do something, you had to put your own money in first. I always did that. I always kept investing back, so we'd make a few bucks, and we'd start the next project. That's what you have to do. Hollywood is a strange town. I'll put it this way: Hollywood is the only town where you have to become a star before you can become a star. You have to become a writer before you can become a writer. You have to create yourself first, and then the town discovers you. A lot of people come to Hollywood and think the town owes them a living. That's one hell of an ego. I've heard in acting school, "I'm going to give them six months." Do you think the town gives a shit about your six months? They don't care. And all the guys who have something to fall back on? Every one of them that had something to fall back on, fell back on it. All of us idiots that had nothing to fall back on are still making movies. That's the difference.

B.O.R.N. [1988] was one of your more interesting films. That had a great cast and a good concept—black market organ sales—that turned out to be ahead of its time.

Isn't that amazing? We kept seeing these different articles, with young people found with pieces cut out and stuff. It was interesting to hear about these guys selling body parts. We kind of developed it from that. It's a very frightening film. The first time we had a screening, this one guy couldn't sleep. He was afraid to let his kids out. It drove him nuts. I felt really bad about that, because normally you want people to leave the theater feeling a little hope. There's not much hope. But it was an interesting concept. I mean, my God, still today I can't believe it.

Was Movie Outfit your company?

Yes.

Were the films you made under that banner all direct-to-video releases?

Yeah, most of them. Today, like the guys that did *Saw* [2004], when they first got their budget, they gave them a million dollars to make the film, but they put $15 million in advertising. Figure that one out! Cruise's films have got to hit $300 million before they break even. Imagine that. The studio could have made 20 or 30 films for $10 million apiece like the old studio bosses taught us. Lou Wasserman, when we worked at Universal, he said, "You don't put all your eggs in one basket." The old bosses would go out and say, "Let's make three detective stories, a western, let's buy a musical," and then they would have a constant flow of films throughout the year. Now everybody comes in and says they've got to have one big film to make us rich. That's stupid.

Then they claim none of them actually make any money.

The bookkeeping system? Today the distribution has changed radically. Starbucks has gone into distributing films. All of a sudden, it's like Garth Brooks made a deal with Wal-Mart; the only place you can buy Garth Brooks CDs is at Wal-Mart. We're getting ready for our new film *Murder on the Yellow Brick Road*. We're finishing that up now. We just got the answer print on it three or four weeks ago. We're deciding if we should open it in theaters because the film turned out a little better than we expected. We've had good test audiences for it. But by the time we put a film in the theater, are we better off just going straight in with television and DVD? So we have to figure that out.

Do you think the Internet has equalized the distribution framework now, since you can buy a movie right from the person who made it?

That's what we're hoping, that we can cut out all that other stuff in between and go straight to the people. In *Murder on the Yellow Brick Road*, we've got Angus Macfadyen in it. SAG came up with a low-budget contract, where we can bring in new talent. Say that you were a new writer. We can bring you into the project without you being a member of the guild. We can bring new actors in without them being members of the guild. So the catch-22 has been broken. We can put them with seasoned actors and professionals on the set, and it gives them a chance to show their stuff. We already know we can get through a film. The new contracts and stuff are allowing a lot of filmmakers to get into the business. Before, they would have had a very rough time.

We cut the film on Final Cut Pro, the new editing system made by Apple. It's absolutely amazing. It literally makes you a studio. Unbelievable. Literally you go out and collect your raw footage, come back to one room and you can put your whole movie together — the music, the titles, everything. You can do the whole thing yourself. It's really amazing.

And you can keep your budget down where you're not going bankrupt. The whole film was shot in L.A., which is one of the most expensive places to shoot. That's why they go to Canada. I said I wanted to make a film at home, on Hollywood Boulevard, with all practical locations, and we did it. We got a nice cast in it. It's a clean film. It's an old Raymond Chandler–type detective thing. I always wanted to play a Raymond Chandler kind of guy, so it's one of those hot, smoggy nights when a dame walks into my office. In the film, she's found dead on Judy Garland's star.

Now that technology can help keep the costs down, maybe we'll see more good low-budget films.

Gary's got his camera set-up now, the new DVD camera with movie lenses on it. It's all about lighting. When you have a great cameraman, then the film is gonna look great. If you have a bad cameraman, then it's gonna look bad. So you still have to have the eye behind the camera. As far as costs, imagine shooting it and you don't have to look at dailies. You've got them right away. It's amazing. Before, we used to have to worry about the lab and answer prints. Now you just shoot your film and go home and edit it.

The big studio films these days are actually like expensive versions of the exploitation movies you used to do, and the independent films are the "prestige" movies.

In other words, we had to go in the opposite direction on *Murder on the Yellow Brick Road*. All the nasty words we cut out. Yet we did a whodunit. Can we do that? It took us ten years to achieve that script. Every movie has the good and bad guy beating the shit out of each other in the end. I said I didn't want to do that. As a director, I don't want to have a big fight between the bad guy and me. How do we solve that problem? We tried it on *B.O.R.N.* We tried to solve it. Hoke [Howell] and I tried to solve that problem where we don't break into the building and have the big fight. We hadn't achieved that state of mind yet.

On *Murder on the Yellow Brick Road*, we went in the opposite direction. I said, "Let's cut all of this stuff out and see if we can actually pull the movie off." And we did it. The good guy and the bad guy do not have that fight, and yet the film ends. We were very pleased with that achievement. We don't care if the audience likes it or not. *We* like it, because it means something to us. I think it works really well. What we do is, we have screenings that are not loaded with our friends. We'll screen the film in different places, and they don't even know we're there. When you see the heads turning or twisting or moving in the seats, you know something's wrong. You go and have a concession stand and feed everybody. I let the crowd drift downstairs and I go to the people serving, and I ask what the word is, because they hear it. The minute they come downstairs, they say, "Oh, what a piece of shit. Let's get a drink and get out of here."

But it held. They said everyone that came down gave it a positive reaction and couldn't believe it didn't have all that normal stuff in there. Because it's very easy to hide behind, "Hey, what the fuck? You got a fucking problem? You fuck!" and to get into that kind of dialogue. But what it does is, it crushes the creative spirit, because you're hiding behind shit words. When you cut those words out, suddenly you, as the writer, say, "Wait, I can't use those words?" It forces you to another level of consciousness, which is kind of weird, man. When you're not using those normal words like from *Goodfellas* [1990]. They used to say, after *Goodfellas* came out, you'd go on any interview in town and all you'd have to do is know how to say *fuck*. "Hey, nice fuckin' day, man. You givin' me a fucking problem?" That's all you had to know how to say.

Do you have a favorite film you worked on?

You know something? Each one that we do at that time is my favorite. If you look back at your work, when you finish a film you're already way beyond it. Never are you satisfied with what you've done. I think if you have reached a point of satisfaction, you might as well retire and grow wine. There's no business that I've ever seen that's more challenging. Imagine you've got to get a hundred people thinking in one direction, and when you're out there it's a war. When you plan a film, you fight the weather, human emotions. You take all the human emotions and put them together like Merlin in a pot, and hope the audience will respond to them.

Each one has its own unique style. If you look at Al's films, some people would say, "Well, what a piece of shit." But is it really? Or does it reflect something about him? It's like art. You walk into a museum and some of this stuff you run away from it, and other things attract. You don't know why. Do you know why you like certain things? Mentally, it's something you can identify with. I cannot identify with Tom Cruise flying through the air like Spider-Man, because I know the stunts are not real. When we did *Action U.S.A.* [1989], those are all real stunts. Those are the top stunt guys in Hollywood doing those stunts. They're real. They're not fake. There's no computer-generated stuff. Did you see *Troy* with Brad Pitt [*laughs*]? Now all the poor guy can come up with is playing Jesse James. The great Hollywood circle, I call it. They just put new faces in the same old, tired roles.

Big, Bad and Bald

SID HAIG

Before he temporarily retired from films in the early 1990s, Sid Haig was one of the busiest bad guys in the business. A veteran of more than 50 features and hundreds of television shows, he worked with some of the most famous (and infamous) directors in Hollywood, from Stephanie Rothman and Fred Olen Ray to John Boorman and George Lucas.

Exploitation fans know him best for the string of women-in-prison films he made in the Philippines, but the chrome-domed Haig is just as familiar to the general public from his TV appearances. He was almost always the villain, of course. Tall, with pronounced features, a rough complexion and a shark's smile, Haig's heavies could exude wild-eyed excess one minute and subtle menace the next. He's a better actor than most people realize, and the nuances he brings to the (mostly) stock roles he plays are frequently overlooked. Perhaps that's why he was Jack Hill's favorite actor; the nuances in Hill's films were frequently overlooked, too.

After studying at the Pasadena Playhouse, Haig (who was born in 1939) made his film debut in Hill's student project *The Host* (1960). From there he appeared in a number of films for Hill and his UCLA crony Bart Patton, including *Beach Ball* (1965), *Blood Bath* (1966), and Stephanie Rothman's *It's a Bikini World* (1967), and played the infantile Ralph in Hill's *Spider Baby* (shot in 1964, but released in 1968).

Despite his long list of credits, Haig's cult status wasn't secured until the early 1970s when he trekked into the jungle with Hill and Pam Grier. For three years, Haig played a succession of comical sleazeballs in more than a half-dozen features filmed in the Philippines. He was in so many women-in-prison films that he became almost a token story element; like the shower scene or the cafeteria brawl, you were almost disappointed if you didn't see Haig's leering face at some point in the proceedings.

Haig's film appearances in the 1980s were a mixed bag of low-budget action and horror films, along with dozens more TV appearances. After *Genuine Risk* (1989) and *The Forbidden Dance* (1990), Menahem Golan's entry into the short-lived lambada movie craze, Haig dropped out of the industry for several years.

In 1997, though, Quentin Tarantino coaxed him out of retirement for a cameo in the Pam Grier film *Jackie Brown*. Five years later, neophyte director Rob Zombie cast Haig as the scene-stealing Captain Spaulding in *House of 1,000 Corpses* (2003), which re-launched his acting career. Response to the character was so strong that Zombie made Spaulding an even bigger part of the sequel, *The Devil's Rejects* (2005), and Haig has since made a number of other genre films.

From left: Beverly Washburn, Sid Haig (as Ralph), Jill Banner and Lon Chaney, Jr., starred in Jack Hill's *Spider Baby* (1968). (Courtesy Jack Hill)

Tell me a little bit about your background. Where did you grow up?

SID HAIG: I grew up in Fresno, California. I had a lot of my initial training there. I went to Fresno City College and Fresno State, and moved on to the Pasadena Playhouse where I finished up and got my degree in theater arts. I started working as soon as I graduated.

What year was that?

'61.

What was the Pasadena Playhouse like then?

At the time, and even before that, it was probably one of the four top theater colleges in the world. Illustrious alumni: Gene Hackman, Dustin Hoffman, Charles Bronson, and people like Robert Preston, Rue McClanahan; it goes on and on and on.

What prompted your interest in becoming an actor?

I started when I was about six years old as a dancer. Because I was real clumsy, my mother decided it was time I learned how to walk and talk at the same time, and signed me up for some dance classes. And basically the first time I stepped on stage I decided that was it. It was a good feeling.

What were some of the first jobs you had?

My very first job was Jack Hill's student film, *The Host*. Then right after that I did a western for the Lippert Company.

What was that?

It was called *Firebrand* [1962, directed by Maury Dexter]. Then a month after that, I did my first TV show, which was the original *Untouchables*.

What was that like for you?

It was pretty incredible, because most of my work was on stage, and the two previous jobs being in film and moving a little slower. For the TV show, to just whip in there and bing, bang, boom, get it out, was kind of a weird experience. Bernie Kowalski was directing that episode, and he was smart enough to realize almost instantly that I had come from a theater background. He just took a minute to pull me aside and calm me down and say, "Don't worry about anything. You know what to do, just do it. Leave the rest to us." And it worked out.

What was your part in that episode?

I played a hit man that Frank Nitti put to work getting rid of some people that had concessions in the World's Fair that he wanted. So there was a lot of torture and mayhem involved. It was kind of interesting because when I saw the show, they cut out the scene where I got shot off the roof of the building across from the police station. I called my agent the next day and said, "What's up with that?" She called the studio and they said the reason they did that was that they wanted to have me back in that role. Then shortly after that, there were protests about the show, saying that it was showing Italians in a bad light. And very shortly after *that* the series was canceled. That's the way that goes.

When you were going to school, were you looking specifically to go into films and television, or did you want to continue on the stage?

I was ready to do anything. I liked stage and the idea of taking the process through and building a performance each night. But at the same time, the challenge of maintaining a performance that was shot out of sequence, and still being able to build the highs and lows and have the whole thing all work out, was a challenge.

What were some stage roles you did at the Pasadena Playhouse?

Oh my God [*laughs*]! You're going back too far now. However, I was fortunate enough to do several Main Stage productions, which were basically forbidden ground to students, but for some reason somebody liked me there and I was able to do several roles with some pretty incredible people. Sidney Blackmer, who was one of the giants of theater in New York, I did a show with him, and I worked with Edward Everett Horton. Several people. The list is too long.

Did you continue with your stage work after you broke into films?

No, I dropped out of it pretty much because at that point in time, theater in Los Angeles was nothing. It was basically workshop- and showcase-type productions where you had to pay *them* to work [*laughs*]. After spending all that money in school and a month later getting employed, I didn't feel that I was ready to get into that. Later on I was kind of drawn back into theater and did several productions.

When did you go back?

It didn't take too long. About '64. I was out of it for about three years. A friend of mine who was a director at the Playhouse was starting a little black box theater in Hollywood, and so we all got together and kind of built the thing from the floor up and did several shows there.

Jack Hill told me that he met you through Dorothy Arzner. Tell me about meeting Jack and doing *The Host*.

Well, actually, I didn't know Dorothy Arzner. She had called one of my instructors at the Playhouse and said that they were looking for someone and gave a description of the character. And Julia Farnsworth, who was a longtime friend of hers and a ballet instructor at the Playhouse, suggested me. She gave me a call and told me to call Dorothy. I went out there and met with Jack and read for him, and I guess he liked what I did and we did it.

What was your character in *The Host*?

I was a drifter who wound up in this Indian village in the 1800s. Their understanding of Christianity was pretty literal, and he ultimately becomes the communion — much like the guy that he kind of took over for unwillingly, unknowingly. It was pretty bizarre. I don't know if Jack talked to you about this or not, but this was basically where Coppola got the idea for the third act of *Apocalypse Now* [1979].

Did you have any particular influences or role models as an actor?

I have people whose work I admire. I never really tried to copy anybody's work, but I just had a lot of admiration for some people. Anthony Quinn, and the *young* Marlon Brando. And the *old* Marlon Brando. The middle-aged Marlon Brando, I don't know [*laughs*]! He kind of lost something. He got it back, though. It was a kick for me to work with some people that I had kind of grown up with. Going to Saturday matinees and watching Lon Chaney turn into the werewolf and all that business, and all of a sudden to be on the [*Spider Baby*] set with him, and working with him ... it was a real exciting kind of thing.

You did *Spider Baby*, but you also did *Blood Bath* for Jack before that. That's a film that's caused a lot of confusion. Did you just work in Jack's segments, or did you film with Stephanie Rothman?

Yes, I worked with both of them [*laughs*]. That was a pretty confusing film, wasn't it? Particularly since — I forget what version it was — but we were running down the street, and turned a corner, and in the next shot I went from clean-shaven to a beard. It was pretty weird.

You developed a very long working relationship with Jack Hill. Tell me what he's like as a director, and how that relationship developed.

I appreciate what he is, not only as an artist, but as a person, and the way that he works. I think that he communicates his ideas clearly to you and then kind of gets out of your way and lets you do your work. There are not a whole lot of people who do that. He's not intrusive as a director. And if you come up with an idea, something that he didn't think about, and he likes it, it's in. Working with someone like him is truly a collaborative, ensemble kind of situation. It's really gratifying to work with people like that. Particularly after you've done as much television as I have, where it's, "Look, we've got 19 pages a day, please don't get artsy with me." I actually had a director tell me that one time on a TV show I was working on. He said, "I really appreciate what you're doing, but I don't have time to cover it. So just say the words and let's get out of here." But that's TV for you, and when you realize that your main purpose in being there is to sell soap, you just kind of go along with it, say the words and get out of town.

Any particular memories of the dinner scene in *Spider Baby*?

It was gross. For the drool, I had to put egg whites in my mouth and I just about gagged. Luckily, body chemistry took over, and after that initial rehearsal I just naturally started to drool.

There were chocolate-covered rubber spiders. For the dead cat we had a roast rabbit. And ... stuff. Just a lot of stuff. Nothing really edible. You could kind of swish it around in your mouth for awhile and then you spit it out after the take.

What about Lon Chaney, Jr.?

I was a little in awe at first. I had seen him on screen when I was a little kid, and now here I was on set with him! I remember at one point Chaney needed to be called to the set, so Jack asked me if I would go get him. So I went to him and said, "Mr. Chaney, you're needed on the set." And he said, "Now let's get one thing straight — Mr. Chaney was my father. Call me Lon." And that kind of set the tone.

One of the things that I think was pretty daring in the film was the weird sexual relationship that develops between Ralph and Carol Ohmart's character. There's an implied rape, and then after that Ohmart runs around searching for Ralph, calling his name like a forlorn lover.

Sid Haig (left) and frequent co-star Vic Diaz (right) appeared as treacherous bandits in Eddie Romero's *Savage Sisters* (1974).

[*Laughs*] That's very perceptive of you. Not many people have brought that up. I had this idea for the scene and Jack just said, "Go for it." My idea was that when he grabs her and has his arms around her, he would have these memories of his mother. And at that point he utters the only word he speaks in the entire movie — he says, "Mommy!"

Did you see it when it came out, or were you aware of the release difficulties?

I remember Jack called me to tell me it was out. I think it was in town two weeks and then it was gone.

You were in *Pit Stop* [1969] with Ellen Burstyn.

A very *young* Ellen Burstyn, then called Ellen McRae. That was a great film. That was a lot of fun to work on. It was just kind of loose, flying by the seat of the pants, let's-do-this, let's-do-that kind of thing. We worked very quickly. We only had Brian Donlevy for I think three or four days, and if you've seen the film he kind of runs through the whole thing. So it was a situation to get that all taken care of, and then the driving and dealing with the cars and all that business. It was really kind of a free-wheeling deal. A lot of spontaneous, interesting things were happening.

Also around that same time you did John Boorman's *Point Blank* [1967].

Well, what can I say? John Boorman was an interesting guy. He kind of knew what he wanted, but then when he got onto a location with all of the elements present he kind of improvised a little bit. It was an interesting deal working with Lee Marvin, who had a phenomenal memory. A couple of years after that I did *Emperor of the North* [1973] with him, and *believe me* I had an extremely small role in *Point Blank*, and he still remembered me from that film. And then about four years later we were both signed to do a Bob Hope special, and I walked onto the soundstage and he looked up from a magazine he was reading and said, "Sid, how the hell are you?" He was just really cool to work with. He knew who he was, and there wasn't a lot of pretense behind anything.

You did a ton of television. You did *Batman*, *The Man from U.N.C.L.E.*, *Mission: Impossible*—

If they go back and look through the records I probably did more *Mission: Impossible* episodes than anybody in town. I did one a year. Actually that's wrong; I did two a year for the first five years of the show. And that was a great show to work on. Basically I'd do one show at the beginning of the season with a beard, and one show at the end of the season without one [*laughs*]! Back and forth like that.

Any other TV moments that stick out in your memory?

Probably the most fun that I ever had on a show was doing *Mary Hartman, Mary Hartman*. I went in to do one episode — this might sound like I'm bragging, I'm not. It was a thing where everything clicked — you know how that happens — and a few dozen episodes later they killed me off. That was truly a talented, talented group of people to work with. They were so on top of everything, and so sharp and witty. That show was so far ahead of its time. That's probably why it never took and became a mainstream, big-time TV show. It was great working on that show.

What do you remember about your *Batman* experience?

This came at a point in time when I was doing a lot of work. As a matter of fact, the week before

I went in and interviewed for that show, I had a guest-starring role in different shows every night of the week for seven nights. Howie Horwitz, who was producing *Batman*, said, "Who the hell is this Sid Haig? How come everybody in town is using him and we're not? Get him in here." So I went in, and he said, "Read the script. Anything besides King Tut you want to do, it's yours." So I read the script and I said, "Okay, I'll play the alchemist." It was really a cool deal.

When did you start working that heavily? It seems like a pretty intense schedule.

My agent and I had a mutual friend. I did not know my agent at the time. And this mutual friend kept telling him that he should take me on. He was a sub-agent for another agency, and he said, "I really can't do anything, but send me his picture and if something comes up and we don't have anybody signed with our agency that can play that particular role, I'll put him up for it." That eventually happened about a year later. I went in to read for a little free-speech kind of guy, and Joe Rich, who was the casting director, saw something happening there and said, "Read this other part." So I read that and ultimately got the job. It was the heavy in the show, on *Laredo*. And then it came down to, "This guy doesn't have an agent." So Ernie Dade, who was ultimately my agent and has been for 32 years, called the guy who owned the agency and said, "I know you said we shouldn't sign anybody, blah, blah, blah, but we didn't have anybody for this role, so I sent this guy out and he's got a guest starring role in this show." And the agent said, "Good, sign him." And that was the start of things

Haig (as Hawk) and Ellen Burstyn in Jack Hill's *Pit Stop* (1969). (Courtesy Jack Hill)

happening. That first season that I was with them, I think I did ten episodes and three films. That all doubled the next year. The association has been great.

It's been kind of tough for Ernie to deal with the fact that I have basically said, "No more." I will not carry the gun any more. It's too heavy, I had to put it down, and I just won't do it. I'll sell shoes in Pacoima before I go back to doing that kind of stuff. It got to the point that I was saying the same lines, just wearing a different costume. Stupid. So I got out.

You did a biker film called *C.C. And Company* [1970] with Joe Namath. What do you remember about that?

When I got that film—I know you should never do this—but I had a real prejudice about athletes just waltzing into major roles in films, and was prepared not to like Joe Namath at all. But we became friends. He was just so real, and so appreciative of everything that he was learning as he was going along, and no pretenses at all. Never threw his weight or his money around, and was just a super-nice guy. I appreciated being able to meet him and work with him, and just hang out with him for that five or six weeks.

That was actually a point in time when I realized what a good actress Ann-Margret was. I thought she was that type of cheerleader person that she always played [*laughs*]. And here's another terrifically warm, beautiful person, who I just fell in love with and I would do anything for. She's just a great lady. And I think over the span of time we've all come to realize what a good person she really is.

You also got to work with George Lucas on *THX-1138* [1971].

That was really an interesting experience, because we rehearsed that section of the film for a week, and then took another three to five days to shoot it. That was a situation where you had six cameras working all at the same time, and you were floating from camera to camera. You might be in a long shot on one camera, but then as you moved across and were doing dialogue with somebody, you were in a close-up on somebody else's camera. Very intricate. Well, it didn't cut together; if people had kind of a question in their mind about what this whole place was about and what was going on, that was why. That section of the film was actually in excess of 20 minutes long, but what you got on the screen was about seven. A whole lot of exposition was cut out. That was really an interesting thing to work on because even though there were 12 people in that scene, there were six different scenes going on all at the same time. It was really wild. It took a lot of concentration.

What about Lucas himself?

Lucas was really cool to work with. Basically, the people that were involved in that scene, except for me and maybe one other person, were the cast of the San Francisco production of *Marasad* which he had seen and said, "God, what a bizarre cast!" and just scooped everybody up for his film. He communicated his ideas clearly and just kind of let us go, and would fine-tune little things that we were improvising.

The one thing I always notice about your films is how you change your physical appearance. Often, even in films you made within the same year, you look like completely different person. Is that calculated?

Most of that stuff was stuff that was thought-out in preparation. I still use some of the techniques that I learned along the way, and animal imagery is a part of that. I try to find an animal character that is residing inside whoever it is that I'm playing and take on that physicality. So, yeah, that was pretty much calculated.

Let's talk a little bit about your Filipino period. How many films did you wind up doing down there?

I think I wound up doing about 10 films.

What was shooting like in the Philippines?

Well, when you get used to the fact that there's eight days in the week down there — the seven that we know about, and tomorrow, which can come anywhere in between the seven [*laughs*]. That part of it you kind of work out. I like working there. It was exciting, it was different, it was definitely guerilla theater. When we went there to do *The Big Doll House* [1971], Jack had a choice of either having a set decorator or a camera dolly. That's your choice. He chose the set decorator and we *made* a dolly.

They're innovative with the way they do things, and some of their special effects techniques are far better than ours. They don't destroy as much stuff as we do. They make it look like it's destroyed. There's not as much of a caste system as there is here. It's much more a collaborative effort over there. The crew really takes care of the cast, and the cast really takes care of the crew. We're all fighting the jungle, and rain twenty minutes every day, and typhoons and everything else, so let's just all take care of one another and we'll get this done. I loved working there.

William Smith confronts wayward biker Joe Namath in *C.C. and Company* (1970). Haig, on the far left, appeared in the film as "Crow." The other actors are unidentified.

You have to be a little adventurous to go there, and not mind the strange odors and the strange things that might wind up in your underwear drawer [*laughs*]. I'd go there and work any time.

You did a half-dozen of those films with Pam Grier. How well did you get to know her?

Very well. You can't hang out together in the jungle for all that time and go through everything that you have to go through to get a film done there, and not wind up really good friends. Either that or going after one another with knives. I really enjoyed all the time that I spent with Pam. To watch her grow through the whole experience was good.

What about Eddie Romero?

Eddie Romero was really an interesting guy. Extremely knowledgeable. A lot of times, actors will link up with the insanity of the director and go with that. Eddie kind of linked up with the insanity of his actors, and used that to communicate his ideas. Really a very classy guy, and it was good working with him.

Twenty years in retrospect, how do you view those movies you did in the Philippines?

It's interesting [*laughs*]! It's interesting to see how some of the people have grown, and also—you know, when you're into a style of filmmaking you really don't realize what's going on as much as you do years later when you look back on it and see the style.

I don't know. The movies in the Philippines were the movies in the Philippines [*laughs*]. That style of film — it's not necessarily something that I would like to spend the rest of my life doing, but it was interesting at the time and I think we made them bizarre enough so that everybody realizes that this was tongue-in-cheek stuff that we were doing, as opposed to bad acting!

Tell me about *Jason of Star Command* [1979–1981]. That show had a really great, weird cast: you, Tamara Dobson, Francine York.

This is one of those cases of never say never. Never say you'll never do a soap opera, and wind up doing *Mary Hartman, Mary Hartman*, albeit it was a bizarre soap opera. And never say you will never do a children's show, and wind up doing *Jason of Star Command*.

It was really a great show to work on because the people that were doing it — Lou Scheimer and Art Nadel, who was directing a lot of the shows—were guys with a lot of integrity and not just there to scoop up the bucks, which are plentiful in children's programming. They wanted to make something as good as they could, and for the time period they were spending a *lot* of money on the show. The effects were all really cool. Basically, the first year of the show they broke some ground. The first year they were 15-minute episodes. They were like the old serials that you used to go to as a kid in the movie houses, they were little 15-minute cliffhangers. The second season we went to a half-hour. I guess the third season we would have gone to an hour, I don't know.

That was really a good show to work on. I got to work with some good people. The residual rewards were better than anything that I had ever done, in terms of all the public appearance and special shows, and all those extra bucks that you pick up doing that. That was pretty wild. At the same time you got kind of an idea where maybe television goes wrong sometimes? I remember we were doing an episode, and Jason had just thwarted my plans again, and I banged my fist on the console and said whatever stupid line I was saying. One of the censors for CBS was there, and he said, "We can't do that. That's too violent." So we did the thing again, and what I did with my voice was maybe eight times scarier than banging my fist on the table. And he said, "Okay, yes, as long as you didn't bang your fist on the table, it's all right." [*Laughs*] So that's why television goes in the dumper sometimes. But I loved that show. I could have done that show for another couple of years.

Another one that I really loved doing was *McNamara's Band* with John Byner. If the network had picked it up, and if we weren't playing network politics, that would have been the first hour-long musical comedy on television. And it all happened basically by accident. We were shooting the pilot, and we were kind of getting into that whole '40s nostalgia thing. You have a lot of dead time on the set, and we were all sitting around singing songs from the '40s. We were doing this little five-part harmony thing, and the producers walked by. And they stopped, and they listened, and they looked at one another and they disappeared. They came back with new pages with a song in the show. Every show that we did had at least three musical numbers in it. As a matter of fact, in one Byner was posing as a Nazi morale officer and had an entire company of Nazis singing and dancing in the mess hall. It was pretty bizarre. I would have loved to have seen that show go on and on.

That was a deal where Fred Silverman loved the show, but it was his last year. The show didn't get signed before he left, and after he left anything Fred Silverman touched was now taboo, and that was it. We were out and *Fantasy Island* was in.

Any more television memories stick out in your mind?

The Fall Guy was a great show to work. Lee Majors was really cool to work with. Another good guy, unpretentious, down to earth, not impressed with his success. I really liked working that show.

You did *Galaxy of Terror* in 1981.

I remember that mountain was damn scary to work on. It was basically this papier-mâché, two-by-four, Fiberglas thing that we had to keep crawling up and down for three or four days, and it kept falling through. That was a pretty wild show. I think the special effects on it were great. Of course, some of the people who worked on that show went on to do much bigger and better things, like most of the people that work for Roger Corman. If you look at the cast and crew list on that, I think you'll see that the second-unit director was James Cameron, and he also designed the costumes. Kind of a long way from *The Abyss* [1989] and everything else that he's done, but there he was doing that. Working with Ray Walston was just such a kick. He's one of those old pros who knows what he's doing, and it's no big deal. "Everybody just calm down, and let's get this over with and go have fun."

I've basically had a lot of fun on all of the shows that I've worked on for Corman. First of all, you know that you're going to be doing a show that's going to be successful. They guy's never lost a dime on a picture in his life.

You did some of Fred Olen Ray's all-star epics in the 1980s.

Fred's an interesting guy. I haven't worked with too many people who can work on the budgets he can and still bring it off. He's got a great ability to get people around him that want to work and do good things, and know that this is a place that you can start from. So they work for next to nothing and show what they can do. He's been blessed by having a lot of really talented people to work with. I don't know if you've seen *Warlords* [1989], but we only had a camera dolly for one day of shooting, and there are tons of dolly shots in the film. He found a guy that was really good with a Steadicam, and did all of these really great camera moves in some pretty inaccessible places, and was able to pull it off. That film I kind of enjoyed, because he actually let me do some second-unit directing on that.

How much behind-the-scenes work had you done previously?

When I first started in the business I was doing a lot of tech stuff. As a matter of fact, I did a picture called *Beach Ball* for Lennie Weinrib, and I started as a set dresser on that show. I wound up in several sequences. I was like the guy who carried the plant through, and the plant keeps getting bigger and bigger, and pretty soon he's walking through with a redwood tree [*laughs*]. I wound up in several sequences. In one I was playing drums for the Righteous Brothers. But I also moved from set decorator to boom operator to still cameraman. I was doing everything. That was really cool.

Jack actually gave me a chance to shoot some stuff when we were doing *The Big Bird Cage* [1972]. The flu had run rampant through our cast, and we were behind schedule, which is something that's rare for Jack. We needed some montage stuff shot, basically of me going through the jungle. He sent me out with a cameraman and a camera. All he could afford to let loose of was one lens, so all we had was a cameraman, an 18mm lens, and me. We went out and shot the jungle scenes. It was cool. I appreciated it, it was fun, and it was something that I had always wanted to do anyway. Basically that's what I'm concentrating on now. I want to direct more. I've directed a lot of stage, and I'm doing mom-and-pop-type cable television commercials. And some really good entertainment pieces, I think. Some documentary stuff. I want to get more into that.

What documentaries have you shot?

I did a documentary on shoot boxing. Basically what I was given to work with was about four hours of fight footage, and that was it. We put a script together and took the footage and cut together sequences. I got a couple of guys to act as commentators as though we were really watching fights that were televised by an American company.

I was working for Diamond Entertainment and Marketing, and we had an opportunity to do a documentary on this Shaolin priest who was in the country for a short period of time. It was pretty wild. That was something where you were really flying by the seat of your pants. You couldn't stage anything because with the things that he was doing, there was no take two. You don't ask a guy to park a truck on his stomach a second time [*laughs*]. You really had to be on your toes and ready with everything.

What was your last film appearance?

Remember the lambada wars? *The Forbidden Dance*. There was actually going to be a *Forbidden Dance II*, if you can believe that. A couple of people got a little too starry-eyed and started asking for unreasonable things, and Menahem Golan said, "You know what, I don't think we need to do this." And that was the end of that. After that I did a picture which ultimately wound up being called *Genuine Risk* [1990], which I haven't seen. It was an interesting film to work on, because it was kind of an organic thing and kind of grew — yes, we had a script, but it just grew out of the moment.

What about on television?

I had a recurring role on *Just the Ten of Us*, and when they decided to cancel that show they moved my character from that show to *Growing Pains*. That was interesting, because Bill Kirchenbauer, who was the lead in *Just the Ten of Us*, was the coach at the high school that Kirk Cameron went to. So they moved Kirchenbauer to the West Coast. Janitor Bob came on *Just the Ten of Us*, that show got canceled, so they moved Janitor Bob back to *Growing Pains*. And then that show got canceled. I have the prestige of being in more canceled shows than anybody!

However, at the same time — God bless him, because he kept food on my table — there was Glen Larson. For some reason I became his good luck piece. Every time I was in one of his pilots, the pilot sold. So that became a rule: "I don't care what Sid Haig does, just make sure that he's in my pilot." So I also have the distinction of having more sold pilots than anybody around.

What kind of role would it take to bring you back to the screen?

It would have to be something that was a people film, where I could get away from playing these characters that are almost caricatures, and written that way. It would just have to be something that hit me as something that I wanted to do. I don't know where that is.

I feel very fortunate in a lot of ways. When I look back at my beginnings when I started at the Pasadena Playhouse, we had a freshman class of 150 people, and two years later we graduated 32, and after that two of those people worked. I feel like one of the most fortunate people in the world to have had the kind of career that I've had. It was satisfying in the fact that people wanted me to work for them.

I was stupid in taking everything that came along. I was so flattered that people wanted me to work for them that I did everything, and I wasn't selective in my work. If I were to do this again, I would be much more selective in terms of what it is that I do. I've had a lot of training, and I think I have much more to offer than anybody has allowed me to deliver. Except for — he kind of gets embarrassed when I say this, but I think Jack Hill is the only guy that knows that I'm really an actor. Maybe I'm one of the few people around that knows that he's really a director [*laughs*]. Except for maybe Tarantino, who realizes that and has been very vociferous about it. But that's what it would take. It would have to be something that you can really sink your teeth into. Even if it's a heavy. It's got to be something that's gonna move people, something that's not cartoonish. I'm not saying that I'm holding out to play Hamlet, because that's kind of stupid. It would have to be something that I really connected to.

But in the meantime I'm still trying to start off like a kid as a director. Sometimes that's even more frustrating than trying to get your foot in the door as an actor. I tried to get into AFI, and was told that if I didn't have a student film they couldn't help me out. At that time I was 45. I said, "You don't understand. I'm 45 years old. I've been in this business for 20 years already. I have a family. I can't afford to go off to UCLA, and tuck my little student film under my arm, and come and impress you. If the knowledge that I have attainted over the past 20 years isn't impressive enough, then maybe what I don't need is to be associated with you." But that's just one of life's little challenges, and we'll meet it and conquer it and move on.

What have you been up to lately?

I'm kind of semi-retired, basically because I just got so heavily stereotyped into those thug-type, heavy roles, and it just became a major bore to me. The idea of getting up and going to work used to be exciting, and after I had done the same part 350 times it got a little boring. There was nothing new happening. I know Jack kind of gets embarrassed every time I say this, but it's the truth: The only guy that allowed me the opportunity to use my skills as an actor was Jack Hill. Everything else was, "You look like a duck, you sound like a duck, you walk like a duck — here, play this duck." It just stopped working for me, so I basically dropped out. That's not to say that I wouldn't go back in, because nobody ever really quits the business.

Sounds of Silence

Monte Hellman

Along with Francis Coppola and Jack Hill, Monte Hellman was one of the most gifted talents to emerge among Roger Corman's protégés at Filmgroup and American International Pictures. But while his contemporaries in the Corman sphere moved either into the commercial or exploitation fields, Hellman carved out a niche making highly personal, unconventional films.

Born in New York in 1932, Hellman was an early graduate of the UCLA film program and, like Coppola and Hill, found his first jobs toiling as an editor on Corman projects like *The Wild Ride* (1960), as well as directing new television footage for Filmgroup properties, including *Ski Troop Attack* (1960).

He made his directorial debut with *Beast from Haunted Cave* (1959), about a group of bank robbers being menaced by the cobweb-covered titular creature. He was also one of several directors who shot scenes for *The Terror* (1963).

Hellman and *Terror* star Jack Nicholson went to the Philippines in the mid–1960s to make the action films *Flight to Fury* (1964) and *Back Door to Hell* (1964) for producer Robert Lippert. The pairing with Nicholson worked so well that the two men headed to Utah together, with financing from Corman, to make the westerns *Ride in the Whirlwind* and *The Shooting* (both 1965). The films, not released until several years later, marked the emergence of Hellman's signature style: unorthodox editing choices, minimal dialogue and languid pacing.

After a nearly five-year stretch without directing a feature, Hellman found himself at Universal during the brief, post–*Easy Rider* period when the studio financed a number of edgy projects by young directors. His contribution was *Two-Lane Blacktop* (1971), a black and white road movie that starred singer James Taylor, Beach Boy Dennis Wilson and Warren Oates, who had appeared in *The Shooting*. He and Oates were paired again on *Cockfighter* (1974), an odd film that was mishandled by Corman's New World Pictures, which attempted to market it as an exploitation item.

His final film of the seventies, and his last with Oates, was the European western *China 9, Liberty 37* (1978). Another decade passed before he returned to directing with *Iguana* (1988), which he followed with the unlikely *Silent Night, Deadly Night 3: Better Watch Out!* (1989).

Although Hellman acted as executive producer on Quentin Tarantino's breakthrough *Reservoir Dogs* (1992), his other projects have remained perpetually in development, in part because he's selective about the scripts he's willing to work with, and in part because contemporary producers are increasingly out of step with Hellman's low-key approach to filmmaking. In 2006, he returned to directing for the omnibus horror project *Trapped Ashes*, along with Sean S. Cunningham, John Gaeta, Ken Russell and Joe Dante.

Warren Oates prepares for battle in Monte Hellman's controversial *Cockfighter* (a.k.a. *Born to Kill*, 1974).

Tell me about your time at UCLA. Those were the early years of their film program.

MONTE HELLMAN: It was a lot of film history. Lots of seeing films from the silent era through the sound era, film theory. Reading critical studies of film. Classes in cinematography and editing, and God knows what [*laughs*].

Did you first get interested in editing while at UCLA?

I don't know. I know that I was really excited by editing at that point. I think the first job I had in the film industry was editing.

What was your first professional job in film?

My first editing job was cleaning out the film vaults at ABC studios.

I read that, at UCLA, your final exam was re-editing the climax of *The Lady from Shanghai* [1948].

Yeah, that's right. I think everybody had the same task.

How did your version come out?

I thought it was pretty good! I thought it was better than the end of the original movie [*laughs*]. That's one of the things that excited me, too. It came out better than the Orson Welles version!

Before the ABC job, you were doing some theater work.

Yes. I did three years of summer stock.

Were you directing or acting?

Both. The ones I directed were *Night Must Fall*, *The Hasty Heart*, *Voice of the Turtle*, *Skin of Our Teeth*, and *Of Mice and Men*.

What was the theater?

The theater was in Northern California in a town called Guerneville. We had a theater that had been built as a WPA project years ago, and was in the middle of a redwood forest. It was really beautiful.

Corman met you while you were doing that, didn't he?

No. I actually saw Roger shooting a film one day in Griffith Park while I was working at ABC. My wife at the time was an actress [Barboura Morris], and she was just coincidentally working on some Corman films. I'd already met Roger through her.

Were you already married to Barboura Morris when she started making films for Corman?

I think I was married to her when she started working for Corman, yes.

What was her background?

I think she was from California. She was from UCLA. I met her in summer stock. I hired her for our summer stock company.

Corman actually put some money into a production you were working on at the theater, didn't he?

Again, that was as a result of my having met him socially. I'd asked him to invest, and he gave me a thousand dollars, which he never saw again [*laughs*].

And the theater was eventually shut down.

Yes. We didn't own the theater. It was sold at the end of our first season and converted into a movie theater. Ironically, it was sold to Robert Lippert, and I wound up doing a couple of films for Robert Lippert [*Flight to Fury* and *Back Door to Hell*].

Were you familiar with Corman's work prior to working with him?

I think I just watched them because of my wife.

The first film you did as director, *Beast from Haunted Cave*, was one of the Filmgroup productions. What did you think of the other Corman films from that period, and what did you think of *Beast*?

What interested me about it was that it wasn't really a monster movie. Roger liked *Key Largo* [1948] very much. I think that was one of his favorite movies. He kept making *Key Largo*, just different versions of it. In this case he added a monster to it.

And he basically did the same thing with *Creature from the Haunted Sea* [1961].

That's right. Which I also worked on.

A lot of those Filmgroup movies were kind of tossed off quickly, but there were all sorts of weird subtexts and multiple levels of interpretation possible with most of them.

In a couple of them he had Robert Towne doing screenplays. They were pretty interesting.

Did you edit *Beast*?

I didn't. I was hired to do it, but it was one of Roger's very few union movies, and it was IA out of Chicago. I think we had Andy Costikyan as the director of photography. Since I was not qualified as an editor in the union (I was an apprentice at the time), I wasn't allowed to edit. He paid me a flat fee as writer, director, and editor, so he got cheated out of a third of his money.

Although it probably wasn't much money to begin with.

It wasn't that much money, right.

Any memories of the how the monster was put together in *Beast*?

Dime store stuff. They literally spent about two dollars at the dime store. It was a mostly angel hair and papier-mâché monster.

I thought the creature was effectively shot, given the budget.

You're being kind or you're having problems with your eyes [*laughs*]!

Any memories of the cast? I think you knew Frank Wolff fairly well.

I knew Frank Wolff and Mike Forest beforehand. I was in school with Frank Wolff. I forget how I knew Mike Forest. I knew him for a long time. I didn't really see Richard [Sinatra] after that. I didn't really see our leading lady, Sheila Noonan, after that, either. I just ran into her son about a year ago. I didn't know where she'd gone or what she was doing.

Were they all fairly cooperative being in South Dakota in the winter?

Sheila had a fear of heights and didn't want to go up on the ski lift. She would call and say, "I'm phoning in my performance today."

You also shot additional TV footage for that film, and several other Filmgroup properties. What would typically be involved in putting that footage together?

Just writing some new scenes and expanding the pictures. Roger Corman had made them as 60-minute programmers, and they had to be at least 70 minutes long for television. I added anywhere from 10 to 15 minutes to not only three of his films, but also to *Beast from Haunted Cave*.

Did you always have access to the original cast for the new footage?

I had all the cast, but it was three or four years later, so the people didn't look very much the same. I just happened to get the DVD that just came out of some of that stuff, and he actually put in the added footage that I shot. Betsy Jones-Moreland, for instance, had a different hair color [*laughs*]. A few minor things like that.

Do you revisit the older films very often?

Strangely, I just bought *Back Door to Hell*, and it was a film I had never been very fond of. I'd kind of disparaged it. But they made it better! They cleaned up a lot of the problems. We had problems with the camera sync. I forget what the reason was. We had to kind of sync up all the dialogue by eye, and didn't do a very good job because of the time limitations and so forth. And they fixed it! It was pretty good.

They just played it on Turner Classic Movies for Memorial Day.

Really? I was just amazed at how much coverage we got in three weeks.

The first film you did with Jack Nicholson was *The Wild Ride* [1960]. You were listed as editor. Did you also act as assistant director?

No. I was an associate producer. I was sent up there on the location to kind of help out the director [Harvey Berman], who'd never directed before. Just to be there in case he needed assistance, and also to kind of protect Roger's interests. He always liked to have a spy on the set, so to speak.

What was your official relationship with Corman at that point?

It was just film to film. I didn't have any continuing role. I wasn't working for him on a continuing basis.

Was *The Wild Ride* the first time you met Nicholson?

No, I think I met him when I had my theater group.

Did he strike you at the time as an interesting talent?

It was apparent that he was a star from day one, mainly because he knew it. He was extraordinary, and I recognized that he had abilities above and beyond his acting abilities. We decided to work together, with him doing some writing. I encouraged him to become a director.

You also first saw Warren Oates on stage, right?

I saw Warren do *One Flew Over the Cuckoo's Nest*.

Can you help sort out for me what work you actually did on *The Terror*?

What happened was, Roger shot on his set that he had left over from *The Raven* [1962]. He shot for two days. Didn't really have a complete script. I don't know what the basis of the scenes he shot was, but he hired Francis Coppola to write the rest of the script and direct it.

Francis shot for five weeks and came up with a storyline. The picture still wasn't done. So Roger hired me to start all over again, write a new script. Jack Hill actually wound up writing the script. We used as much as we could of the material that Francis had directed, but wound up, I think, with considerably more of the picture than we were able to use of his footage.

Did you work on the editing?

I wasn't the editor, but I can't remember if I actually edited my scenes or not. It seems to me that I did.

Did you watch the finished product?

Sure. I think it's pretty bad [*laughs*]. We didn't think about those things then.

I always thought it came off like one of those books where a different author writes each chapter.

We only shot for five days. It was pretty intense because the first day — kind of typical of the situations with Roger — nobody had bothered to get permits. We got stopped before we could shoot. We spent the first half of the day down at the city hall trying to get a permit. It really clobbered our shooting schedule.

Did Jack Nicholson direct any scenes in *The Terror*? Corman says he did; Jack Hill says he didn't.

Not that I know of. There were only Francis and myself and Roger.

Did you work with the full cast on *The Terror*?

I worked with probably everybody except Boris Karloff. I think somebody who just did a book about my movies figured out that I did something like 40 percent of the movie.

How did you get involved in the war movies you made in the Philippines, *Flight to Fury* and *Back Door to Hell*?

I guess it was Fred Roos who had seen *The Terror* in Hong Kong, and he knew that both Francis and I had worked on it, so he cabled Robert Lippert and said, "I'd like either Francis Coppola or Monte Hellman to direct." They couldn't find Francis, so that's how I got the job.

Was *Flight to Fury* the first script you'd worked on?

Well, I'd worked on *Beast from Haunted Cave*. I supervised the writing of *Back Door to Hell* and *Flight to Fury*. Both were written on this ship that we sailed to the Philippines on.

How was your experience in the Philippines?

It was interesting. I learned a valuable lesson, which was you couldn't really depend on anything being done without checking on it numerous times, and even if you did that, you were apt to find out once you got on the set that nothing was there that should have been there. That proved to be true in the Philippines and every place else I ever shot. It really made me hands-on in terms of following through on every aspect of every production.

Do you remember much about the Philippines cast members like Vic Diaz or Joe Estrada?

Joe Estrada became president of the Philippines. They were terrific. In fact, I was just watching some of *Back Door to Hell*, and the Philippines actors were very good. They had a very lively film industry at the time, and they had a lot of experience.

After that were the two westerns you did in Utah. Those came together after you had pitched a script called *The Epitaph* to Corman.

You know more about me than I do!

What was the plot of *The Epitaph*? I know there was an abortion mentioned in the script.

It was a very simple story. A young actor, who was going to be Jack, finds out his girlfriend is pregnant, and spends three days running around trying to raise money for the abortion. We were going to intersperse this with scenes from some of the actor's movies. Of course, they would have been scenes from Jack's movies. It was kind of interesting. I don't think it was what Roger had in mind. I thought it would have been an interesting film, but he didn't want to do it. He gave us a chance to do the two westerns as an alternate.

Were you a fan of westerns?

Absolutely. Those were the first films I saw when I was a kid. To me, that's what a movie was. They were the *real* movies.

Millie Perkins in *The Shooting* (1965), one of two westerns Hellman shot in Utah with Jack Nicholson.

Were there particular films that you had in mind as you were trying to craft the scripts for those?

Not the stories, but just in terms of research for the work of directing. I guess maybe the stories, too. Jack and I watched a number of westerns including *Stagecoach* and *My Darling Clementine*, *One-Eyed Jacks*. *Shane*, I think.

Paul Lewis and Gary Kurtz worked on those films. How did you know them?

I can't remember how I met Paul Lewis. I think Gary had contact with Corman, so he was suggested by Corman. Paul, I can't remember.

By the time you'd done those two films, how had your approach changed? Did you feel you had more of a handle on what you wanted to do as a director?

I think on *Beast from Haunted Cave*, I didn't know anything at all, so that was ground zero [*laughs*]. I think that I kind of gradually learned the craft of it, but I was kind of surprised at what a big difference there was between *Beast from Haunted Cave* and *Back Door to Hell*. That was a major leap, and after that everything was small increments.

How would you compare the two westerns, in terms of what you were trying to accomplish? *Ride in the Whirlwind* is considered the more traditional of the two.

I worked on those scripts in different ways. I worked all day with Jack; we were really just locked into this tiny little office in Beverly Hills. We knocked out *Ride in the Whirlwind*. I was pacing and he was sitting at the desk writing in longhand.

Carole Eastman I would see every night, and read her pages. Jack I think had laid out a kind of outline of the story. I think Carole worked one scene at a time. She would just kind of work in a very organic way, and see where it took her. It was very interesting to see that process, and then to read her pages. At the end of the day I would either say yes or no, right direction or wrong direction. Some days she would go back to the point she'd been at before, and some days she would just go back to where that day's work would end.

Did you like one better than the other?

I liked them a lot. It was the first time I really was doing material that I had selected. *Back Door to Hell* was from a screenplay Richard Guttman had written. We just pretty much threw that out and wrote a new script from scratch. That's been kind of an M.O. that I've utilized ever since. I've been given material, and then thrown out the script and written a new script. It's kind of worked for me. I like doing that [*laughs*].

The release of both of those films was delayed quite a while.

Jack took the pictures to the Cannes Film Festival and had a very successful screening. A lot of interesting people came, like Godard. He established a lot of personal relationships and a lot of relationships that were good for the films. He wound up selling the pictures, and the company that bought them went bankrupt. The pictures were kind of locked up in court proceedings for three years. They couldn't be released in France until at least three years after he had originally sold them.

The final French release led to them being sold almost every place in the world except the U.S., because Roger had sold them to Walter Reade-Sterling. They had lied and said they were going to release them in theaters. We assumed they would because they owned a lot of theaters, but instead they just put them in a TV package and sold them on TV. So their chance of being released into theaters disappeared.

So there wasn't a theatrical release?

I think they played for about a week in some place in Texas, but that was all.

You used cameraman Greg Sandor on several films. Did he shoot *Two-Lane Blacktop*?

Yes. He got a credit as photographic advisor because he was promised to get into the union on that picture and they wouldn't let him in. They had to hire a stand-by union cinematographer who stayed at the hotel.

Can you tell me anything about him?

He was a Hungarian from Cuba [*laughs*]. Aren't they all?

Pretty much all cameramen seemed to be Hungarian back then.

I guess so. He was the only Hungarian who never got into the union. I don't know why. I guess he didn't have the right connections.

You then wound up working at Universal for a time.

I was hired as a contract director, believe it or not, for the princely salary of $250 a week, and developed a script with Carole Eastman. They decided not to do it. My contract was not picked up after six months or something.

After that, you worked as an editor for Corman for several years.

I worked quite a bit for Roger. I worked as an editor on *The Wild Angels* [1966]. I worked as an editor on another picture that Roger was doing for Columbia [*A Time for Killing*, 1967], then he got fired, so I left that picture.

I worked as a dialogue coach on *The St. Valentine's Day Massacre* (1967). Roger was producing a picture called *Explosion* for AIP, which I was to direct. Actually, we cast it and we were three days from beginning to shoot when the picture got cancelled.* I got paid in full for that and got into the Directors Guild.

What was that film supposed to be about?

It was about a black sheriff in the South. It was about racial prejudice. We met with Samuel Arkoff a few days before we were going to shoot. This happens sometimes. A lot of studios start looking at what it is they are making at the last minute. They don't pay much attention until then. We said it was about tension between whites and blacks in this town. Arkoff said he grew up in Missouri, and there was no such thing as prejudice in Missouri. He thought it was totally fictitious, and an impossible story. He cancelled the movie. He said, "We had one black in our town and everybody liked him." [*Laughs*]

You have an acting credit in the James Frawley film, *Christian Licorice Store* [1971].

That was a picture that was produced by Michael Laughlin, who was the producer of *Two-Lane Blacktop*. He offered me both pictures to direct, and I picked *Two-Lane Blacktop*. I wasn't interested in directing *Christian Licorice Store*. He was a very funny man. I remember a conversation we had where he was trying to convince me to do it. He said, "What is it you don't like? We have a scene in Laurel Canyon. You can change it. You can make it Benedict Canyon. Beverly Glen. Anything you want!" That obviously wasn't the problem I had with the script [*laughs*].

But you did do *Two-Lane Blacktop*.

That was one of those scripts that I said yes, and then threw it out.

You filmed that in sequence, moving cross-country, right?

It was one of the best sales jobs I ever did. Universal was convinced that since the whole picture took place inside a car and mostly at night, we could shoot the whole thing in the Fernando Valley. I somehow convinced them that it would be much better to shoot it in the real locations.

This was part of a clutch of "youth films" being made at Universal. Peter Fonda directed one of the others.

Ned Tanen was one of the executives who convinced them to do these five pictures, *Two-Lane* and *The Hired Hand* [1971], *Taking Off* [1971], *The Last Movie* [1971] and *Diary of a Mad Housewife* [1970]. It was one of those kind of insane projects that, really, Lew Wasserman didn't have any faith in. He was just doing it to be nice to Ned, but he really didn't believe in these pictures. Then he did his best to kill them when they came out, just to prove that he was right. "You've had your fun; let's get serious and make real movies." That was the extent of it.

---

*AIP eventually used the title *Explosion* on the 1969 Jules Bricken film about a hippie and a draft dodger fleeing to Canada.

Musicians Dennis Wilson (left) and James Taylor hit the road in Hellman's *Two-Lane Blacktop* (1971).

That had to be a frustrating experience.

Yes, it was. One of the things we had in our contract was final cut, which I'd never had before. So it was kind of interesting.

How so?

I think it's nice knowing that you're going to get the movie you want to make. It's your vision, not somebody else's vision. Today it's getting worse and worse, because producers have access to digital editing and there are too many possibilities and choices they can make. It's not a lot of fun. I don't think it leads to good movies.

I was watching *Two-Lane Blacktop* again this morning, and I'd forgotten all the little things in it that were so funny, like randomly offering someone a boiled egg through the car window. Were those types of things in the script, or was there much improvisation?

I think everything was in the script other than the a couple of scenes we improvised. One was the cicada scene, and there was another tiny little one-line scene.

Did you use a lot of locals for the extras?

We brought Alan Vint in from Hollywood. I brought Bill Keller in from Utah, because he'd been in the westerns. We brought Harry Dean, obviously. Most of the real smaller roles, all the people seen doing things like the people working at the gas stations, people working in restaurants or shops, they were all the people who actually did that.

Was that difficult to manage or to direct?

It was great, because they knew exactly what to do. I didn't *have* to give them direction.

You use a lot of quiet spaces in your films, where there is no dialogue or minimal dialogue. When did you first discover how useful that technique could be?

Well, I don't know when I discovered this or that. I do know that I've just been having some arguments with my producers on the current movie about the use of music over a scene that's literally supposed to be silent. It's supposed to be archival nitrate silent footage. One of the things that occurs to me, and it's something that I discovered along the way (I think maybe I discovered it doing the westerns), is that an audience can't really absorb oral stimuli and visual stimuli simultaneously. If you want them to see something, you can't have anything distracting on the soundtrack. If you want them to hear something, you can't have something distracting on the screen.

It kind of became clear when Roger was completely convinced that one of the problems with *The Shooting* was the fact that nobody would understand that his alter image was his brother. So he wanted to repeat three times in dialogue, "His brother, Coin." He was adamant that we say this at least three times or the audience wouldn't get it. Well, the audience still doesn't get it, because they're *watching*. They aren't *listening*.

There really aren't quiet spaces in films any more.

With the new film, I saw what happened as soon as the silent footage began. The audience became so absorbed. It just commands their attention in a way that sound and pictures together never do.

Why do you think people *aren't* quiet in films any more? There are never any pauses.

I think that it's not new. It's not something that just happened. Maybe it will never come back, but there was a very destructive aspect to sound. When sound came in, suddenly these tremendous visuals—the complicated camera moves of the Germans and all kinds of brilliant stuff that was beginning to happen at the end of the silent era—stopped, because in the early days they couldn't move the camera with sound. It became talking theater. Obviously that's changed, but I think the idea that it's drama as opposed to moving pictures maybe hasn't changed so much.

One of the films where you again used minimal dialogue was *Cockfighter*, which was a property Roger brought to you.

Yes, he had bought the novel and commissioned Charles Willeford to write the screenplay. I had been off in Hong Kong working on a movie that I got fired off of.

That was *Shatter* [1974].

Yes. When I came back, Roger called me and said, "I'm doing this picture. Do you want to direct it?" This was maybe the first time I had ever been involved in something where it was ready to go, the script was completed and I didn't have to start from scratch on the screenplay. It was difficult for me. I had a lot of problems with the script and I got Roger to agree to hire Earl Mac Rauch, who was either a disciple of Terry Malick's or they were both disciples of somebody else. He was from Texas. Roger agreed that Mac would do this rewrite, and after a week he saw his baby literally being taking away from him. He said, "Okay, you have one more week." We had started out the first week just working from page one, intending to go through the whole script. So the second week we kind of had to concentrate on the most important scenes. He did some wonderful stuff, including the scene by the river, including the scene where Warren steps on the rooster's head and hands it to his girlfriend, things like that.

Warren actually took the head off the rooster, didn't he?

Yes he did. It *was* dead [*laughs*].

Once it was finished, Corman began tinkering with it because he didn't think he could market it correctly.

That's right. He became concerned, first of all, because there was a tremendous backlash by animal rights groups and so forth. It looked like it was going to be very difficult to get any kind of real distribution. So he tried changing the title and tried to make it seem like something that it wasn't. He created a trailer that was very deceptive. Then he insisted on putting some of the footage from the trailer into the movie because he said it would have been dishonest not to do that [*laughs*]. So he added these dream sequences, tits and ass and car crashes, stuff that had nothing to do with the movie, just because it was in the trailer.

There was a great tagline for that film: "He came into town with his cock in his hand, and what he did with it was illegal in 49 states."

That's a good one [*laughs*]! I wish I'd thought of it.

You shot that in Georgia. What was Georgia like in '74?

Georgia was wonderful. It was really, first of all, a physically beautiful area. Atlanta is a very interesting city. Very cultured city. The people that I was working with were all professional cockfighters. They were the best people on Earth, just wonderful. I had a very strong negative reaction to the sport itself, but the people were wonderful.

Did they have any reservations about participating with the film because of bad publicity?

Just the opposite. They were real enthusiasts. It's more than a sport to them; it's kind of a philosophy of life or something. Some of them wrote poetry. They were very different from what you would expect. Not the kind of typical concept of the redneck or anything like that.

Tell me about *China 9, Liberty 37*.

On *China 9*, I was working with Elliot Kastner over a couple of years trying to find a project to do together. We had agreed on a picture, I can't remember the title, but it was about a race-car driver who has to drive across Europe with a body that's being preserved in extremely cold temperatures because there's a time limit to how long you can stay alive like that. That got cancelled. I didn't hear from Elliot for about a year, then I got a phone call from him. He had given me a script called *A Man for Deejum's Wife*, which I had rejected. I got a call from him, he was in Rome, he was meeting with some producers there and they wanted to do that film. I said that script had a lot of problems, and I didn't see how it could be made the way it was. He said, "No, no, maybe it needs a little polish, but can you come right over to Rome?" This was like the day before Christmas. I said I had to spend Christmas with my family, so I couldn't come until after the New Year.

He said, "Fine, get here as soon as you can." As soon as I hung up the phone I called up a friend of mine, Jerry Harvey. I said, "You have to help me out. I just kind of committed to doing this movie, and I know this sounds strange because my career hasn't even begun, but I think this will end it if I do this picture. You have to write a new script."

He looked at it and he called a friend of his, Doug Venturelli, and the two of them knocked out *China 9* in eight days. I arrived in Rome with the new script in hand and the Italian producers loved it. Elliot Kastner hated it. He dropped out and I wound up making this movie for two of the biggest scoundrels! He just called a few minutes ago, and he said, "Whatever you do, don't talk about me." Here I am talking about him [*laughs*]! That was the happiest movie I ever made in terms of how much fun we had while making it.

The unhappiest movie was the one I made again in Europe, and again in Spain, this time in the Canary Islands. *Iguana*. That was the worst experience. *China 9* was the best experience I ever had.

How did the *Iguana* project come together?

It was offered to a friend of mine. He didn't want to do it. He recommended me. The producer, who is Italian and who didn't and doesn't speak a word of English, was in New York and he had about four or five directors that were recommended to him. I was on the list, and he called me first because I had two threes in my phone number. He believed in numerology. I went to New York and met with him, and I read the script that he had. As has been my experience, this was an unbelievably bad script, all in the form of a diary, which I guess had been taken direct from the novel. Had no dramatic structure. Just an impossible script to ever shoot.

I decided to turn it down. So he came to L.A. and I had a meeting with him, with a friend of mind acting as translator. This friend had spent ten years in Italy becoming an Italian movie star, so he spoke perfect Italian. I said, "Tell him that I regret that I'm not able to do the movie." So he translated that as, "Monte would like to do the movie, but he has some reservations and he'd like to make some changes." At the end of the meeting, I thought I'd said one thing, but I was really saying something entirely different [*laughs*]. So there I was doing the movie.

Despite the problems with making it, *Iguana* is one of your favorites, isn't it?

It looks like a primitive, because it is a primitive. Because of really incompetent production, we didn't have lights for three weeks, and many days we couldn't begin shooting until four in the afternoon. A scene that I may have had five different shots to cover, I had to shoot in one shot. Looking at it now, compared to *Back Door to Hell*, it looks like it was Grandma Moses. How do you make a movie if you have no props, no sets, no lights and no time? It becomes very primitive. I still like it. You take the problems and you make an asset out of a liability.

What about *China 9*?

China 9 I like. I feel that it's disappointing as a western because it's so lackadaisical, and not very much action. But there are some things about it that I like.

The producers altered that film after it was completed.

They did a lot of things. First of all, they recut it for Italy because there are scenes in it that they said there was a superstition against them. They took out the circus, they took out a lot of the jokes because they didn't understand them. They cut the picture considerably. It was after the picture was sold, and I was the one who arranged the sale because they had been about to make a deal in 1978 at the Cannes Film Festival with a schlock distributor who was going to release their cut version in kind of a cheap package of TV/video/whatever pictures. I felt I had to stop this, so what I did was, I asked to borrow the one video they had that they were using to sell it. I said I had somebody else who was interested, which was kind of a lie, and I just kept it for three days. They kept saying, "Where's the video?" I gave it to Lorimar and they agreed to buy it in my version, and that's how I saved it. Otherwise that version would have been destroyed.

You then made the third film in the *Silent Night, Deadly Night* series, which was a bit of a departure for you.

That was another one where I kept saying no, no, no, but the producer was one of my best friends, and finally I just said, "Okay, but we have to start all over on the script." Again, we wrote the script in eight or nine days, and began scouting locations even before the script was finished. From the time that we began writing the script to the time we began shooting was about five weeks. The picture was shot in four weeks, it was edited in ten days, then I went to Cannes again. I came back and we mixed the picture, and we had a print by the first of July. By the fourth of July we were in Spain showing the movie.

Were you familiar with the other two films?

I incorporated some footage from both of them, I think. At least the first one. I'd seen them both. I guess they're supposed to be scary. They scared me — they scared me away from the project [*laughs*]!

The first one was very controversial at the time because of the killer Santa.

Of course we subverted that idea. We were castigated by the true believers.

On *Silent Night*, you used some footage from *The Terror*.

Yes we did, just for the fun of it. I thought it was also interesting to have scenes of a blind girl watching television [*laughs*]. And watching a scene about a man having his eyes clawed out!

Tell me about the new project, *Trapped Ashes*.

There are five directors. The piece that I did is kind of a speculation on the reason why Stanley Kubrick never came back to Hollywood. Why he stayed in Europe. It's kind of a vampire movie, I guess. He falls in love with this girl who turns out to be a 400-year-old vampire. It was very satisfying because I always think it's luck if you find really terrific actors who are the perfect actors for the role. I found the perfect person to play a young Stanley Kubrick [Tygh Runyan], and all the other people were great as well. It was shown as a stand-alone short at the Cannes Film Festival.

How was it received?

It was very well received.

It was an interesting collection of people: Joe Dante, Sean Cunningham, Ken Russell. How did you get involved?

The writer-producer Dennis Bartok is a good friend of mine.

Until you did *Trapped Ashes*, you've mostly just had projects in development. What's the status of those?

The Payoff is still floating around. Another one was *Ghost of a Chance/Ever After*. Plus I had a picture called *Secret Warrior* that I worked on for a long time. I've got a closet full of projects that are in various stages of abandonment or revitalization. My favorite of them is a picture called *Dark Passion*, which I won't give up on as long as I have the strength to make it.

In terms of the types of films you would like to make, how receptive or unreceptive has the industry been? Has that changed over time?

I think the one film that I have that generally is seen positively from a commercial point of view is *Ever After*. It is commercial. The problem with it is that the script is just not as good as it needs to be. Nobody is in the development business any more. You can't make a deal and say you'll make the script right. You have to somehow get it right, then set it up. I just haven't had the means to get that work done on it. The rest of them, the projects themselves like *Dark Passion*, from the very beginning — and it's still true today — it's just too dark. People think you can't make a movie about a lead character who's not instantly likeable. If he's dark and if he does things that are considered unpleasant, studios don't want to make the movie.

That seems to be changing somewhat.

Well, the easiest way to make a movie is to make a deal at a studio. That's one entity that makes a decision. At one point in time, that entity was really one person who made a decision. Now, it's got to get past ten readers and another dozen junior executives who want to put some input in it. If you do make a development deal, which I did on a picture during the '90s called *Freaky Deaky*, the chances of it getting made are next to zero, because there are just so many people who are trying to make it into something different from what it really is.

When I sold *Freaky Deaky*, they wanted to make it into another *Good Will Hunting*. Well, Elmore Leonard is not *Good Will Hunting*. There's no way you can make that into something that's so fundamentally different from the source.

Do you think digital filmmaking will help remove some of those obstacles?

You can make a movie now for $60,000 that will have some rough edges, that's one result. Despite the success of my past films, I really want to reach a large audience. I'm not interested in making a movie just for iPods. At least not yet.

It's Not Nice to Hate

JACK HILL

When Jack Hill walked away from filmmaking more than twenty years ago after his disastrous experience filming *Sorceress* (1982) for Roger Corman, it looked like the director of *Spider Baby* (1964) and *Coffy* (1973) was hanging it up for good. After two decades in the movie business, Hill had finally had enough. Disgusted with the jealousy, the back-stabbing and the cutthroat competition, he waved the rat race goodbye.

When I first spoke to him in the late 1990s, however, Hill was experiencing something of a renaissance. His films with Pam Grier had gotten a well-deserved second look, and the cult audience had re-discovered *Spider Baby*. More astoundingly, Hill's seldom-seen *Switchblade Sisters* (1976) was re-released in *theaters* in the summer of 1998 via Quentin Tarantino's company, Rolling Thunder. Along with all of this attention came the opportunity to direct again, and Hill—who told *Variety* in 1994 that he simply wasn't interested in movies any more—said he would be more than happy to take it.

Unfortunately, the new Jack Hill film still hasn't materialized, but Hill seems to have taken this in stride, as he has most of the other twists and turns in his career.

Talking to Hill today can be a bit disconcerting. To most film buffs, he is Jack Hill, Exploitation Director, the man who made nudies with his UCLA classmate Francis Coppola; who reinvented the women-in-prison film with *The Big Doll House* (1971) and *The Big Bird Cage* (1972); who introduced the world to Pam Grier.

But there is another side to Jack Hill. Unlike the more gregarious Hollywood hucksters who were his contemporaries, he's mild-mannered, witty and refreshingly frank in his appraisal of his films. It's almost hard to believe that this is the same man who conceived the infamous penis-in-a-jar gag for *Foxy Brown* (1974).

Hill was born in 1933 in Oxnard, California. His mother was a music teacher, and his father was a set designer for Disney. At UCLA, Hill and Coppola toiled on each other's student films (Hill's *The Host* has long been cited as the inspiration for the ending of *Apocalypse Now*), then found themselves part of Roger Corman's first generation of film school recruits.

After he made *Pit Stop* in 1967, Hill directed Boris Karloff in the horror's king last four films, the Mexican co-productions: *Cult of the Dead* (a.k.a. *The Snake People* and *La Muerte Viviente*), *Dance of Death* (a.k.a. *House of Evil* and *Macabre Serenade*), *The Torture Zone* (a.k.a. *Chamber of Fear* and *La Camera del Terror*) and *Alien Terror* (a.k.a. *Sinister Invasion* and *Invasion Sinestra*).

Switchblade Sisters was Hill's last official directing credit. He worked (uncredited) on the scripts for *The Bees* (1978), *City on Fire* (1979) and *Death Ship* (1980). In 1980, Hill and his second wife, Elke, began practicing Siddha Yoga under the guidance of Swami Baba Muktananda.

Beverly Washburn (left) and Jill Banner prepare to cut loose in Jack Hill's *Spider Baby* (1968). (Courtesy Jack Hill)

Hill continued writing scripts after the *Sorceress* debacle, but eventually turned his attention to a series of novels. Most recently, Hill appeared in the films *I Pass for Human* (2004) and *Sugar Boxx* (2007), a women-in-prison film that also featured Tura Satana and Kitten Natividad.

What was your reaction when Miramax contacted you about *Switchblade Sisters*?

JACK HILL: Well, I was astonished. That's about as understated as I can get. But I knew that it was a favorite of Quentin's [Tarantino], and when I realized that they had made an arrangement with Quentin to release pictures of his choice, then I realized what was going on.

You actually found the negative yourself, correct?

Yeah, almost by accident. The original distributor of the film gave me some clues where I might look for it, and one of them turned out to be a film warehouse in North Hollywood. There was a bunch of stuff on a shelf there that they didn't know what it was, and there it was, among other things.

There's been quite a bit of interest in your work lately. You were quoted in *Village Voice* as saying, "The films I made in those days are really just trash —"

I don't think I put it that way. I said they were *considered* to be trash, and I went on to say that now critics are taking them seriously and writing profound things about them, and seeing things in them that they didn't notice before because they didn't look at them. They were kind of lumped together with other movies of that type.

Then what's your actual opinion, since you've been misquoted?

The movies I made in those days? I think they're *classy* trash.

Why do you think there is such a fascination with these types of film?

Well, people have asked me that question, and it's kind of hard to give an answer. I suppose they were really kind of outrageous, because all we had to sell, really, were strong ideas. We didn't have big budgets or big stars, so we had to go for really kinky ideas. There's a certain kind of liveliness and vitality to them that you don't find in most movies today. Because they have so much money at stake, everything kind of gets canceled out.

You started out as a musician. What prompted your interest in directing and writing?

I just kind of fell into it. I had been a musician, I had a career as a concert artist and an arranger, and I was interested in composing for films. I went back to school to finish my degree in music, and I got into the cinema department in order to learn a little bit more about how I could score films. In fact, I did score a student film while I was there. Then I took a writing course and they encouraged me to do more, and I ended up writing and directing a student film. I kind of got odd jobs as a cameraman and as an editor, and writing, and then ended up starting to direct and kind of changed careers.

How did you first meet Roger Corman?

I was a student at UCLA, and Roger in those days, when he needed some cheap work done or he needed to find some new talent, he would ask around at places like UCLA or USC, places like that. I guess mostly UCLA, because he had been a student there himself. They would recommend somebody, and so that's what happened to me. I went there, at about that same time Francis Coppola was doing some work for him.

A lot of those early films that you did for Corman were paste-up jobs, where you were re-editing existing films, like the Russian sci-fi movies. How did you approach that type of assignment?

I needed the money [*laughs*]! Well, with different things it's kind of hard to say how you approach any type of assignment. You just get something that it looks at first glance like it's gonna be impossible, and you try to find a way to do it. That's why it's such a wonderful training ground. For the Russian films, since you mentioned them, Corman had purchased the rights to a couple of Soviet-made science fiction films, which had wonderful special effects. Since the actors were wearing spacesuits half of the time, he got the idea that we could duplicate the spacesuits, put our own actors in there and shoot a lot of extra material to make sense of it. It didn't really work, but it was releasable.

You first used Sid Haig in *The Host*, and he's a wonderful character to watch onscreen. How did you meet him?

My supervisor — the teacher that I was working under when I was doing my student film — was Dorothy Arzner. She was a great woman, the only woman A-Hollywood director all through the 1930s and 1940s. She was coaching at the Pasadena Playhouse, and Sid was a student there. She recommended that I see him. When I first saw him I thought he wasn't really the right type for what I had in mind at all, but she told me to have him read and I did, and he was just really great.

Francis Coppola has sometimes said that when he went to work for Corman at AIP, he took some flak from some of his classmates about "selling out." Was that your experience?

No. I don't know why they would have thought he was selling out. He always had in mind exactly what he was going to do with his career. He had a lot of experience in theater already, he'd gone to a theatrical college in New York, and he had written and directed plays (his father was in the theater). He knew from the very beginning that he was going to win the Goldwyn Award and that he was going to be the biggest, hottest director in town. He took the steps that he had planned, and did it exactly right, and that's what happened.

I guess he was puzzled because some people were upset with him for being successful at what he wanted to do.

Jealousy. A lot of jealousy in this business. It's unbelievable.

You made a few nudist films in the mid-sixties — *Tonight for Sure* [1962] and *The Playgirls and the Bellboy* [1962] with Francis Coppola, as well as *The Raw Ones* [1965] and *Mondo Keyhole* [1966]. Was it awkward filming them in the nude?

Do you mean nudie cuties or nudist films? I did some shooting with the things that Coppola worked on, but I also did nudist films. They're two entirely different things: Originally, non-theatrical 16mm films for mail order, based on the nudist movement as a respectable thing. That's how they got away with it, basically. Then we assembled a lot of those together and opened a full-length feature in the theaters. It was the first time full-frontal nudity had been shown in a theater. We were all standing around expecting the police to come in any moment. They didn't, and it sort of freed that whole area.

But was it awkward for me? The only thing that was awkward was when you're running a camera, I usually had my pockets full of stuff, and when you don't have any pants on, it's a little difficult to do that.

When all was said and done, and the movie came out, what did you think of *The Terror* (1963)?

[*Laughs*] Well, it's hard to say. I mean, I didn't have anything different to think of it when it was released than what I'd been thinking of it every step of the way, working on the editing. I had seen it hundreds of times by the time it was released. I thought it had a great score, I'll say that for it.

We always had trouble trying to make sense of the story. I was the last person to actually do any writing on it, writing some new scenes and putting it together and organizing it so that it would make sense. I tried to make as much sense out of it as I could, and basically tried to put in some good scenes in order to take your mind off of the fact that the story wasn't making sense.

You also worked with Karloff on those four Mexican films. Was it difficult working with him when he was so ill?

First of all, I didn't work directly with Karloff during the making of *The Terror*. He finished whatever he shot before I ever became involved. On the Mexican films he was an absolute sweetheart. He knew that he did not have long to live, and he loved working and he was anxious to work. The way he put it was: "I want to go out in harness." That's the way he felt about it. It was a difficult shoot, and I felt kind of sorry for him, too, because it was very disorganized. But he liked the scripts, and he liked the idea of playing four different characters on four successive weeks. He was in a wheelchair then, and when he had action to do he'd breathe some oxygen, get up and do his action, and then he'd come back and sit down in the wheelchair and have his oxygen again. That's the way he got through it. He was quite a sweetheart.

Spider Baby **stands apart not only from the rest of your work, but also from about anything else that was out at that time. Where did the idea for the script come from?**

I don't know. I don't know where ideas come from. The idea just came to me for the story, and I wrote it out as kind of a brief outline. A friend of mine [Karl Schanzer] who was an actor — he was working as a private investigator for two guys in the real estate business who had been at UCLA at the same time I had, and wanted to get into the film business with a low-budget horror film. They were actually looking for a full, written-out script, and when they read this, it was so different from anything they had read they talked to me about it. I showed them some work that I had done for Roger, and they decided to put up the money for me to write the screenplay and direct the picture.

When you were developing the story, did you have any idea how off-the-wall it would be?

Well, we didn't use that expression in those days. I don't know. It doesn't seem that way to me. It was just something that everybody sort of liked, and was fun, and I thought would be an entertaining movie. Movies kind of take a shape of their own as you get into them, both in the writing — the initial idea as you write it out it tends to take on its own kind of life, different than what you anticipated — and also when you start shooting, it takes on a different form than what you originally thought it would be.

Do you have any particular memories of shooting the dinner scene?

The art director was a gay guy who was into cooking, and he cooked the food, which everybody said was delicious. He made a big thing out of cooking that; he wanted to cook up something special so the people could really enjoy eating it as well as shooting the movie.

Jill Banner gave the most striking performance in the film.

Yeah, just an amazing talent. She'd never done anything before. She came in for an interview hoping she might get some kind of little small part. We were all just so struck by her, we had her read and we just felt she was perfect. She did her homework, she came prepared. She was just a wonderful talent. It was a real loss that she didn't get the right breaks.

Do you know much about her background?

No, I don't. Her real name was Mary Molumby. I know that she was very close friends with the actress on *The Mod Squad*, Peggy Lipton. She and Peggy Lipton were very close friends, and Peggy was absolutely devastated when Jill died. In fact, she can hardly even talk about it. I gave her the videocassette of the movie, and she hasn't been able to watch it. At that time, Jill Banner was Brando's girlfriend.

Did any of you keep up with her after the film was completed?

No, she was always a very private — if not elusive — person. She was very mysterious. I didn't keep up with her, and in fact I never saw her again after that. I did have a project that never got made when I was under contract at Universal. I tried to contact her and I couldn't reach her. She would not return my calls. It was a very funny thing. She was always very shy with me. That's about all I could tell you.*

One of the most striking things about the film is the sexual subtext. How much of that was in the script, and how much just grew out Jill Banner's performance?

---

*Jill Banner gave up acting in the early 1970s after becoming romantically involved with Marlon Brando. She died in an automobile accident in 1982.

It was obviously kind of implied in the script, but only in the one scene with Peter [Quinn Redeker] in the chair. The idea is that after she sees whatever it is off-screen that Ralph [Sid Haig] is doing with Emily [Carol Ohmart], it gives her ideas from that point on. I don't know if people ever make that connection in watching the movie. Immediately after that, she starts looking at Uncle Peter wondering what this kind of thing could be all about. So it's only from that point on that I think there's an implied sexuality in it. That's implied in the script and in the subtext, but she brought it to life in a way that was beyond anybody's expectations [*laughs*].

Sid Haig told me that in that scene with Ralph and Emily, he had an idea that Ralph saw his mother in Emily, which prompted some kind of sexual response.

Well, I don't recall, but that sounds like Sid's way of thinking.

Was there ever a moment during filming, particularly in those scenes we just discussed, that you thought it was too far over the top?

No. Quinn [Redeker] just brought that character to life in a way that I really hadn't anticipated. He kind of brought something to it that was beyond what I really had been able to imagine. Of course, the chemistry between those two was so interesting. I don't know. You can't explain things, they just kind of happen like that.

How did you get Lon Chaney, Jr.?

We were looking for a star to play the leading role, and he was the most obvious choice. It was quite a tricky negotiation, because we really didn't have as much money as his agent wanted for him to do a horror picture. But once he read the script he just fell in love with it, so we were able to get him to do it for a very low price. He really liked it.

You can tell that he liked the character. He gave a very natural performance.

He was wonderful to work with. He was an extreme alcoholic at this time, but he wanted so badly to do this and do it well that he stayed on the wagon for the twelve days of the shoot. He made a schedule: In order to make it through the day, at three o'clock in the afternoon he would have a glass of beer. That would get him through the day. It was very difficult for him.

How did he wind up singing the theme song?

That was the composer's idea, Ronny Stein. By the way, that's the same Ronald Stein who wrote the score for *The Terror* and many other Corman pictures and AIP pictures. When he saw the finished picture he just loved it, he really wanted to do it, and he just came up with the idea and wrote it out. We went in with Lon and recorded it.

Where was it shot?

A little sound stage in Glendale. I don't remember the name of it. The wonderful thing about that stage was that in earlier years it had been an automobile garage, so it had a pit in it. Or a low-budget picture, it's very difficult to have a pit, because in order to have a pit you would have to build a false floor and put the pit underneath it. But I did use the same pit in *Blood Bath*, so I knew that this stage existed with the pit, and that's one of the reasons that I wrote the pit into the script.

Who did you get to play the uncles and aunts in the pit?

I know that one of them was the makeup man, and the other was the girlfriend of the cameraman, and who the third one was I have no recollection. It was not exactly problem casting.

The film was shot in 1964 or 1965?

I have a hard time pinning it down. I remember it was in August, it was extremely hot and there was no air conditioning on the stage, and the producers were the only people who had their hands free to be able to move the fans around all the time.

What happened to the movie in between the end of filming and the actual release date in 1968?

This is something that I haven't told anybody before because it's a little complicated, but if you really want me to give you the details it's kind of scary, actually. Here's what happened:

When the picture was first finished, we wanted to set up a sneak preview for it, and so we screened it for the theater owners. As it turned out, it was set for screening late in the afternoon, after some other movie. So these guys sat through this other movie, and then it was almost five o'clock in the afternoon. They screened *Spider Baby*—it was called *Cannibal Orgy* at that time—and very early on in the picture, these guys all got up and walked out. The producers almost had a heart attack. They thought that they hated the picture, and so we were not going to be able to get a sneak preview. In fact, it was just their dinner time. These guys see hundreds of movies, they had seen all they needed to see to know what kind of movie it was, and they got up and went home to dinner. But the producers got into a panic, and said, "This is terrible, we've got to do something." So they wanted to cut off the whole first part of the movie, the whole Mantan Moreland sequence. At first I said no, we can't do this. So they said, "If you don't do it, we'll get somebody else to do it." So I said, "All right I'll do it" because God knows what somebody else would do with it; they might destroy negatives that might otherwise be put back together someday. That was my feeling, but I felt they were totally wrong. It was a total mistake to do this. I thought the picture would make no sense to anybody without that opening scene.

We did, and we screened it, and everybody knew in watching this version that the picture was gonna make no sense at all. Anyway, the picture went out and was screened for distributors in New York and they didn't pick it up. About that time, the producers were in serious financial trouble because the real estate development business was collapsing, and a lot of developers went under because they were very highly leveraged. When the boom collapsed, all that leverage came down on you.

We had gotten into a little bit of financial trouble on the movie itself, because of things that happened. For example, the soundtrack came out all out of sync. The sound service that we used recorded on quarter-inch tape that had a synchronization pulse on it, then they sent that to another lab to synchronize it with the 35mm. And that lab then sent it in to do the optical track, then the film lab synchronized the optical track with the picture. When we first screened the answer print, it started going more and more out of sync. So the whole answer print was a loss, and it was very expensive to do an answer print. That was money down the tubes that we couldn't recover. The sound service blamed the transfer service, and the transfer service blamed the sound service, and it ended being a very expensive situation. But by that time, they had spent a lot more money on the picture than they intended, so they brought in two partners, and the partners were the guys who were named on the screen as associate producers.

The picture went to New York, and nobody would pick it up in that cut version. David

Hewitt, who later became the distributor of the picture, had a company called American General. He saw one of our original screenings, liked the movie, and he wanted it for distribution. By that time the bankruptcy was taking over, and the picture was locked up because it was an asset and had to be determined by the bankruptcy court. It was four years before Hewitt could acquire the picture. He just kept track of it and watched it all that time, and when the bankruptcy was cleared up, he acquired it for distribution. He gave it the title *Spider Baby*, and created the campaign, and did very well with it.

The scary part of it was, when he first got a-hold of the print, he was appalled to see that the whole opening scene was missing. So he had somebody go back and check in the lab, and he found the missing footage. Why he didn't contact me and ask for my help at that time, I'm not quite sure.

When did you first become aware that it had gained a cult following?

About three years ago when I began to get calls from people like yourself who were interested in finding out something about it. I didn't even know that there was a videotape of the picture in existence. I heard from somebody that there was a tape and I acquired one from Sinister Cinema, and it was so bad that I set my heart on generating a really good one.

I guess this is one of those "now it can be told" stories, since it's too late for anybody to do anything about it. When I first tried to acquire a print from the lab, they wouldn't let me have a print because there was some question that I didn't have the right to order materials from the lab. I was not listed as one of the owners of the picture. The distributor, as it turned out later, left about a $30,000 bill owed to the lab back in the sixties, so there wasn't anybody that could touch it. So I bided my time and waited, until about two years later. I had talked to somebody in the vault who had the access list of people who had a right to order the materials. One of the people, of course, was the distributor, Dave Hewitt. So I managed to find him after quite some time, and he gave me his permission to do what I did: I made up a purchase order from his company, which has been defunct for many years, and I just Faxed it in to make a one-inch master tape off of the negative. I kept my fingers crossed, they called me up and made an appointment, and I went in and made my tape, paid 'em cash and ran out the door. When the front office heard what I'd done, they went ballistic, but there was nothing they could do about it. So now the picture's available in its beautiful, pristine original form for everybody to see.

What do you think the appeal of the movie is now, 40 years later?

Two things. First of all, it's different. So many of the movies that are out today are just clones of each other. Crude as *Spider Baby* is, it's different. It has a liveliness to it, and a kind of vitality that I think is missing from a lot of movies today because they're just looking for ways to spend money. We didn't have money to spend. We had to come up with ideas. The other thing is that everybody likes the feeling they've discovered some long-lost gem. Otherwise, I'm baffled.

I was talking to Quentin Tarantino—he loves the movie, too—and he was saying that he and some of his friends can watch it over and over again, and each time they see something that they hadn't noticed before. I find that a great compliment, because I did try to put all kinds of little subtle touches in the movie as it went along. Of course there's lots of stuff in it that I wish I could do over or just cut out. But when I suggest that, people say, "Oh no, don't touch it!"

Like what?

Oh, I think there's too much wandering around in the hallways there at one point. But that's the nature of horror pictures, isn't it? Roger Corman was even worse; he's got people wandering up and down hallways in his movies, on and on until you wonder if you can stand it any more. And then it ends with some kind of a shock. The idea is that you push the audience almost to the point of boredom, and then you hit 'em with something.

The film reminds me a lot of James Whale's *The Old Dark House* [1932].

You know something? I had never seen that movie until recently because Carol Ohmart was in it —

You're talking about *The House on Haunted Hill* [1959].

I had never seen it before, and I saw it on American Movie Classics the other day, and oddly enough Carol Ohmart falls into a pit at the end. She was very good about it. She knew her way around pits!

After *Spider Baby* and *Pit Stop*, you wound up at Universal for a short time. How did that happen?

Well, I had shown them *Pit Stop*. I was looking at the possibility of Universal distributing it, and there was a fellow there who was sort of in charge of finding and setting up a department to encourage new, young talent and put them on contract. When they saw the film, they were very impressed with it, so they asked if I had something else that I would like to do. I got very excited because they wanted to do a picture with me, and I brought them a story. They said, "Love the story," but it was a little too ambitious for me to do for my first movie. They wanted me to take something a little bit smaller. So they said, "We'll put you under contract and you can come up with something."

I remember that's the way he put it: "You can come up with something." And I spent the next six months reading things and submitting them, and I might as well have thrown them into a hole. I never heard a thing. It was like Kafka. I realized that my six-months period was up when I came to my office and found somebody else's name on my door, and somebody else lying on my couch. That was my experience with the major studios.

When did you first meet Pam Grier?

I was preparing to do a picture called *The Big Doll House*, which was an ensemble picture with a group of women, young actresses, to be shot in the Philippines. We had kind of a cattle call, we just put the word out, and she came in on a general call. She had never done anything in pictures before except a walk-on in a Russ Meyer movie [*Beyond the Valley of the Dolls*, 1970]. I was immediately struck by her — what we used to call "authority." The kind of person that walks in the room and you feel right away you want to look at them. This was somebody that I should give a chance to, so I had her read, and I felt she could do it. She just had this striking personality, and I thought it was quite remarkable. She ended up practically stealing the movie, and singing the title song, and from there the rest is history.

What was the arrangement in the Philippines that brought so many producers down there?

Well, you could get a lot for your money. The costs were very, very low. Basically, you could take your time and really do something good if you had the patience to do it. Nobody knows how much *The Big Doll House* actually cost, because the whole financial arrangement was so complicated. Nobody really ever understood it, but my reckoning was about $150,000, which was pretty good.

Brian Donlevy (left) and Sid Haig in *Pit Stop* (1969), Hill's racing film. (Courtesy Jack Hill)

When the black film boom started in the early 1970s, how cognizant were you or the other people at AIP that there would be such an explosion of activity in that genre?

Like anything else in the movie business, one person makes a movie that's a big hit and everybody jumps in on top of it, and they keep doing it until that particular cycle fades out. In this case, the seminal film — which opened the same year as *The Big Doll House*— was *Sweet Sweetback's Baadassss Song* [1971]. That kind of took everybody by surprise, and there were a few more, and then AIP knew a good thing when they saw it and they jumped into it and started making them. What put an end to it, eventually, was the fact that the rest of the industry saw that there was a market in African-American theatergoers, and they began to put black scenes and black players into mainstream movies. Once that happened, there was not much market for the little pictures any more.

Were you surprised by the high returns you got on a film like *Coffy* at that time?

I was surprised by it. I wasn't nearly as surprised as AIP was. Most of the people at AIP just thought that it was crap. They had nothing but contempt for the movies they were making, and contempt for the audience they were making them for. There was a lot of racism there. It was really quite disgusting. I felt — and all of the actors I was working with felt — that we had something really good going. So I had very high hopes for it. I was probably the least surprised of anybody, although I was surprised that it did as well as it did.

Pam Grier (bottom) and Roberta Collins display the subtle charms of the women-in-prison film in Hill's *The Big Doll House* (1971). Hill directed Grier in four films.

There was a lot of criticism among black intellectuals about white directors and white producers making black-themed films. Did you feel any of that?

Well, yes. In fact, just at the time we were doing *Coffy*, some articles had come out in *Time* magazine on that very subject. AIP was very sensitive about it. Some of the actors that came in to interview were downright hostile. We made every effort to find black technicians to work on the crew, and the fact is there simply were none. The closest we could come was a black stunt gaffer [Bob Minor], who was our stunt coordinator, but that was basically like being an actor. At that time, it wasn't racism that kept black people out of the technical areas, it was the unions. AIP had union contracts, and in order to get into the union in those days you had to be the son of somebody who was already in, and that precluded by definition anybody other than white people. That changed eventually, of course.

Were you aware of the assorted anti-blaxploitation groups that sprang up, like the Coalition Against Blaxploitation?

No, but I can tell you that I felt pretty good about the whole thing myself, because we were putting a lot of black actors to work who certainly loved the opportunity. They were delighted to have a chance to work, and many of them broke through. It affected television; there was more and more black subject matter on television. I think it was, on the whole, a very positive thing, and I think anybody who would criticize that on any such grounds would simply be misguided.

What do you remember about Antonio Fargas in *Foxy Brown*?

Well, I don't know what I can tell you. He's an extremely talented actor. I had seen him in *Putney Swope* [1969], and he made a great impression on me. I said, "If I ever get a chance to use this guy, I'm gonna do it." So when I was writing the script I had him in mind, because I felt there was a certain family resemblance between him and Pam Grier; they looked like they could be brother and sister. I'd always had him in mind for the picture and I was delighted that he accepted the picture. He was great to work with.

During the years that you were out of the thick of things, what did you miss the least about the business?

What did I miss the least? Not getting my phone calls returned [*laughs*]!

What were your fondest memories from that period?

Oh gosh, that's a tough one. I don't know. Fondest memories? Well, working with wonderful players like Ellen Burstyn and Brian Donlevy and Lon Chaney and Boris Karloff. I guess I could say that. And wonderful actresses I kind of discovered like Jill Banner and Pam Grier.

In recent years you've been concentrating on your writing. Can you tell me about what you've been working on?

That depends on what you mean by recent years. I've been working on a novel — actually a series of novels — which I undertook with the idea of just doing one, but then the subject matter kind of grew and required a lot more than that. I put a lot of work into it, but I had to put that on the back burner recently because there's much interest right now, kind of a window of opportunity, in doing some films. So I'm very much occupied with that at the moment.

Will you be directing again?

It looks like it. I've turned down a few things that were wall-to-wall car chases. That's not what I'm interested in doing.

What kind of film do you want to do?

Well, the number one thing I have on the top of my pile at the moment is a sophisticated comedy called *Julie McGriff's Difficult World of Sex*. That tells you kind of what it's about. It's a tough sale because it's not only offbeat, but also it's actress-driven, and those are two of the hardest things to sell. We have a very fine actress that wants to do it, Sheryl Lee, who was the Laura in "Who Killed Laura Whatever-Her-Name-Was" on *Twin Peaks*. So we're trying to get a package together.

Was it a difficult decision to return to directing, or had you been thinking about it for awhile?

It's not really a difficult decision if it's an opportunity to do something I really want to do. So, in that sense, it's not a difficult decision at all. Of course, the movie business is so difficult no matter what you want to do, you're never really sure if you want to spend a whole lot of time that could end up being just time wasted, when you could have done something more rewarding. Right now, things are kind of shaping up interestingly, because I've been invited to screen five pictures at a film festival in Paris in August, and a similar one in London. With all those kinds of things going on, it's kind of encouraging. It's always a choice of whether you want to devote a lot of time to something that might never materialize, and that's kind of why I got out of the business before. But the movies I made before that were not really considered quite respectable are now being talked about as classics, so I'm in a different kind of situation. That makes it more interesting.

Karl Schanzer mentioned you might be working together again.

Yeah, you know how it is in this game. You have to throw a lot of things on the wall and hope that something will stick. I can't give you a definite title yet. We keep changing the title. When you submit a script to the studio, they have a reader and they do a reader's report, which may be negative because readers are all assholes and they don't know how to read a script. I mean, they all turned down *Pulp Fiction* [1994]. So much for readers! If you submit a script to a different producer at the same studio at a later time, they'll always pull the reader's report first. If you have a negative reader's report, they won't even read it. What you do is you change the title, and that way they think it's a new script. That way if it goes to a reader, it will go to a different reader. So much in this business is just like playing roulette.

And readers sometimes don't even read the script. In fact, Karl told me this because he was, for many years, a reader himself. He said the readers are encouraged to reject as many things as possible so that other people don't have to read them. So quite often they don't even read the script. One time I had submitted a script to Columbia some years back, and I got a call and they asked me to please re-submit the script because they discovered this reader wasn't reading them. That's Hollywood. That's what we all have to struggle with.

When did you first begin practicing the type of yoga that you're involved with?

In 1980. That's when I met Swami Muktananda. Muktananda was great saint, a living saint, and he was a meditation master. Teaching meditation in the real Indian tradition — and he was the real thing, not one of these screwballs like Rasnish. When you come into his presence you know immediately there's somebody very out of the ordinary here. What happens with someone like this is not exactly in the normal way of teaching. Once you make contact with someone like this— and you know this is what you want to be like — you meet someone who has reached a mental state, you immediately say to yourself, "I want to gain that; I want to attain that." Having made that contact, they work on you from within, and things happen spontaneously if you do the practices. The practice is mostly just meditation. It's a long path, but the goal is the highest goal you can attain in human existence. It takes awhile.

It's interesting trying to reconcile the image I have talking to you now — and knowing where you seem to be spiritually and professionally — with the image I had of the man who directed *The Swinging Cheerleaders*.

Look, I would go and shoot *The Swinging Cheerleaders* in the daytime, and then go home and read Strindberg and Shakespeare. It was a job and I was having fun with it. You can't really get an idea of what a person is like from the work that he does necessarily, when you just kind of work for hire. I'm very much changed in that respect. I'm not interested in doing those kinds of films. I'm only doing the kinds of films that people feel, when they walk out of the theater, they've gained something instead of feeling they've just been assaulted.

How is the Jack Hill of today different than the Jack Hill of 25 years ago?

Well, I never took myself or anything I did very seriously in those days. I didn't think of myself as an auteur or filmmaker or anything like that, I just kind of fell into work little by little. I'd make a movie that was successful, and somebody else would hire me to do another one, and I didn't do the steps that you normally take in order to have a career in movies. You're supposed to take a step up when you have a success, and instead I would just kind of take off on a long vacation, most often with a beautiful woman.

The difference between me today and then is that I'm not interested in just playing. I'm interested in doing work that will have meaning for someone. I need to do something. I need to do some kind of a picture. I need to get something going. It may not be exactly what I want to do, but hopefully it will have some of the values that I want to get in it, at least not be negative. There's the difference, I suppose, if that answers your question.

The Tough Guy

GARY KENT

Gary Kent arrived in Hollywood at a fortuitous time. The old studio system was falling apart, and the new generation of independent filmmakers were coming to the fore could provide plenty of opportunities for a hard-working actor like Kent who was willing to do his own stunts and lug equipment.

Born in Walla Walla, Washington, in 1933, Kent had done a stint in the Navy as a journalist before he caught the acting bug and joined a theater group in Austin, Texas. A lifelong movie fan, Kent was soon drawn to Hollywood, where he landed a few small roles at Allied Artists. But it was with the independents where Kent built his reputation, working alongside almost every low-budget director in the business. Over time, Kent would be cast has both heroes and heavies, in bit parts and leads, and slowly built his résumé to include work as a stuntman, special effects artist, writer and director.

Kent's first indie was the odd western *Run Home Slow* (1965), followed by films for Ray Dennis Steckler (*The Thrill Killers*, with his then-wife Laura Benedict), Ted V. Mikels (*The Black Klansman* and *One Shocking Moment*), David L. Hewitt (*The Girls from Thunder Strip*, *Hell's Chosen Few*), and Monte Hellman (*Ride in the Whirlwind*, *The Shooting*). But he's best known for his work with two very different directors: Richard Rush and Al Adamson. Kent appeared in Rush's *A Man Called Dagger* (1967), *Hells Angels on Wheels* (1967), *Psych-Out* (1968), *The Savage Seven* (1968), and *Freebie and the Bean* (1974), working closely with legendary stuntman Chuck Bail. At the same time, he was part of the regular cast and crew on Adamson's cheap exploitation films, taking the lead in what was probably Adamson's best work, the biker film *Satan's Sadists* (1969).

Kent also worked frequently in the burgeoning world of adults-only cinema, and had a hand in films like *Suburban Confidential* (1966), Steckler's *Sinthia, the Devil's Doll* (1968), Gary Graver's *The Hard Road* (1970), and *One Million AC/DC* (1969). Along the way, Kent collaborated with such disparate figures as Peter Bogdanovich, Brian De Palma and director (and close friend) Donald M. Jones.

After years working as a production manager and stunt man, he moved into directing with the surreal *The Pyramid* (1975), which he made with his wife, Tomi Barrett (since deceased).

Kent now lives in Texas, and has continued to work as a stuntman and production coordinator, with one of his last credits being Don Coscarelli's bizarre Elvis-vs.-mummy flick *Bubba Ho-Tep* (2002). When we spoke, he was working on a book about his movie experiences called *Shadows and Light: Journeys with Outlaws in Revolutionary Hollywood*.

Gary Kent prepares to menace Maray Ayres in David L. Hewitt's *The Girls from Thunder Strip* (1968).

You were in the press office for the Navy in the 1950s. You thought you were going to Korea, but wound up serving in Texas, right?

GARY KENT: Corpus Christi. And I lucked out because they needed a J.O., a journalist, right away. I was sent to the headquarters flight unit as a journalist. I was actually two days A.O.L., absent over leave, because I had stayed for a football game in Washington! I showed up late and they threw me in the brig, but they then sent a special thing out to get me because they needed a J.O. They figured they'd better treat this guy nice, get him right away to write for the Blue Angels.

What sort of things did you do?

I wrote publicity and hometown stories. The headquarters flight unit was where a lot of the pilots, after their training at Pensacola, came to because that's where the Blue Angels were training. I covered the ceremonies when they got their wings, and I wrote stories that went to their hometown newspapers, and then whenever they were going to come to a town I'd write their press releases. At that time they were just great guys, seat-of-the-pants pilots. You just had to love them. Now they're just so hi-tech it's hard to even talk to them. Then, they were the kind of guys who were like, "Give me a pair of wings and some gasoline, and I'll fly this sucker."

When did you leave the Navy?

I left the Navy in 1954.

You started acting while in Houston.

I had acted in high school and majored in drama in college, although I'd only gone to college for a year and a quarter when I got called to active duty. In the back of my mind I was interested in two things: writing and acting. I ended up acting in Texas, and the big place to go was the Alley or the Playhouse Theater in Houston. At that time, Off Broadway was just terrible. The Off Broadway that was Off Broadway in New York wasn't really doing great stuff. The great stuff, believe it or not, was being done in Texas. It was being done by two women, Joanna Albus and Nina Vance. They both are legends in theater. They had two theaters, the Alley and the Playhouse in Houston. I was dying to somehow get there and find out what that was all about, because I knew their reputation.

I got to Houston and I was working as a radio announcer. I was doing news announcing in Corpus when I go out of the service. I couldn't wait to get to Houston, though. I got there, and drove a friend to a reading at the Playhouse. The director was a guy named Adrian Hall, who (if you don't know him) is a giant in the theater circles, Broadway included.

Actors loved him. He's the kind of guy you'd die for, kind of like everybody wants to work for Robert Altman or Woody Allen. That's the way they felt about Adrian, and there he was at the Playhouse. He saw me in the lobby and said, "Are you here to read?" I wasn't; I had driven a friend there. But I thought, "Wow, grab this chance." I read and they signed me on. The ingénue lead was Katherine Helmond, who later made a name for herself on *Who's the Boss?* and in *Soap*. She was the one that played opposite me, and in my first play I did a love scene with her. We were both just kids getting started!

When did you decide to move to Los Angeles?

The Playhouse broke up. Joanna Albus sold it. She was getting in ill health, and no one liked the new guy, so everyone was leaving. We were a family. You know how theater people are; they're worse than movie people, and consider themselves so. They were all going to New York. In fact, a lot of New York actors were hired to come down and be guest stars in different plays that we did, so they all were going to New York. But I had just seen Brando in *On the Waterfront* [1954], and it blew me away. I thought, "That's what acting's all about. Screw New York, I'm going to L.A." I grabbed a Greyhound and came to L.A. True story.

You loved movies, and got to work in film when the film industry was going through some intense changes.

Right. I was green as grass and didn't know much about the film industry. I thought it all came from the major studios. It pretty much did. It was sort of like corporate America before corporate America. The studios were nation states. They decided what went out, who saw what, who was a star, who wasn't a star.

Then all of a sudden, the drive-in theaters happened in the 1950s. When the drive-ins happened, at first the majors totally ignored them because they thought they were low-class. But it was a place for mom and dad to go with the kids. So that was their big thing. Then TV came in, so mom and dad could stay home with the kids and save money. They didn't even have to go to the drive-ins. So the drive-ins were looking for product. The only product they could get were these wild, crazy independents that were being made that broke every rule Hollywood ever had.

They smoked pot, sex was happening, people actually slept together, cursing actually went on, and the drive-ins opened up that venue. I fell in love with it, because the exciting people were making the independent films. They were just hitting the streets. John Cassavetes started it in New York with *Shadows* [1959]. He started the whole independent scene. Peter Bogdanovich feels the same way. In the book *Easy Riders, Raging Bulls*, he gives the credit of that whole movement to Cassavetes, and I have to say the same. He got a camera and some kids and said, "Let's hit the streets." It inspired a lot of other people to do the same thing. By that time I was working at Allied Artists in the mail department, and conning my way into movies however I could get in them.

Still, it was studio movies. I thought, "This isn't exciting like I thought. This isn't art. It isn't anything but some sort of a system." Here were all these guys like Ray Steckler and Al Adamson and Richard Rush and Brian De Palma, at that time really out there taking some chances, and that's who I wanted to work with.

One of the westerns you did at Allied Artists was *Battle Flame* (1959) with Scott Brady, who you worked with later. Did he remember you on *Satan's Sadists*?

Absolutely. Yes, he did [*laughs*]. I love Scott Brady. I remember sitting on the set and hearing this big booming voice that he had, and of course everyone knew Scott and his brother Lawrence Tierney as the best barroom brawlers in L.A. He walked on the set and said, "Gary Kent — if any name sounded like a made-up movie star name, that's one right there!" And that's how he started his introduction to me. "Who the hell made up that name?"

Years later we did *Satan's Sadists* together, and I reminded him. He turned out to be, to me, just a wonderful guy. We threw a party for a theater group, and leading up to where we had the party to raise funds for the group, we had tiki torches. I needed a celebrity, and he said, "I'll be your celebrity." But he showed up with all his Notre Dame football buddies. They got drunk and they stole all the tiki torches. The next morning I hear *knock, knock, knock* on my door. I get up, and there's Scott, looking like his dog had been run over. He had all those tiki torches and brought 'em back. He apologized. I couldn't believe this was the big, tough Scott Brady, who would go to that much trouble and apologize for doing that. He was a sweetheart.

One of your first films was *The Thrill Killers* [1964]. How did you meet Ray Dennis Steckler?

I was writing a script with a guy named Gene Pollock. We wrote the famous movie that never was, which was *Devil Wolf of Shadow Mountain*. Gene was a friend of Ray Steckler's, and he said, "I want to introduce you to this guy that lives across the street. He's got a camera and he wants to make a movie." That's how we got started. Ray was another one of those guys that was gonna make a movie on pocket change or whatever, but he was going to make a movie.

Was that your first independent production?

No. My first independent production was *Run Home Slow*.

How did that project get started? It's a pretty odd film.

It is very strange. How I got involved was, there was a girl in a drama group I was in. Back then, everybody in Hollywood belonged to a group, Players Ring or something. We had a group called West Coast Repertory. In that group was a young girl named Dayle Rodney. She said, "I'm going to read for a movie tonight after the group, about 10:00. Would you mind going with me because I'm a little afraid?" I thought, "No one legitimate reads you at 10:00 at night." Dale was really nice-looking, and I thought she surely was headed for danger. But it turned out to be this nice, funny character you would have loved. He was the character of all characters. Tim Sullivan [a.k.a. Ted Brenner] was the director of this movie, and he was doing a movie called *Run Home Slow*.

At first, he cast me in a bit part in it, and then they went out to shoot and Dayle, who was playing the lead, had a miscarriage, so they had to postpone the movie. He didn't pick it

Kent co-starred with Mercedes McCambridge, Linda Scott and Allen Richards in the peculiar western *Run Home Slow* (1965). (Courtesy Gary Kent)

up for maybe three or four months. When he picked it up he had recast it with Mercedes McCambridge playing the lead, and he cast me as her brother, the other male lead. He moved me up a notch. I loved Mercedes McCambridge, and Tim was just such an original character. It's hard to explain. He'd been a big star on Broadway, been an alcoholic. Couldn't get hired. He'd been a star, but by the time he was 40 he was burned out, living in the park. He couldn't make it across the street one day because he was too drunk. He knew if he tried to make it, this cop would see he was drunk and he'd go to jail, and if he went to jail he was gonna commit suicide.

So he said, "Well, that's just jake." In those days "jake" was an expression like, "That's just swell." Believe it or not, this voice said, "I'm Jake. What's going on? What's the matter?" This voice from out of nowhere. He said, "Jake, I can't make it." Jake said, "Give me your hand, and I'll walk you across the street if you'll quit drinking." In Tim's mind, Jake was God. He was seeing all of this in his head. He took his hand and walked him across the street, totally sober, and he never drank again. True story. Strange story.

Did *Run Home Slow* get much of a release?

No. It came out and that was about it. It just disappeared forever. Somebody sent me a copy in the mail. Here were all these weird comments from different reviewers that had seen it.

Some of them compared it with Buñuel, and some of them said this was the worst piece of shit ever made. Frank Zappa did the music.

How did these films compare with the experience you had at Allied Artists?

Much different, because it was so loose. First of all, you had no money. You had baloney sandwiches for lunch, whereas at Allied Artists they had caterers and studio kinds of things. But they also had this systemized way of making the film in which if you were an actor, you didn't pick up a piece of equipment. On the independents you did everything. It didn't matter if you were starring. You ate your baloney sandwich and then picked up a reflector. That's the way it was done.

To me it was more exciting. As bad as the movies were, there was something more exciting about them and more vibrant. It was like guerilla warfare. No one had a permit. We always said we were students from USC, just making this film by accident. I don't know how many times we used that excuse, but I probably heard it on every film that was made out there that was independent.

Devil Wolf of Shadow Mountain **was a project you were going to start with Bud Cardos, but it never got made.**

We started, and I think we did a couple of days on it. Gee whiz, one of the guys that had been hired as the stuntman — Bud and I both had experience with horses, so we were okay with that. I was going to direct it and also play in it. So we had this scene where we were to come riding out of a barn that was being dynamited. The effects guy was using real dynamite.

Horses can smell gun powder. They know what's going on. So inside the barn the horses were jumping around already; they were spooked. I looked behind me, and this young kid — John Carpenter, who was directing that scene (he was actually a producer), he'd hired this kid, and I could tell he couldn't handle his horse. His horse was already getting away from him and nothing had happened yet. All of a sudden, boom! There went the barn, we all went riding out and did our falls that we were supposed to do. I heard Cardos yell. I looked back over my shoulder, and this kid had gotten his foot caught in the stirrup. The horse just took him and slammed him against all these fence posts. There must have been fifty of them. It just took all of his skin off, broke every bone, whatever. Bud and I were exhausted because we were doing falls all day long for nothing almost, and the next day we found out that Carpenter didn't have any money to do the film.

What he was doing was shooting the film, the action first, and then using that to try to raise money. Bud had taken it very seriously because he really wanted to be the werewolf. One of Bud's dreams was to be the werewolf, and I wanted to direct, of course. We would take any abuse to get this going, but to fall all day long and not get your paycheck was too much. We said, "That's it," and as far as I know he never did get it made. But I keep running into people that swear they've seen it. It's the phantom film that never was!

How did you land your job on the Monte Hellman westerns, ***Ride in the Whirlwind*** **and** ***The Shooting*** **[both 1965]? How did you get involved in stunts in the first place?**

I had noticed that every time I went on an acting interview there'd be these huge lines of actors out of work, just like me. But the stuntmen, they were a mystery to me. Even though Bud and I were doing stunts, we weren't really "stuntmen." We were just doing it. I was having coffee with a soundman named Art Names, and he said he was going to Utah on these two westerns. He said he wanted to get me on, but they were looking for a stuntman. I said, "Well, I'm a stuntman."

He gave me a number to call. It was Jack Nicholson. I went out to this weird office he had out in Beverly Hills. It was more like an office supply room. There were a bunch of shelves. I don't even think he had a desk. It was like somebody donated a back room or something to them. He and Monte were in there, and the first question they asked me was if I could make a horse gradually get sick and slow down, drop its head and then fall down. I said, "Sure, that's no problem."

I thought, "I don't know how to do that. That's gonna have to be a good actor, that horse!" On the basis of just pretending I knew everything, they hired me. Of course, the first thing I did was call a vet and asked how to do this. They said, "Just give him a shot and drug him." Jack thought I was a genius. Monte said, "That's beautiful, Gary." I was falling all day long off a stagecoach without pads. I didn't know stuntmen wore pads. I didn't know how you dig up the ground. I was coming in every night just bruised. They said, "Man, you're really tough." Tough? I was stupid!

Not that I don't like Ray Steckler, 'cause I love him — he's a crazy con artist — but the difference between him and Monte Hellman is just night and day. Monte really is a director. He really does know what he's doing. The moment I got on that film, independent or not, I knew these guys were doing great work. It wasn't about cowboys in shiny shirts playing guitars and rescuing girls from all the bad guys. It was about real people and real situations. Those two movies I just thought, "Boy, how did I luck into this?"

Those were shot in Utah, which I think is how you wound up working on *Daniel Boone*.

They came to town and they were looking for another stuntman. They didn't want to call back to Hollywood. So Cameron Mitchell recommended me, and Cameron was staying at the same hotel they were at. The rest of us were at this little postage stamp thing. There was one big hotel in town and that's where all the 20th Century–Fox people were. Cameron said, "Yeah, I've got this great stunt guy. He doesn't wear pads or anything." On *Daniel Boone* were the good stunt guys. So the minute they heard *that*, they knew I didn't know shit. "Send him over and let us have a look." So Jack cleared me to take some time off for *Daniel Boone*. After they razzed me and put me through it, they started showing me the ropes. I just lucked out, because they were the greats like Charlie Horvath, who wrote the original manual that the Marines use to this day on hand-to-hand combat. Ted White was the stunt coordinator; Roy Jensen was one of the all–American tackles for California when they had that great football team in the late 1950s.

You worked as a bouncer and private investigator during that period.

Absolutely. Anything I could get to. I had a family, and I had kids that I dearly loved, and I didn't want them to suffer because I wanted to be in the business. I made up my mind I didn't want to have to go out and go work in aerospace like everyone else. I would take whatever I could get in the movies, and anything where I could make use of what I could do, which was fight and jump around and make a lot of noise.

How did you get acquainted with Dave Hewitt?

There was a big soundstage on, I believe, Santa Monica Boulevard called Hollywood Stages where Al Adamson had his offices. David Hewitt was a friend of Al's, and had offices there also.

***The Girls from Thunder Strip* (1968) may be David Hewitt's best film.**

Ha! And what's-his-name was in it, Casey Kasem.

Jack Starrett was in that, too, and he gave a really incredible performance.

Oh, I loved Jack. By the way, I was just a special guest of Quentin Tarantino. He was just in town and showed *Savage Seven*. I didn't know Quentin, but he called me on the phone and said, "You and Chuck Bail are my favorite stuntmen. Would you come and be a guest?" So I went down, and I wasn't sure I was gonna like him, but I loved him because it was all about the films. It wasn't about Quentin. He said, "Guess what? I just saw *Girls from Thunder Strip*, and I loved it." So there you go. It's one of Quentin's favorites. I couldn't figure it out. I thought, "Why would he like that movie?" I guess it's because it's weird.

It's also one of the only biker films where the bikers ride around in a car, which I assume was because Hewitt couldn't afford to rent the bikes.

That's it [*laughs*]. You got it.

Where was that shot? Just around Los Angeles?

Yes, and this is kind of interesting. The Spahn Ranch, we shot a lot of it out there. It was always interesting, because no one knew what Charlie Manson was up to, but he and his crowd were always hanging around. They would come over at lunchtime and try and borrow your lunch, because they were always hungry. If we left a sandwich or something around, they would grab it and eat it. You kind of felt sorry for them because they were these scraggly kids that hung around there. We shot several things out there.

You did *Lash of Lust* [1974] with Al Adamson there, and Bud Cardos worked on *The Female Bunch* [1969] with Al there.

I was not on *Female Bunch*, but we also did *Angels' Wild Women* [1972]. We shot part of that out there.

Bill Bonner was in that. Do you know what happened to him?

Bill Bonner, yeah. I have asked so many times and I cannot get an answer. I understand he became very bitter. I heard that from Don Jones, who was directing the film Bill got hurt on. I loved Bill Bonner. He was just a great guy. I've said constantly that I want to go see Bill Bonner, and Don kept saying, "He won't talk to anyone. He doesn't want to see anyone." That was years ago. Then I asked recently, and someone had heard that he was living in Compton and his sister was taking care of him, but that he was still more or less bitter about those old days and didn't want to see anyone.

Harry Woolman, the special effects guy, worked on *Thunder Strip* as well.

"Three-Finger Harry," we called him, which should give you a clue. "Hair's Breadth Harry" was the other name. I have a collector's item on Harry. He was a motorcycle daredevil, and some old stuntman sent me a tape of Harry when he was a young man riding his bike, doing stunts on a beach. I liked Harry. He was a crazy old guy. He'd pick up a stick and hold it up in the air and say, "You know what this is?" And we all had heard it a hundred times, but we'd go, "No." He'd say, "This is a stick up!" That was his famous line, and he'd do that forever.

How did you all wind up working on so many films together? Did you just call each other when something came up?

Yeah. It was either that or go work construction or something, and Al at least would pay. He didn't pay a lot, but you'd get your check. A lot of people said they didn't, but I always got mine. If you should have gotten $150 a day, he'd give you $50 a day, but at least it would be $50 and you'd get it.

His lunches were terrible. On *Satan's Sadists* I talked him into using my girlfriend as the cook, because she could cook anything, and on the budget she just cooked these gourmet meals. It pissed Al off. He wanted baloney sandwiches. "Where's the sandwiches?" She was cooking crepe suzette and all this stuff. The crew loved it, but Al wanted baloney sandwiches. Dave Hewitt, I don't think we even got that. But that's how it happened. Dave or Al, once you got to know 'em, they'd just call you themselves. Usually there wasn't a script, just part of one.

You also worked on *The Black Klansman* [1966] with Ted V. Mikels.

Ted Mikels I met on an earlier film, I hate to admit, which was a nudie cutie, where guys could get money for a film because they could get a girl to take her blouse off. *One Shocking Moment* [1965]. I went on the interview and he cast me in the lead.

I kind of liked him. Strange guy, if you know Ted. To me, these guys were not good directors, but they were always directing. Somehow they would get a few bucks together and get something going.

***Voyage to the Planet of Prehistoric Women* [1968] was directed by Peter Bogdanovich. You did special effects on that film, and also worked on *Targets* [1968].**

We had a theater group at that time called West Coast Cinema Workshop. We changed it. I forget what it ended up being. We ran an ad, and we had pooled our money and bought a camera. We were going to shoot scenes. We wondered, "Why are all the groups constantly just doing stage work when we're in a movie town? Let's shoot movies." We ran an ad in the trades for a director. Here came this guy — we were holding a meeting at John Parker's, which was down several flights of stairs. I smoked at that time, and I was out having a smoke break. Here came this guy tumbling down the stairs. Talk about the absent-minded professor! He had an armful of papers, and they all spilled. He'd bend over to pick up a paper, and his glasses would fall off. I thought, "Who is this dork?" It turned out to be Peter Bogdanovich.

He was there to audition as a director. He came and we met with him, and for some reason we didn't go with him. The next thing I knew he was shooting this movie called *Targets*, and called up and hired a bunch of people from the group, which I thought was wonderful considering we didn't hire him. I actually did a small part in it, but I did the effects and didn't get credit. I did all the shooting, the whole end of the film which has been called brilliant by some people. I staged all that. I had great pride in doing the effects. Instead I get credit as "oil tank worker"! But that's the nature of the game.

It's a great movie.

It was a good movie. My respect for Peter shot up from the day I saw him tumbling down the stairs.

The sci-fi film I mentioned was shot around existing Russian footage that Roger Corman had purchased.

[Peter] called us, me and Don Jones and Walt Robles. He said, "Can you come out and do some effects?" We pumped all the mist and the haze. Mermaids jumped around in it.

You started working with Richard Rush on *A Man Called Dagger*. Can you contrast him as a director with Monte Hellman?

Absolutely. I had just gotten off the Monte Hellman pictures, and I had met the wardrobe woman [Vana Carroll] for Monte Hellman. She had gotten a job on *Man Called Dagger*. We were kind of friends, and I liked her husband, a great guy named Brandon Carroll. She said, "I'm doing a film with this guy named Richard Rush, and they're looking for someone to do stunts and effects combined."

I had helped Harry Woolman on the two Nicholson movies in Utah, and had learned a little about effects. I said, "That's what I do, stunts and effects." I went over and in walked Richard Rush. I liked him immediately. There is something about Richard that I think is top drawer. I knew I was in the presence of someone I was going to really like.

Monte was a good director; nice, but aloof and removed to a degree. Very caught up in his movie and where he was going. A lot of times he would just take off with his viewfinder and everybody would have to grab a reflector and follow him. None of us knew what we were doing or where we were going. It was all in Monte's head.

But Richard just communicated with everybody. He had a way of making everybody feel important. The guy getting the coffee, Richard would listen to him. Especially stunt guys. He loved stunt guys. I think he always wanted to be one for some reason. He'd let you pretty much do your own fights. It was a chance to get your hands on the camera, which a lot of us guys that later on went into directing were grateful for, because it gave us a chance to learn staging. It was obvious right from the start, the way he handled people, he was just a master at being kind and good to people. And sensitive with his actors.

He could take really standard exploitation material and make it more than the sum of its parts.

That's a great comment, because when they first sent me the script on *Hells Angels on Wheels*, I thought, "This is terrible!" When we did it, Dick was just changing it. It was becoming this other thing that actually had a class and a style and a mood to it. I thought it was going to be another Dave Hewitt picture. Not so.

Did you meet Joe Solomon?

He was producer on a lot of those things. He'd usually sit in his motel room and read *The New York Times*. He'd show up on the set every once in a while and growl at Dick. "You're over budget! You're over time! You're taking too long!" And then he'd go back to his motel room. Dick would always say, "You're right. You're right, Joe. I am over budget, I am taking too much time. Good comment." Then he'd leave, and Dick would go back to what he was doing.

You were injured on *The Savage Seven*, weren't you?

Yes I was. We were riding our bikes down the street doing second unit, and I was standing on my seat, and a great biker named Alan Gibbs, a stuntman, was right next to me. For some reason he lost his bike. He'd never done that particular gag. On his way down he hit the handlebars, which threw his bike right into mine. I'm headed down the highway with nothing under me, going about sixty. The first guy to hit me was Joey Bishop's son, Larry Bishop. They just wiped out my whole left side. All my ribs broke.

There's a psychic thing I must mention. Max Julien was on the show, and he and I were good friends. In fact, he and I and Penny Marshall got stoned one night on *Savage Seven* and saw a genuine flying saucer, I swear to God. Max was over with the first unit, and the word came back that Chuck Bail had been hurt. Max said, "No, it's not Chuck Bail, it's Gary Kent." Max said he always knew that psychically.

The biker films usually had some combination of actors, stuntmen and actual bikers riding. Were those difficult conditions to work under?

Only in this way: They all wanted to do stunts, and they were all terrible at it because they were always wiped out on reds or black mollys or six beers. They could ride, but that was about it. Talking them out of participating was the thing, because they all wanted to be in the fight scenes. They just couldn't be relied on. The trick was trying to get them not to participate without pissing them off, so we could have the real guys come in.

At what point did you start directing second unit? Was directing a goal of yours in the early years?

I started with Dick. Richard Rush was the one who let Chuck and me start doing that. We both coordinated a lot for him. He would give you the chance to pretty much set up. Like in *Psych-Out*, I said, "Let's do a scene in a junkyard," just because I always wanted to do one in a wrecking yard. We manufactured that whole scene about Bruce Dern living in a car and that whole thing, based on my decision to do the fight there. That's what I loved about Dick. If you had a creative idea, he might run with it. With Steckler and everyone, they just didn't know what they were doing, so of course you got a chance. You could do whatever you wanted to do.

You continued with David Hewitt on *Hell's Chosen Few* (1968) and *The Mighty Gorga* (1969), which is a very bizarre film.

On that, Dave Hewitt called me and asked me if I'd come in and do a day's work. I went in and did it. *Gorga* was Dave in an ape suit running around. And he had his usual guys, Greydon Clark and some other guys. Anthony Eisley, Scott [Brady] and those fellows, a lot of the Al Adamson guys. I just worked a day.

Did you ever watch it?

Never did.

It's really funny, especially Bruce Kemp as the witch doctor.

That's funny right there [*laughs*]!

Some of the special effects shots for that film ended up in *One Million AC/DC*.

Is that right? Oh, that picture just haunts me to this day.

That was an Ed Wood film, right?

It's very strange. No one knew who Ed Wood was or what he'd done. He used to hang around the editing rooms, and he'd always have a vodka in a Styrofoam cup. He'd be drinking and helping people edit. He changed his name to Akdov Telmig, which is vodka gimlet spelled backward. He wrote it, and much later on, all of a sudden he's an icon. Wow, I did an Ed Wood film! Unfortunately, it was *AC/DC*. Great title, but is that a good film [*laughs*]?

Where was it he was hanging out?

There was a company—I can't think of the name—that did a lot of nudie cuties. It was Jay [Fineberg], the guy who did *One Shocking Moment*, and the Little Chef. I wish I could remember these names. They were classic L.A. kind of characters, Damon Runyonesque in their personalities. The Little Chef had been from some country and ended up in L.A. He opened a bunch of little coffee shops—Vince Miranda! He opened up the Pussycat Theater chain. They had a bunch of editing rooms, and if they weren't making a film, a lot of the other people could go over there and use their editing equipment. That's where I met our friend who made *AC/DC*, Ed DePriest.

You also did *The Hard Road*. You play the sleazy guy with the two-way mirrors in his office.

Paul Lewis had become a good friend of mine, and was an excellent production manager. He taught me a lot about production management. Gary Graver hired me as production manager on *The Hard Road* because I knew something about it. I production managed it, and ended up playing that part. We had a ball on it. One of the great actors of Hollywood that was terribly wasted, wasted himself and his career, was Johnny Alderman. I guess booze and a lot of the stuff that did in our friend Jack Starrett also did in Johnny Alderman. But he was someone who really did have talent, who could have gone on and done much better things.

Did you get to know some of your female co-stars in those films like Maria Lease, Bambi Allen, and Connie Nelson?

Sure. First, I liked them all. Second of all, I felt enormously sorry for Bambi Allen, because she was this nice person who had had a lot of breast augmentation surgery, and it was already giving her trouble by the time we were working. She was already having severe illness, and it related directly to that operation. Connie Nelson was Gary Graver's girlfriend, and ended up being his wife, but they eventually split up.

Maria Lease was, again, like a Damon Runyon character. Maria and I never dated, but we constantly acted opposite each other. A couple of times she called me for jobs when she was editing and they needed voiceover work. She liked my voice. So I worked with and around Maria a lot and got along with her real well. She dated good friends of mine. Now she owns a hotel in Palm Springs, and from what I understand it's a pretty good place. She just absolutely loves doing it. I never knew much about Maria's background, except Don [Jones] was always telling me it would make a story in itself. But I liked Maria and always thought she was a good person, although I heard wild stories about her. She was always dating a buddy, and I never knew what the stories really amounted to.

Secret Places, Secret Things **[1971] was another film you directed, correct?**

God, would I love to find a copy of that. Again, I was working as production manager for the Pussycat chain, but they weren't doing anything. Gary Graver got to be a pal, and we were writing a script called *The Moonshiners* for them. The next thing I knew, Vince Miranda called and said there was a guy named Mike McFarland that wanted to do a movie, and he was looking for a director. They told him I was a good production manager, so he wanted to hire me.

I met Mike at a sub sandwich shop, and he sat down and I thought, "Well, if I'm ever gonna make the jump, do it now." I said, "Don't look any further for a director. It's me." I talked him into letting me direct. But he had no idea what he was doing. He wanted to make nudie cuties. I said, "Let's make an art film. It will be a nudie, but it will be art."

I wrote the script with one of the partners from the Pussycat. Mike produced it. I co-directed it with this other fellow. At the time, I had already worked with Laszlo Kovacs and [Vilmos] Zsigmond. I thought you had to have a Hungarian cameraman or you were not a director, so I hired a guy named Louis Horvath. I think it was his first job in L.A.

Part of the film had this great camerawork from this Hungarian cameraman. The other director had his own cameraman, and I don't know what he did. I thought my part of it wasn't too bad. Of course, what did I know? I have never seen it. Don't know what happened to it or where it went.

How long did you work with the people who owned the Pussycats?

Probably five or six years, off and on.

What was that like? Eventually, that became a pretty rough business to be in. In the 1970s, a lot of theater owners wound up getting shot.

I was out of it before then. I liked Vince Miranda. Jay Fineberg was his partner. I liked Jay, but there was something very strange about him. He'd cut his hand severely at one time, and so he was always washing them. He never got over washing the blood off his hands. Every three minutes he had to find water somewhere and wash his hands. It was the first time I ever met an obsessive-compulsive person. Plus, he was always trying to get girls to undress.

Vince Miranda just wanted to make movies, and maybe even do something serious. He started a Shakespeare stage company in San Diego. He and Maria and other people got involved in it. He did at least try and get out there. There were people that didn't like him because they thought he was a thug. He could have been, but if he was, he was a nice thug. You'd think there'd be this wild sex going on all the time. There would be Maria and a few women that would undress for the parts they were playing, and I guess Jay and Vince auditioned them, but I was always production manager or actor. No one in our group was really into drugs at that time. I didn't really want to be a part of it, but I did want to production manage. I loved Gary Graver and Don Jones, but it was always kind of on-the-edge. By the time it went hardcore, and really got into the bad scene when Bob Cresse got shot, I was out of it.

In *Satan's Sadists* you got to be the hero. Al Adamson had a habit of giving people one good role, then just letting them do supporting roles in other films.

Very strange. I got that role and I didn't even read for it. I just met him with Bud, did that little thing where I ran around in Pacific Ocean Park [*The Fakers*, a.k.a. *Hell's Bloody Devils*, 1970]. Al was on the phone saying, "Would you like to do the lead Vietnam guy?" I had no idea what he was talking about, except that Bud was gonna be on it.

He said, "Well, Scott Brady's gonna be on it, Kent Taylor, Bob Dix." Wow! Of course I want to do this. Never thinking it would ever get out. Thinking, "This is gonna be a bad movie." Oddly enough, Sam Sherman, his partner, said that's the movie that started their whole company. I've read here and there reviews that said this was the *Citizen Kane* of biker movies. You and I know it's not, but somebody got drunk on Chevas Regal and wrote that!

You've described Al as a "white soxer," and a guy who wanted to make movies like they did in the 1940s, which must have created an interesting atmosphere with all of these hard-drinking old-timers and pot-smoking kids working together.

Al *was* a white soxer. Al was that kind of guy. His pants were always a couple of inches too short. He'd be the last guy to get a date for the prom. Which made him kind of surprising. I hate saying this about him, because he did so many nice things for me, but a great director? No. But his relationship with Scott and those fellows, I always respected. They did too, because he would give them work, and they would get their health benefits. They were all at that age where they were starting to lose them. Al would give them jobs where they could feel like something again. I think that's why he did it, in a way.

The younger guys, we were into pot and just anything to get wild and crazy. He hired us because we did all the work. We were the young turks. We'd do anything, fall off anything. He brought us together with the old-timers, and it actually worked out well. I loved listening to their stories. There's a bit of professionalism that went on that is missing now. Scott was never late, whether he partied all night long or not. He was a heavy drinker, and he would show up just reeking of alcohol, but he'd have his lines and do his part, never complain, never ask for special treatment. Same with Carradine; same with all those guys.

I was discussing Gregory Peck the other day. When I was an electrician, he'd show up on the set and say hello to everybody. He never had an entourage like Bruce Willis. There were never twelve guys carrying him half a block. He'd walk it and greet everybody. When it ended, he'd always thank everybody. There was some of that same kind of professionalism still going on with the old guys like Scott Brady and Kent Taylor.

The Incredible 2-Headed Transplant [1971] was made during that same period, with many of the same people you worked with on Al's films.

Somehow or another they changed my name, which pissed me off. I had to sue to get my residuals. They denied I was even in it. Then I found out they did it a lot, changed names so they wouldn't have to pay residuals. I had to take in stills from the film, and my contract, which I didn't have. I had to get someone, the director, to write me a letter. Finally, I started getting residuals.

You did two Robert Vincent O'Neil films, Psycho Lover and Blood Mania [both 1970].

Robert was a prop man to begin with. I had no idea he was a director. The next thing I knew he was doing it, and called me as a production manager. It was fun. He took it seriously, so you never got the feeling he was in it just for the bucks. I thought it just took him forever to get a shot. He was always fussing over it. It was murder. His movies were long and arduous, but nonetheless I had some affection for Robert.

You appeared in The Forest [1982] and Schoolgirls in Chains [1973] for your friend Donald Jones, who has a reputation for making pretty weird, sick films. Were those films odd to work on as an actor?

Don Jones and I met when he was an electrician. Don was a boxer originally. He fought under the name of Irish Frankie Conway, I think. He was very good. He had 21 pro fights, and won 20 of them, if I remember correctly. In one of our theater groups, he ended up being the electrician, handling the lights. From that he sort of worked his way into being part of it.

I knew Don well as a friend, and he's not that odd. He's just a great guy with a lot of energy and a sense of humor. In fact, I mentioned to him once what you just said, that he made odd films. He said, "I do?" He was shocked. He was such a likable guy that it was easy for him to attract help. So even though the budget was extremely low, Don took them very seriously. And, for the most part, the people acting in them took them pretty seriously.

You would get a Don Jones script, and go, "What is this? People don't talk this way." Then we made a rule. All the actors got together on one film and said, "What we're going to have to do is, let's not change one line; let's find out a reason the character would talk like that." So you'd get all these bizarre performances. What you run into with actors all the time anyway, even on the big budgets, they all want to change the lines to fit what *they* would say. It's only a very secure actor that's just gonna take what's there and make it work.

He told me that he lost his house making The Forest.

Yes. There you go again. He hocked his house to make the film. He's one of the few directors ever that I know of, besides myself, who actually paid his deferments. We all worked for a deferred amount of money, too. When he finally got money from the film, he paid us first before he paid off his house, which was really honorable. Not one out of a hundred would do that, and Don did. So he had that kind of standing with his friends and pals. They knew he was going to be very honest and above board.

You directed *The Pyramid* in 1975. Did your experiences with Richard Rush and some of the other directors influence the way you directed?

A little bit. *Pyramid* was my total chance to set myself free and do what I wanted. I wasn't working for anyone but me. Mike McFarland, the guy who had put up the money for *Secret Places*, put up the money for *Pyramid*. I was going through the whole thing where you took a little blue Cheer and thought you saw God. I wanted to do a story about consciousness, if there was such a thing.

Did I use other stuff? No. I was just kind of out on a limb and decided, "I'm gonna get these people to go with me." Edgar Mitchell, who was one of the astronauts; Thelma Moss, who was head of neuropsychology at UCLA; I had all these people in my film. I just had them interact with my actors. I had actors, psychics, scientists, interacting with each other. I thought it was a great experience. Some people saw the movie and just went, "Huh?" And some people said this was the greatest thing they'd ever seen.

It's either way ahead of its time or way out there. It was my chance to do something totally original. I guarantee you will never ever see anything like *Pyramid* anywhere else.

Chuck Bail was in another film you directed, *Rainy Day Friends* [1986].

A much more conventional film. The picture was relatively successful. It sold in 42 countries. My wife and I lived off it for four years, so financially it did pretty well. Generally, 98 percent of the critics raved about it. About 2 percent hated it. Kevin Thomas was one. The other guy that hated it was the critic from Seattle, my hometown. That happens to be the review they run on the Internet Movie Database all the time. Why couldn't they pick one of the great ones [*laughs*]? When Arnold Kopelson bought it and changed the name to *L.A. Bad*, I thought that was the worst title. He wanted to sell it as a gang film, which it's not at all.

How did the book project get started?

How this all came about is that I sat around with my good friend Chuck Bail and drank a lot of coffee and bullshitted about the old days. A lot of different people would join us from time to time, and several of them said, "Gary, you ought to write a book." Then my wife really got on me about it.

I managed, because I do a variety of things, to work with a tremendous amount of talented people, both from the top to the absolute bottom. The more I thought about it, the more I thought, "Well, maybe there *is* a book here." But I didn't want to just write about what I did. So I was looking for a tapestry that could bind the book, sociologically and culturally. I don't want to sound hifalutin here, but I wanted to somehow combine what was going on in the street and in the corporate office, as well as what was going on at the movie set, in the minds and psyches of the people I worked with.

In the meantime, I kept running off and doing stunts. Then on *Bubba Ho-Tep*, I broke my leg very badly—stupidly so—and it sort of put an end to my stunt career. I had a lot of time to sit while the bloody leg healed, and I started writing. Out of that came the book.

What happened on *Bubba Ho-Tep*?

It was toward the end of the filming, and it had rained the night before. This rock on the edge of the cliff that everybody had been standing on for the previous day had been greatly loosened

Kent's wife, the late Tomi Barrett, in a publicity still from *The Pyramid* (1975). (Courtesy Gary Kent)

by the rain. They called lunch, and I know as a stuntman when they call lunch, don't go to it, because when they get back from lunch is when they're gonna want the stunt and you'll be full of food. Nevertheless, they called lunch, and I stepped back on the rock, the rock gave way, and I just tumbled down the cliff.

When you were working on the book, did you go back and reconnect with a lot of the people you worked with back then?

I did, and that was interesting too, because I'm one of the few people, I guess, that loved Hollywood. I had few bad experiences with people, so I was on good speaking terms with so many people, and as you know it's like a big family anyway. A lot of people you lose touch with. You're close friends on one picture, and they you don't work again for ten years.

Did you discover a lot of things during your research that you didn't know, or that you'd forgotten about?

Yes. The strangest thing was the way other people remembered things that had the same experiences I did. I ran into people that thought they did things they didn't do at all. I knew they didn't do it. I have a pretty clear memory of things, and kept notes through the years on different things. I keep having to go back to *me* as the main librarian and say, "Was that true?" For instance, stunt people taking credit for stunts they didn't do, yet by now they are thoroughly convinced they *did* do them. In some cases, they're talking to me and I'm the guy that did the stunt!

Most of the things I found out were about the problems that the filmmakers had getting a film going, and getting it released. I didn't realize that part of the motion picture business until I made a couple of my own films, and then I said, "Gee, I've got these films, what do I do with them?" I just wasn't aware, and neither are students today. They all want to make a

Gary Kent (left) and John "Bud" Cardos at the 2000 Bicknell International Film Festival in Utah, which presented a tribute to the films of Al Adamson. (Courtesy Gary Kent)

film, but that other end of it, they are all convinced that somehow if they just get it made, it's going to be easy to get it played. Which is not true.

When I finished those two westerns [for Monte Hellman], I thought at last I'd done something I was proud to be a part of. Roger Corman looked at 'em and said, "I can't make any money off these things. Get 'em out of the office!" So he sold the rights right away. Jack worked hard putting those two things together, and had a terrible time getting them distributed. Even to this day, probably an awful lot of people that are not connected with the film industry have no idea there even *were* pictures called Ride in the Whirlwind or The Shooting. Which again is the problem today with the kids saying, "Come on, Gary, how do you do it? How do they get their picture out after they've been to Sundance?"

If you put together a good group of actors, you can walk into a studio and say, "I've got this person and this person," and the studio has already figured what those people are worth in certain countries. If you just have a really good script, not true. It's better that you get some name that has enough power, or find your financing elsewhere. Don Coscarelli, who is a good example of a successful outlaw filmmaker today, works his butt off and finances his films through friends and relatives and so forth. He's yet to walk into a studio and say, "Here's what I want to do," and they love it.

Can you imagine the response if he pitched *Bubba Ho-Tep* at a studio?

Right [*laughs*]. "Get out of here!"

Beyond the Call of Duty

JOYCE KING

Behind every successful (and not-so-successful) low-budget film is a dedicated crew working long hours (often without pay) under grueling conditions. In California, those crews often included Joyce King, a busy script supervisor who got her start on independent productions with director Burt Topper (*Hell Squad, Tank Commandos*), eventually working her way up to big-budget projects like *Nashville* (1975) and *Grease* (1978).

In between, King provided support to everyone from Al Adamson and Ted V. Mikels to Richard Rush, Monte Hellman and Peter Bogdanovich. She also took part in the rollicking productions of Dennis Hopper's *Easy Rider* (1969) and *The Last Movie* (1971). On several of these films, King would often appear in small roles (for instance, as the cranky librarian in *Race with the Devil*, 1975), and frequently found herself drafted into being a stunt double.

A California native who originally hoped to be an actress, King first met Topper when they worked together at the Horseshoe Stage in Los Angeles in the mid–1950s. After a brief career detour working as Eartha Kitt's personal assistant, King spent the next four decades collaborating with directors of every stripe. Here, she shares some of her memories of the exploitation films she worked on.

Did you grow up in California?

JOYCE KING: I was born in Hollywood, grew up in Eagle Rock, which is a sub between Glendale and Pasadena. I went to Glendale J.C. and I'm a graduate of the Pasadena Playhouse College of Theater Arts.

I ran into Burt Topper, and he took me to the theater first, the Horseshoe Stage, 1954, and then one day he said, "Let's go make a movie." I thought he was full of shit. What is this movie crap? Is he gonna chase me around the office now? No, he meant it. And for six months, with about 50 guys (there were only three women ever involved), we'd go outside of Barstow and go up in the hills and sort of build a camp, and we shot a picture called *Hell's Angels*. I know that it was released because I saw it on Hollywood Boulevard. It was made in 16mm, and like I said, it took six months, working on weekends only. Everybody contributing everything. To the best of my knowledge, Burt Topper paid every single person every single penny he had coming.

Was that the war film? I think it was called *Hell Squad* [1958].

Hell Squad. Thank you, sir. I'm getting old. There was another one, but I can't think of it right now. We were on the Italian Street at 20th Century–Fox doing a war movie in the '40s. I can't remember the title of that one. My name should have been on *Hell Squad*, but on the other

An impromptu biker dance party was a highlight of *The Rebel Rousers* (1970).

one, I was at that time called an apprentice script supervisor. Then they [the union] spring the thing on me that you have to have 90 paid shooting days as a script supervisor, somebody hires you and pays you, and that was totally insane. All the time I was working under those conditions, I only got 13 days. It devastated me, really. It had a bad effect on my ego and spirit.

I had an opportunity to go to work with Eartha Kitt, and I was with her for three years. Of course, she took me to Europe and South America and all over this country, and showed me things that I had no idea. I was a lily-white little girl in Eagle Rock, California. When I went to Miami with her, I said, "Eartha, why aren't the guys with us?" The trio. That was in '58, and they had to stay down the road a piece in a black hotel. I had no conception. I was really pretty isolated as a child. My mother was a schoolteacher. My father was kind of an itinerant trucker. This sort of thing never crossed my doorstep until then.

What got you interested in theater?

When I was about nine, my mother took me to see Tallulah Bankhead. My mother took me to every touring company that came into the Biltmore Theater. You know where the Biltmore Hotel is? There was a theater there. In fact, my mother [went] the night before I was born to see Jeanne Eagels in *Rain*. She took me to the theater, and I was fascinated.

There wasn't any arrow to follow. There wasn't any yellow line down the middle of the road. I was totally unprepared for all the stuff that happened. When I got angry, I got angry. I probably shafted myself more than I want to know.

Did you want to be an actress?

I had long red hair and gorgeous gray eyes, and an adequate (I would say) figure. But the face was not there. No Julia Roberts in this corner!

How did you meet Burt Topper?

At the Horseshoe Stage. We helped open the Horseshoe Stage in 1954. We did the Julie Harris–Ethel Barrymore thing about a kid in the South [*The Member of the Wedding*]. That was our opening show. We had James Edwards, who was my favorite person in the whole world for as long as he was alive. James Edwards played the guy that just came in with the horn every once in a while. We opened the theater. I was the stage manager, and Burt was the "when something had to be done" person. One night he said, "You wanna make a movie?" We went out and made a movie for six months on weekends.

The other film was *Tank Commandos* [1959] and then he did *Diary of a High School Bride* [1959].

I may have done a day or two on that last one. But on *Tank Commandos* we were out in Pomona, and guys in German uniforms and black boots and helmets came up out of the sewer. The town went wild! They called the FBI, and it was traumatic for everyone. But visualize a sewer pipe with a diameter of, say, 12 feet, and that's where we worked. We were able to bring Burt's homemade dolly down there. His homemade dolly worked just as well as the ones that cost $20,000 today. What was I doing down there? I was trying to do my job. He said, "We're out of money, we're out of food and you've got to do something." I went to the Pomona Fairgrounds, where my adopted aunt, one of the greatest ladies who ever lived, gave me $50. I went back and got hamburgers for everybody. We finished the day, but we were out of money and out of gas and out of everything.

I take it since you worked with him quite a bit that you got along well with Burt.

I 99 and $^{44}/_{100}$ percent adore and admire him immensely. He never asked anybody to do anything that he wouldn't do himself. I find that very nice in a man or anyone.

You did another Burt Topper film, the one with Fabian, which was called *The Day the Lord Got Busted* [1976].

We shot that in San Diego. I photographed the car going off. I was one of the cameras on that. He had a camera that would accept 50 or 90 feet of motion picture film, and so I had it, and when the thing happened, I just let it go through my frame and I started down, down, down, and I got the explosion from one angle.

It was all bad luck. The damn picture came out somewhere, it was released down South in so many theaters. There was something going on at the time that just took all the publicity. It had no publicity. The guy that played the crazy preacher was a friend of mine from the Pasadena Playhouse days. It was a good picture. It should have made it. It makes you mad when that happens.

I always liked his movies.

They are right out in front of you. You don't miss a trick. Don't blink and you won't miss anything.

On the low-budget films, were you asked to go above and beyond what a script supervisor would normally do?

That may be an understatement. It's like in the theater, you get involved. You're doing a show, and somebody needs something, you get it. You need the hamburgers, you get it. I think I wasn't called upon, but I volunteered most of the time.

How did you wind up working with Eartha Kitt?

James Edwards was working with Eartha Kitt on *Anna Lucasta* [1959], her one and only starring movie. He took me and his girlfriend to Tijuana to the bullfights, and when we came out and were inching our way toward the gate, this convertible pulls up next to us. Eartha says hello to Jimmy, and Jimmy says hello to Eartha, and Eartha says to the guy she's with, "Screw it!" She jumps out, jumps in our car in the back seat with me. By the time we got to Hollywood, she hired me.

What was your job with her?

Well, secretary-slash-gopher-slash-try to avoid anything that you can. On your toes. It worked sometimes. One time it didn't work. We were in the Waldorf-Astoria and the phone rang. It was Joseph Papp, the guy that produced Shakespeare in the Park [in New York]. He said he'd like to speak to her, and I didn't put my hand over the mouthpiece, and she yells out, "Tell him to go fuck himself!" So I never got to meet him [*laughs*]! I don't know what she was mad about, and then she was mad at me because I hadn't been smart enough to get my hand over the mouthpiece. It was a lesson learned. I don't think it ever happened again.

You were with her for about three years, then?

She was pregnant when I left. I can't remember at the moment, but I had something to go to. But that was an education, you know. Think about this for a second. You're in a top floor suite at the Waldorf-Astoria on Christmas night. The next night you're in the Apollo Theater. And I have to tell you that my sensibilities were jarred a few times. The drink backstage at the Apollo was 150-proof rum.

From what little I know about Eartha Kitt, she sounds like she led a pretty wild life.

She is brilliant, and like I said, without the three years with her, I'm sure I wouldn't have been able to accomplish half of what I have. She taught me to think on my feet. I wish I could see her. I love her.

Another one of your early credits was the Curtis Harrington film, *Night Tide* [1961].

I never had any rapport with him at all. I understand that some people like his stuff. It was a hard shoot, and like I said, no rapport.

How did you get that assignment?

Somebody asked me. That's the way it is. You're working on one film and something may be coming up to overlap. You can't quit the one you're on, but you say, "If something happens and you're going to be delayed a couple of days, I'd be happy to do the show."

Did you appear in the film?

I may have. I honestly don't know.

That film had Dennis Hopper and Luana Anders.

I'm not telling this out of school, but it's such a reflection of his lifestyle. Dennis went to lunch one day and came back in a cast. He had picked up this girl on Santa Monica Boulevard, and he had somebody's scooter. He "liberated" it. He drove it into a tree or a wall. I don't know. This white sailor in a white suit, and he's got a white cast on his right foot!

We had to block things [to hide the cast], like ladies being pregnant today. Moving furniture and whatever it took. Curtis Harrington, like I said, we weren't enthused with each other, but there were some moments in there that were really quite nice. Like the seagull landing on the railing? That only took about half a day!

What did you do between *Night Tide* and the Monte Hellman westerns?

I did a film called *Futz!* [1969], the man who loved his pig. It was a Broadway show that was then brought out here to a pretty big cow town between here and San Francisco. They brought the entire crew or cast from New York, and you walked down the hotel for half a yard and you were zonked, there was so much stuff going on.

The Monte Hellman films were shot in Utah.

Yes, for like $35,000 each. Roger Corman financed it [*Ride in the Whirlwind*, 1965]. The one that I worked on was with Cameron Mitchell. It was a tragedy, you know. It was like when the drama starts happening, there's no stopping it. I thought it was a very good film. You had Cameron Mitchell and Jack Nicholson, Harry Dean Stanton. Just a terrific cast. I was very happy to be part of it. I loved Cameron. When we were on the western, he had one of the biggest horses I've ever seen. He used to come by and pick me up with one hand and throw me on the back of his horse. Which was very nice. It doesn't sound like it was so nice, but it was terrific.

You didn't work on *The Shooting* [1965]?

No. That one I did not work on.

What was Hellman like to work with?

Very reclusive. I would sit in the back of the car next to him, and if he dozed off I'd grab his notes and see what the heck he thought he was doing that day, because he wouldn't tell me! I found that a little difficult, a little disturbing, and a little embarrassing, because I want to help when I'm working. There are some pictures I've been on where people have told me it wouldn't have been half as good if I hadn't been there. That's what I aim for.

What were a script supervisor's duties on these types of films?

After the war movie, Burt Topper got a contract with AIP, so he wanted to help me, thank me for my six months of servitude. He got me hired as an apprentice script supervisor for a picture called *No Place to Land* [1958] — John Ireland, Mari Blanchard, Gail Russell, Robert Middleton. We got to Holtville, California, and it was a 13-day shoot, three of those days being second unit. Second unit goes before the first unit, which is unusual, but that's the way they did things.

I ended up being a stunt double for Mari Blanchard in a 1918 biplane. I think that's above and beyond the call of duty. I got out of the plane, and my legs were rubbery because that guy had done it all. And he was the epitome of Errol Flynn in one of those war movies. When I was able to walk, I was walking along the side of this hangar, and I turned the corner and I literally bounced off the chest of this very big man, who happened to be the SAG representative. He said, "Was that you up there?"

I was terrified. I was just beginning to hear about crap that unions can and will do. They let me stay, and I worked as an apprentice the rest of the show. The producer, or probably Burt himself, paid whatever fine there was for letting a non-union person fly as a double.

I'm looking at the credits of that film. It was made by Albert Gannaway.

I loved him. He was an old charmer, a southern gentleman. He was married to an actress who put him through the ringer. I can't think of her name right now. Some very frenchy lady. He and Burt were like hand-in-glove. That movie was made in 13 days. John Ireland was always professional and right on his mark. Gail Russell had been one of the most beautiful women in the world. But she had just come out of some sort of rehab.

Did you do *Las Vegas Hillbillies* [1966], the Larry Jackson film?

I used to live with him and his wife. We were pretty good friends.

Can you tell me anything about his background?

I don't know how to figure this out or prove it, but I think he was a tank commander in the war, and I guess it would have been the Korean War. He was a ballsy, fearless guy, another charmer. I don't know anything other than he married a girl I was very friendly with, and they had a beautiful baby.

So you knew his wife.

That's how I met him. We worked for an independent director who made documentaries. I remember doing one that I directed, for the Woman's Christian Temperance Union, anti-smoking, that type of thing. I got to photograph and direct an autopsy. That was charming. I think that was with Burt Martin, around 1958 or so. I can't remember. We went to White Memorial. There was one scene with the one leading man and his girlfriend that took place in an autopsy room. We had a doctor and a heart, donated that day. It was a matter of about four hours that I had the wheel.

How did you get involved in those documentaries?

The director had a long list of documentaries that he'd done. I worked with him on two or three pictures. One was anti-smoking, another one was anti-booze, that sort of thing.

Did you do any other type of directing?

Second unit on a Larry Jackson film. Second unit, driving stuff. One night when we were all so zonked from having worked too long and not eaten properly, I designed a shot that saved us three shots, so that made me a hero for that day.

What film was that on?

Bob Dix was in that.

That was *The Road Hustlers* [1968], shot in South Carolina. I talked to Bob Dix not long ago.

He's alive? Oh, I'd love to see him. He saved my life. On that movie I was stunt doubling. Don't laugh, but I did it again! The boat wiped out at 75 miles per hour, and Bob dove in off the second story of the chase boat and pulled me out.

Were you the one on the boat when it blew up?

Yup.

Larry Jackson was in the boat, too, wasn't he?

No, it was the crazy, crazy man whose property we were shooting on that was driving the boat. It was a racing boat.

Bob told me Larry got hurt in that, too.

I'm sure there was more than one accident. I came home after mine.

Did you also work on *The Black Klansman* [1966]?

I don't even think it's on my résumé. We had our wonderful 24-hour days on that show. Don't laugh.

Ted Mikels is quite a character.

Don't know, don't remember. Some of the stuff has been pounded out of my head from all the different bangs I've had. I'm like a football player; I've been hit one too many times.

How did you get talked into doing all these stunts?

Well, I don't know if this sounds stupid, but after you've been working on a sequence and the schedule says you're supposed to do this and this and this, and you're coming on the twentieth hour and there's nobody there to do it, somebody always says, "Okay, I'll do it." Unfortunately, I was that stupid person.

You want to hear a cute one? I think it was *Blood of Dracula's Castle* [1969]. The ingénue, who wasn't even qualified — she was just somebody's cutie that they picked up off the street. Here it's January in 20-degree water. She wouldn't do it, couldn't do it, really. Bob Dix takes me, strangles me with back to camera, strangles me and shakes me and throws me out, and then Laszlo Kovaks frames it so that my limp body floats into the frame and out of the frame. I'm wearing Levis but no top. That was the worst.

I remember that sequence. There's just a random girl sitting in the middle of the stream when Bob Dix is escaping from prison.

That was me doubling her. He saved my life before, but that time he killed me!

You did a couple of Richard Rush films. Was he a lot different than Monte Hellman?

They partied together on set more.

What did you think of those films?

I had a couple of lines in *Psych-Out* [1968].

Which part?

The guys are coming out of a church for some reason, and a tourist-type person is coming up the steps and says something like, "I never thought the reverend would allow this sort of people in."

And then they cut to the portrait of Jesus, after you talk about their long hair and sandals or something like that.

Probably. Susan Strasberg was quite a find for that show. Bruce Dern was on it. *Psych-Out* was a well-done mystery-murder type thing.

Were the sets on these films pretty loose by that time in the sixties?

Yes. A lot of partying. *The Savage Seven* [1968], oh, it was so cornball. He got Robert Walker

Jr., with blue eyes, to play an Indian. We laughed ourselves silly. I did five motorcycle pictures in a row, it seems like.

They frequently used actual motorcycle gang members on those films.

Well, the guys on *Easy Rider* were my friends and my neighbors up here where I live in Chatsworth. Really tight friends. They had a work ethic that was bar none. Get the job done. Really good.

Do you remember much about *Hells Angels on Wheels* [1967]?

Actually, right now I'm fuzzing out on that. I know it was a hard shoot, but I can't think of anything right now.

You mentioned *Blood of Dracula's Castle*. You did a few films with Al Adamson. How did you meet him?

Same thing. Burt Topper, same bunch of people were around that part of Santa Monica Boulevard, near Vine Street. There was a studio or stage a couple of blocks west [Hollywood Stages]. I spent a lot of time there. I was next to Mr. Boris Karloff when he said to Peter Bogdanovich, "You don't treat people like this." That was a 20-hour day. He was the second person or something to ever get a SAG card. He was, needless to say, a great experience. And his wife was just fabulous. Glad I didn't miss that.

That would have been on *Targets* [1968], which was an excellent film.

And it was not easily made. It was a tough shoot.

Did you get to speak with Karloff much?

Yes, I did. I loved him. His wife the most beautiful lady. Charming, warm, wonderful.

What about Bogdanovich?

Like I said, Mr. Karloff said to Peter, "You don't treat people like this." Peter went on doing everything the same.

You also worked on *Vampire Men of the Lost Planet* [*Horror of the Blood Monsters*, 1970) for Al Adamson.

I'm sure you know, he would buy these pieces of film from the Philippines and then come over here and think of some way to put them together. It was bad.

***Blood of Dracula's Castle* was shot at Hollywood Stages, and partly at an actual castle.**

I was in the castle.

Do you remember anything else about that?

It was just painfully uncomfortable, as most of those sorts of things were. Cold. No hot food. No accommodations of any kind. That sort of thing.

You said you did the stream sequence. Did you do any of the dungeon sequences?

I was there as a script supervisor, but I didn't get hung on the wall, thank you!

John Carradine was also in that film.

I must have done four or five with Mr. Carradine.

From what I understand, he had a photographic memory.

Seven pages he could do. Unbelievable. Absolutely unbelievable to me. The only other person like that is Cicely Tyson.

Do you remember anything about *The Rebel Rousers* [1970], which was filmed as *Limbo*? Martin Cohen directed that, and he had produced the Dracula film.

Okay, then here's something for your memory. Things were so bad that the cinematographer and the gaffer would wrap up the film, give it to me and I'd take it home. Until our checks cleared, they didn't know where the film was. But they brought it on themselves. They treated us like shit.

They seemed to have trouble paying their bills on a few projects.

That's the word, paying. You write a check and you give it to the guy for having spent 14 hours that day. And then when it bounces, and his wife yells at him....

In *The Rebel Rousers*, Cameron Mitchell and Diane Ladd are involved in this traditional plotline, but it looked like all the bikers were just improvising in the background.

That's right [*laughs*]! "What script? What pages?"

Cameraman Glen R. Smith (left) and Bruce Dern on the set of *The Rebel Rousers* (1970). Script supervisor Joyce King has less-than-fond memories of the production. (Photograph by Hedy Dietz/Courtesy Gary Kent)

Did that make your job more difficult?

Can you imagine this dirty little town, and the cameraman is standing right in the middle of this intersection, like a five-way intersection. The cameraman, I think it was Leslie [Kovacs], he's doing hand-held, doing a 300-degree shot with the bikers coming around, kicking dust in his face. And then the check to the town bounced. And we'd been drinking their water. It has to be trucked in. How to make friends and influence people in the small towns of America! Yes, we're a movie company. "Get out of here right now!"

I take it you all made it out alive.

Yeah, but that was not the only situation like that.

You worked on *Easy Rider* after all of that was over.

Night Tide was with Dennis Hopper, so I knew him. Actually, I knew Dennis Hopper from the La Jolla Theater and Eartha Kitt. They were friends. Peter [Fonda] was a surprise. Peter was a big surprise. I thought he was going to be a pain in the ass, and he was just a wonderful guy. Whenever he could make things better for us, the crew, he did. He came in one night and moved us out of one hotel and moved us into a better hotel, and ate the cost.

Was that film challenging from the point of view of the script, or lack thereof?

Excuse me [*laughs*]? No pages! Whatever they said, I tried to get the essence down on paper. That one campfire scene—come on, tell me you don't know everybody was zonked! Yes, it was difficult.

Was the shoot as crazy as it's been described?

We were doing five hundred miles a day, and we were just being eaten by southern bugs. It was a difficult shoot.

What about Hopper?

He has a funny sense of humor. He can be absolutely Prince Charming, and then forget what he said. I remember being in Peru with him on the picture that Universal let him direct. I'd ask him a question, and he'd just glaze over and walk away. I said, "You've been shot in your left shoulder. Doesn't that mean anything to you?" And he walked away. I guess it didn't mean anything. I think it shows.

That was *The Last Movie*. I imagine that film was an even crazier production than *Easy Rider*.

We were living in Cuzco, which is at 9,000 feet, and we were driving an hour and a half in the morning to go up to Chinchero, which was 12,000 feet. Does that give you a hint of how the day would be? The sun would go behind the cloud, and you'd have to put on a parka, because the temperature would drop so fast. And then pretty soon the sun came out again and you were burning.

How long were you in Peru?

Three months. And that's how I got my IA card. After 15 freaking years, I finally got my IA card because of that picture, because of Dennis, because of Paul Lewis, who was the production manager–producer. Paul Lewis is probably the only reason I survived in this business. He kept hiring me.

Did you ever feel like that movie wouldn't get finished?

No problem about that. I never worried about it getting finished. Just, what was it gonna be?

Did you get to see it?

I think I saw it twice. I was sad, because, my God, look at the elements that we had, and the beautiful place. The place was fabulously beautiful. The sunsets and sunrises. I have a picture that I got by getting on my hands and knees early in the morning and hunkering across this meadow until I got within ten feet of a pair of young, young llamas. One was white, and she was folded up in the grass, her legs tucked in, and he was standing guard. He was brown. I still have it on my wall.

You mentioned Paul Lewis. He probably would have been the one who got you on to Werewolves on Wheels [1971].

I remember we were way out in the boonies in the desert on the way to Barstow, and all of our actors that were Hell's Angels were buck naked on their hogs, driving up and down this sands park, with people from Iowa watching. I remember that! I remember one scene where the [marijuana] smoke was so thick that I know I probably don't remember getting home. That was Werewolves on Wheels.

Did you ever work at the Spahn Ranch?

I did one nudie, because that's where I found out that when a girl has had implants, they don't go flat anymore. They just go ping! Just standing there. It struck me as so funny. I was hard pressed to keep my laughter to myself. I didn't have any background in that. That was my first nudie, and I was not script, I was shooting stills.

What was the film?

It was cowboys coming into town, and lots of shooting, and cowgirls who were doing a lot of shooting when they could get up off their behinds. I remember being uncomfortable. That was before we found out what had been going on there. There was something that was very uncomfortable. I guess maybe it was the guys that they hired to be wranglers. They were kind of weird. It was an unpleasant situation. I'm glad I was only there for a few days, got paid cash and kept moving.

But the Manson people were still there?

Some of the people were there, living on the ranch.

Did you do any other nudies?

Oh God, I did one called *Kama Sutra '71* [1970]. It was at that stage on Santa Monica. It was supposed to be the Indian exotic lovemaking, the Kama Sutra. We came in and there was this lady, who was the producer, she was a high mucketymuck, and she was literally stomping around on the stage and rattling strings of beads in her hand. I was making some notes on my script, and she walked up behind and gave me a shot in the shoulder, like pow! I looked up and she said, "No dirty feet! No dirty feet!" Then she walked away. So when they put the people in the bed, I saw dirty feet. The guy was on top, his feet showed. Dirty feet. I went over to the first assistant director and said, "I think we have a problem here if you can't get this nerd to go wash his feet."

At that particular time in my life, I had eleven dollars in my bank account. So three days at $75 a day, cash in my hand at the end of the day, was blissful. That's my other nudie.

King had her work cut out for her on *Easy Rider* (1969), starring Dennis Hopper (left) and Peter Fonda. She later accompanied Hopper to Peru for the equally raucous production of *The Last Movie* (1971).

Can you tell me what else you remember about Al Adamson's films?

I admired his chutzpah. He'd get on the phone and he'd get Mr. Carradine, he'd get all of these people, and he'd get 'em for five hundred bucks a day, sometimes less. He could be charming in his alligator shoes. I guess that always annoyed me: a guy who's not paying your check, who's not getting the money to you, is wearing alligator shoes. That's why when the guys [on *Rebel Rousers*] told me to take the film and hide it in my icebox, I did it. How dare they sweat us like in a coal mine, and then not pay us?

You did *Race with the Devil* [1975] in Texas.

I had three or four lines in *Race with the Devil*. In the library when the girls [Lara Parker, Loretta Swit] are looking for stuff, I was the librarian and I was such a bitch. Then at the end, there's this big parade of the vampires or whatever they're supposed to be. I was involved in that, whether or not I was legible on film I don't know.

I'll have to go back and look at it.

I hope I don't scare you!

Were you on that film during the portion that Lee Frost shot?

Yes, I was on the whole thing.

How much did Lee do?

Oh boy, I don't want to say because I remember it was quite a shock. Maybe a week. I couldn't swear to it.

The change was very abrupt, and from what Paul Maslansky has said, the crew was not happy about it.

You're never happy when that happens. Particularly when you're tied with the director. When they get fired, you get fired, too.

Was it a difficult shoot?

I broke three ribs.

How?

We were in the Winnebagos. We had to have two, because one would get shot, and we'd have to have the one that wasn't shot. In those days, that particular model had a pointed corner on it. It was not curved like they do today. I was inside, and once again I had volunteered. So I reach out and I slate, and within seconds somebody slams on the brakes and I go right into that corner and I cracked three ribs. And Peter, dear man, gave me his pills.

I've interviewed Bud Cardos, who was a stuntman, and I think you got more banged up back then than he did.

He's much a better stunt person [*laughs*]. He analyzes these things. He plans it out. He does not jump in an icy stream half-dressed.

At that point in the 1970s, you started moving on to bigger films. How did you make that transition?

Go to work. Nobody hires you, you go to work and see if you can help the problem or not *be* the problem. I was lucky to have done *Nashville* [1975]. That's one of the greatest experiences of my life.

How were the larger budget films different that the independent films you did?

You get to go to the bathroom, you get to eat, you go home once in a while [*laughs*].

And you don't get blown up in a boat or thrown in a stream.

There you go. You got it. That's the difference. Then, once in a while you have a big hunk of money.

So you actually got paid, too.

Thank God. I would probably be dead by now if I didn't have the kind of health insurance that the studios give you. If I had worked all of those pictures under union conditions I would not be talking to you. I would be in Maui or someplace.

Of the films that you worked on over the years, do you have a favorite?

Nashville.

Why?

Everything. It was crazy. Again, you let these people go. One actress would go home at night and write her own scene, and the next day she'd give it to me. Therefore I had something to incorporate into the script to show the editor where the heck we were at. God, I loved her. Everybody else just went off the top of their head, which was fine, but it's very demoralizing to work that way.

Are you still working now?

No. I would if I could.

But you don't consider yourself retired.

No, I'm afraid I haven't retired. I have macular degeneration, which is being held in abeyance with pills, so I'm kind of a pillhead now. You never know when that stuff can go back on you. So I'm paying now for floating down the stream at seven o'clock in the morning with not enough clothes on.

Put Your (Other) Head on My Shoulder

ANTHONY LANZA

Anthony Lanza was not a prolific director, but his short list of credits is certainly memorable: Dennis Hopper's first biker film, *The Glory Stompers* [1968], Arch Hall Sr.'s talk show spoof *The Irv Carlson Show* [1971], and the legendarily deranged *The Incredible 2-Headed Transplant* [1971].

As an editor, though, Lanza had a hand in dozens of exploitation films throughout the 1960s and 1970s. Born in Lake Charles, Louisiana, in 1936, Lanza studied filmmaking at University of Southern California, graduating in 1959. His first jobs out of school were cutting Ray Dennis Steckler's *Wild Guitar* (1962) and working on Timothy Carey's infamous *The World's Greatest Sinner* (1962). From there, he worked as a script supervisor and editor on most of Arch Hall's Fairway productions, including *The Sadist* (1963), *What's Up Front!* (1964, which he also produced), *The Nasty Rabbit* (1964), and *Deadwood '76* (1965), and as assistant director on the Coleman Francis-Anthony Cardoza production *The Skydivers* (1963).

Frequently working out of a cutting room at Ray Dorn's Hollywood Stages studio (where Al Adamson and David L. Hewitt held court for many years), he also provided support on James Landis' *Jennie: Wife/Child* (1968), *Cycle Savages* (1969), *Scream Free!* (1969), the racing documentary *Hot Rod Action* (a.k.a. *Follow Me*, 1969), *Bigfoot* (1970) and Dorn's *Is This Trip Really Necessary?* (1970).

In the 1970s, Lanza directed at least three more films that either weren't completed or didn't receive wide release: *Desert Gems*, *Freedom Riders*, and *Squeeze Play*, a troubled production that starred members of the Dallas Cowboys football team. He also directed *The Man of Kingwood*, a short documentary about the Imperial Potentate of the Shriners. In later years, he worked as an editor and/or production manager on *Dangerous Love* (1988), *Victor One* (1994) and the Brigitte Nielsen film *Codename: Silencer* (1995). Lanza is now retired, and is living once again in Lake Charles.

What got you interested in working in the film industry?

ANTHONY LANZA: I always loved movies since I was a kid. I made movies when all we had was a 16mm camera, and it was very [difficult] to get film for it. I used to do my own movies whenever we could afford it. There wasn't very much to them, but the first thing I did that was sizable was my father, who was an electrical contractor at the time, was doing the Bull Shoals Dam in Arkansas, and he wanted me to photograph it for him. So he bought an Auricon 16mm sound-on-film camera, and I was able to, with the help of one other person, to kind of cover it for him and photograph it. So that was about all I did before I went to school.

Once you got out of school, was your first job working on the Timothy Carey film?

Oh, *The World's Greatest Sinner*! I helped him with that, but I guess I did do that first. I was still in school or finishing school. I helped him with it and did some re-editing, I believe. I didn't do much on it.

You had an assistant producer credit, but I wasn't sure what that meant.

It means that I put some money in it, probably [*laughs*]. I think I did make an investment in it, but I never made a dime off of it.

How did you meet Carey?

I met him through a friend. I took a look at the picture. He had it pretty much already cut. He wanted to see if I was interested in investing in it, which I wasn't at the time, but I later on did. Then they needed some re-editing, and they couldn't afford to have anybody else do it, I guess [*laughs*]. Ray Steckler had a feature going at Fairway, which was Arch Hall's studio, and he asked me if I would cut it for him because he didn't really have anybody else to do it. I was right out of school, and I said, "Well, sure I'll go ahead and do it for you and get some practical experience." So that was really the first feature I cut—it was called *Wild Guitar*. It was a little black and white quickie film, low-budget, that he directed and Arch Hall produced.

Once you took a look at it, what did you think of the Carey film?

Well, it was different! I think most critics looked at it that way, as something different. It got good reviews, and got some really bad reviews. My own personal opinion was that it was interesting. I did cut a trailer for it—that's what I did on that one—and looked over some of the other editorial stuff that he had already done, was basically what I did.

Do you remember much about Carey? From what I know, he was pretty odd in real life.

Yeah, he was. I don't particularly like to talk about the dead, but he was quite a character. For his type of personality, he was the same onscreen as off, I always felt. He was—how would I say it?—a little bit disgusting sometimes with some of the things he would do to get attention. I remember him telling me one time that he was in a car with some other actors during a scene, and he wanted to be seen. He was in the back seat. So he started picking his nose. He felt that would get him some attention, and somebody would notice him back there. There were little odd things that he would do like that. The director probably never let it go by, but he put himself on film like that sometimes.

From there you worked on several films for Arch Hall. Can you tell me about him?

I found him very easy to work with, and he liked what I was doing, and the directors from then on liked what I was doing, so I just kind of stayed on there for a few pictures. *Wild Guitar*, *The Sadist*, which I think was the second one I cut for Arch, and then one called *What's Up Front?* It was a comedy, which I also cut for him and produced. It was very low-budget, and we had some big people on it for the time. We had Vilmos Zsigmond and Leslie [Laszlo] Kovacs on the same show as his assistant. We had some terrific people on that.

We did a Technicolor picture for probably around thirty or forty thousand dollars, which you couldn't make a trailer today for that. Then we did one called *Nasty Rabbit* [1964]. I think the title was changed to *Spies-a-Go-Go*.

The massive John Bloom and a reasonable facsimile of actor Albert Cole's head make their escape in Anthony Lanza's *The Incredible 2-Headed Transplant* (1971).

The western was *Deadwood '76*, which we shot in South Dakota. I went up there and did script supervising for the director, then came back and cut it.

Were you typically on the set of the Arch Hall films that you edited?

Oh yeah, I did script supervising on some of those, which they kind of wanted me to do, because by doing that I was more familiar with the film, and I could cut the film faster. That's what they're thinking was, and it worked out fine.

Did you work on *Eegah* [1962]?

No, he had done that before I got there, thank God. It wasn't too much to look at. I think he had done one other one with his kid, some kind of racing picture [*The Choppers*]. But I had nothing to do with that one either.

Did you get to know Arch, Jr.? The general consensus is that his father was more enthusiastic about his film career than he was.

I thought so, too. He never really was that interested in the movies. He was more interested in his music. He had a little band.

He's actually turned up again, playing with his band.

I thought he was a pilot. I thought that's what he did for years. That surprises me, but I guess nothing surprises me. I haven't talked to him or seen him in years. I wouldn't recognize him, probably.

Were you able to support yourself entirely with film work in those days?

It was touch and go. I didn't really have that much money coming in from these pictures, but I figured I liked the directors that were on two or three of them, and I decided to get as much knowledge as I could first hand. You don't learn everything at USC. You don't learn the practical things. That was then. I don't know what they're doing at SC now.

Actually, I freelanced for years. I never worked for one company. I think a year and a half was about the longest I stayed with one. Most of my work was all freelance, low-budget pictures. At the time, when I first started, it was difficult to get into the IA union. In fact, it was almost impossible. They just didn't want to take anybody. So we — Leslie Kovacs and Vilmos and myself — all joined NABET, which is the other union. I got some work out of it, not a lot. I think Zsigmond got more than I did.

After that, I really didn't even try to get into the IA union. I just kept on doing what I was doing. A lot of these, you couldn't be union and work on a non-union picture, so I figured at least I could work on something and get a living out of it.

Did you get any sense of how Kovacs and Zsigmond felt about the movies they were working on during that period?

Well, we were working for money. I know they were. Zsigmond was probably getting a hundred dollars a day and very happy that he could get that when he first came over here. So as far as their feeling about the movies, Zsigmond was into some bigger stuff, at least mentally, already. He was contemplating wanting to do some bigger shows. In fact, we did do a show called *Tender Grass* [a.k.a. *Jennie: Wife/Child*], and he invested in it and the director of several of those pictures invested in it, and they tried to make something that was really artistic and good. Photography-wise it was beautiful; it was black and white and very well shot. It was one of Zsigmond's earliest black and white movies that was so beautiful. As far as Kovacs, he usually worked with him as his assistant on the early pictures. I remember him working with him. So there were both of them on set sometimes if I were there just doing script, or in the case of *What's Up Front?* I did producing too. I had a very small crew, but we got a picture made in Technicolor for about thirty thousand dollars.

Were you primarily interested in editing, or did you want to direct?

I always wanted to direct, or try it at least. The first opportunity I had was *Glory Stompers* in 1967.

How did that happen?

One of the producers [was a guy] I had kind of done some work on the side for. He was making some of these softcore films, I guess you call them. They weren't even softcore at the time. Right now you'd probably see them on television. At the time, they were considered softcore, and they had comedy in them. He wanted me to kind of go over it for him.

Was that John Lawrence? I think the film you're talking about is *Tales of a Salesman* [1965].

Yes, he's the one who hired me to do some work for him. He liked my work and had the opportunity to start getting some investors to put together *The Glory Stompers*. He wanted me to direct it, and I had never directed before. I said, "Well, sure I'll do it, but my background is editing." He said that was good [*laughs*]. So I did *The Glory Stompers* for him. Actually, my name's not on it as an editor. My assistant is on there, Glenn Miller. I decided since I was getting director credit, I didn't want two credits on the same picture, so I gave the credit to him.

How did you know Lawrence?

I had done some editing for him on another little movie he was putting together. I don't know how he ever got my name, but he did. Maybe through a friend. But he wanted me to go over his film with him and make some changes. It was one of those little girly things, it wasn't much of a story to it. So I did that for him, and then he got interested in my background at USC. He was contemplating doing a movie, and he wanted to know if I would possibly direct it and edit it. That's really how we started talking to each other.

Did working on Lawrence's nudie film bother you at all?

That was really the first thing I worked on like that. Arch Hall had one that was looking through magic spectacles or something [*Magic Spectacles*, 1961]. I didn't do it, it was done probably before I got there. That was about this guy that every time he put spectacles on, girls would lose their bathing suits. It was comical and cute. It wasn't vulgar, I didn't think.

What was it like directing for the first time?

It was difficult because of the circumstances. We were making it with hardly any money. We were shooting crazy, for a low-budget picture. We had to shoot in two weeks. After we shot the thing, they were running out of money. That's when American International came in and said they'd put up the rest of the money and release it for us. The bike pictures were very hot then, and they were trying to get two or three of them out as quickly as possible.

We shot the two weeks and got principal photography, or most of it, done. We didn't shoot the big party scene, because we couldn't afford it at the time. When they put the money in it, we were able to do another one or two weeks. I think it was three weeks for the whole show.

We were having some problems with Dennis [Hopper]. He's a very good actor, really adding a lot of things to the film that were great. But many times we didn't have the time to do these things and have the rehearsals that he wanted to have. We were lucky to get it in the can, which is what my job was. I kept falling behind because he kept wanting to do this, or wanting to listen to a soundtrack back, and wanted to listen to hear how he sounded, or check what he looked like or whatever. He was doing a good job, though. That's when I just told Norman Herman, who was our producer from AIP, that he would have to control him or I could not finish the picture. Everybody knows he was on weed; he was high all the time. He was just very hard to control. Other than that, we had a lot of good actors on the picture, and they did the best job they could under the circumstances.

Did your editing background help you when you were directing?

Oh yeah, definitely. Before I was on the set I did a breakdown of the kind of shots we would need. I went over to the director, and some directors knew what they wanted to do and all I had to do was just make sure we got the coverage. But some of them didn't know beans about what they needed. They were just trying to make a movie and they just set the camera up. So yeah, it was it was a big help, knowing how to put a movie together. Editing is a highly recommended background.

Casey Kasem was in that, as well.

Yes, he was. Jock Mahoney, Chris Noel, Lindsay Crosby, Jody McCrea. John Lawrence always wanted to put as many so-called names or partial names in a picture to help the advertising and to be able to play drive-ins, which is where most of these pictures went. That was my first experience as a director, and I didn't direct anything else for a while.

I did another one for John Lawrence, *The Incredible 2-Headed Transplant*, a science fiction one. That was a little more expensive to do. We shot ten minutes of the film that was action-packed. After those ten minutes he was able to raise the money.

AIP picked that up, too.

Yes, they did. That's their kind of picture! I never made a dime off of it. We were supposed to have points, but I never saw a point. With *Glory Stompers*, I did get a few dollars out of it. I had three and a half points. Some of the other people had some points. Dennis also had three and a half points, and I think Casey and Mike Curb had points in it.

When he offered you *The Incredible 2-Headed Transplant*, what did you think of the overall concept?

Well, I wanted to make sure it was going to work a little bit with our budget. We didn't have a budget to do a good head, and I didn't think it would look realistic. We had to use a fake head, and the makeup kept changing on it, the color kept changing. It was really hard to do. I told him if it worked camera-wise, if we got low angles, then possibly we could put the thing together. So we did some early photography just to see how it would come out. We discovered [we had to get] down low enough with the camera angle, which was kind of hard to do, but we would follow him for a few seconds at a time.

On *Transplant*, there were some pretty good shots of John Bloom running, and Al Cole's head is clearly on his shoulder. How did you achieve that?

We experimented with that for a long time before we started shooting. I thought unless we can get this thing to come off somehow — because we didn't have a good head to begin with — we'd have to try different angles. I wound up trying a real low angle and John Bloom was able to hold the guy on this back. With the low angle you could only see his head, so it worked out. For some shots where they were running, it was very hard to do, so you couldn't keep the shot going for very long. That's how I got by. Some of it, at the time we just didn't have the money to make a credible, good-looking head.

Do you remember much about the "two heads" in the film, John Bloom and Al Cole?

John Bloom was not an actor, he was just brought in because he was so big. Actually, he proved himself to be a pretty good actor. He didn't have any professional experience. With Cole, he was an actor, and I guess John Lawrence cast him. But he fit the part pretty good, and he was small enough that he could get on the big guy's back and do the necessary head shots.

What about Bruce Dern?

Again, this is one of those pictures that he took because he wanted the money [laughs]. I think he got like $1,700 or something like that. A low figure at the time. Maybe it was a slow period for him and he just took it. I liked working with Bruce. He never gave me all he had until we were shooting. He wanted to make sure the camera was rolling, and wouldn't rehearse at his full potential. He's a very fine actor. I've always liked his work.

I always thought he seemed kind of subdued in that movie, compared to some of his other films in that era.

Jody McCrea (left) and Dennis Hopper in Lanza's *The Glory Stompers* (1967).

Right, he did a lot of those bike pictures. I cut a couple of them. He was a brilliant actor. He just was himself, to me, on the screen and off the screen. Always himself. I didn't have any scenes in that picture that I remember him being different than he was in real life [*laughs*]. Some actors are that way. John Wayne is always John Wayne, you know?

What did you think of the finished film?

I guess some disappointment, and yet, at least I tried to make the film a little light, and not too heavy. It wasn't really supposed to be a real heavy, scary picture. It was more a fun picture. That was the way we thought about it. It got a couple of reviews that I remember being favorable, but it got some bad ones, too, like with most pictures.

It, to me, was just a fun picture. I didn't try to put too much into it except for a few scenes where John Bloom is making the change. The subtle changes that John Bloom is going through throughout the thing, and trying to stay as a good guy, and trying to keep the bad guy from overtaking him even though he was supposed to be retarded. That part worked for me, but some things didn't work at all. As a director, I wouldn't do another one like that, I don't think.

I saw an interview with Ray Dennis Steckler, where he said he was offered the chance to work on that film, but turned it down because he thought it would be bad for his reputation.

Incredible Transplant [*laughs*]? Well, he was welcome to it! It's not really my type of picture. He directed one for himself—what was it called? *Incredibly Strange Creatures*. John always wanted me to do *Incredible Transplant* after *Glory Stompers*. He was very happy with *Glory Stompers* and the money it made.

What was it like working at Hollywood Stages? Do you remember much about Ray Dorn?

You know that's not there anymore. It was gutted and torn down. The inside of it was torn out just a couple of years ago. Anyway, in its heyday, it was a great place to work. I had an editing room upstairs for a long time. Several pictures were going on and I just happened to be up there, and I'd go from one to another. I was real busy for a while with different projects. Ray wasn't always involved in the projects, but there were several that he was. I guess he even put money in some of them, or at least built sets for some people. I loved Ray. He was a great guy.

I also found an editing credit for you on a film called *Dinah East* [1970], about a transsexual actress.

Dinah East was made over at the old Culver City Studio. I got on that picture because we had two or three people that were in the NABET union. We only had two or three editors, and [producer-director Gene Nash] was going NABET on that show. I went out for an interview. [The other editors] came in and interviewed for the show, and he liked what I had done in the past, so he hired me. So I cut *Dinah East*. I wish I could find it. I wanted to see it for years, but I've never been able to locate a print of it. I'm sure it exists on video.

Mae West allegedly filed a lawsuit to get the film pulled from release.

Well, it was really based on her. They never came out and said that, but that's what it really was about. The picture wasn't bad; it was a good little story. I enjoyed cutting it. We cut it pretty fast at the Culver City Studios. After Gene died, I tried to find a copy. Let's see, he must have died, probably, in the early 1980s. When I went back here, I called and tried to find him, and they said he had passed away. I enjoyed that picture and I thought it was good.

You did one more Arch Hall production, *The Irv Carlson Show* [1971].

I think they changed the title of it. Yeah, it was like a comeback Arch Hall was trying to do. I think I directed that, didn't I? I don't see it on my résumé here. Must not have been something I wanted to keep! It was [also] called *The Beautiful People*. It was shot on 16mm, and it was kind of a takeoff on *The Tonight Show* type of thing, which I think they did another one later that was better. They never got a good release on it. It never played very much. But it was a fun thing to do. It was the first thing I ever did in comedy.

You also worked as an assistant director on Anthony Cardoza's *Bigfoot* [1970], which was directed by Robert Slatzer.

Again, as friends we're trying to help each other out, I guess [*laughs*]. I worked on it as an assistant. I tell you, I better not say very much about that picture!

Did you know Cardoza very well?

Oh yeah, I knew him before, and he knew my work and he wanted me to try to help.

Do you remember much about Bob Slatzer?

Yeah, he directed that. I really didn't work *with* him on that. I was trying to not get bogged down. I guess he was okay as an actor's director, but he didn't really know how to get footage and get the right angles and stuff. That's what I was trying to do mostly for Cardoza — try to keep the show on time.

After *Two-Headed Transplant*, your filmography gets a little sketchy. What did you do during the 1970s?

As a director or editor? Back to the 1960s, we did a picture called *Tender Grass*, which was the same director [James Landis] that Arch Hall had used on *The Sadist* and *The Nasty Rabbit*. We did it in a studio down close to downtown Los Angeles. It was almost all interiors. The picture was really financed by the group. You ever hear of James Enochs? He was one of the investors. Zsigmond put money in it himself. They had some other investors. We did the picture, I was on set as the script supervisor and the picture, when it was finished, was cut according to the director. He seemed to be happy with it, but I was never happy with it. It was not a very easy picture to watch. It was interesting, but it was too slow for my editing style. That picture never got a release. I wound up later on, much later, having it put on video and giving everybody copies, and that was the last I heard of it.

That was retitled *Jennie: Wife/Child*.

Yeah, that's right. I don't know if it ever got much of a release.

It's out on DVD now.

It's a black and white movie. Beautifully photographed. Zsigmond was unbelievable, even then. The story was okay, but it was a child bride story.

I did a lot of pictures, usually called in to fix things. I did another picture called *Questions* [a.k.a. *Doomsday Voyage*, 1972], another low-budget picture. It was shot all locally, and had Joseph Cotten in it. That was probably back in the early 1970s.

Al Adamson was involved in that.

Yeah. It was cut over at Hollywood Stages. I used to do a lot of work off and on at Hollywood Stages. Some people would come over there and they'd see me working, and just ask if I could help them with this, or help them with that. I would get some of these pictures and try to fix them. I did a lot of that.

As far as directing, what else did I do after that? I only did a half a dozen shows as a director. *The Beautiful People*, I did direct that. One called *Desert Gems*, which never was finished, I don't think. I was directing that for a company called Cinema 35 on Western Avenue in Los Angeles. Another one called *Freedom Riders*, which was done in Dallas, which was never finished. And *Squezze Play*, I think I did that one in '78 or '79. It was supposed to be an action comedy, but it never really came off. I don't think they got much of a release on it.

I did some documentaries. I did one called *The Man of Kingwood*, which was actually about the imperial potentate of the Shriners. The Man of Kingwood was a gentleman right here in Lake Charles who had become the imperial potentate of the Shriners, and I did this twenty-minute film of his life and put it together, and we showed it at the Las Vegas convention. At the time, all we had was one-inch tape, so we had a projector and projected it onto as large a screen as we could get. I did another one, a series of pictures. Twelve one-hour shows called *Star Power*, for Mutual General. We did that for television. That was in ... I'm not sure.

What was *Desert Gems* about?

The producer used his kid in it. As I remember it was a kid going out in the desert and looking for certain rocks, and there was some kind of drama in it, but I don't remember.

What about *Freedom Riders*?

Freedom Riders was something we tried to put together in Dallas. That was a Bill Collins production. It was bikers getting together and riding across the country. I guess it was kind of a similar premise as *Easy Rider*. *Freedom Riders* was made in '78 or '79.

And *Squeeze Play*?

That was a movie we did finish. That was in Dallas. It was a bad movie [*laughs*]! Just a bad movie. It didn't get much play. I think it played in Texas. It was a 35mm film that was budgeted at around $800,000, I think. It had four Dallas Cowboys in it. At the time they were very popular. Too Tall Jones was in there. I can't remember all the cast right now. It had two or three people that were starlets that were just starting out, didn't really have any background, didn't want to be told what to do or how I should direct them and the action. It was just very unprofessional, and I didn't enjoy putting that together at all.

Who produced it?

The guy went to jail, as I remember. He had somehow swindled the company out of some money. That's what I heard. He had some prison time. I think his first name was Bill. It was shortly after the film was finished that he was indicted, I think.*

When did you leave California?

I left in, I think, 1975. My father passed away. I had three kids by then. I came back and wanted them to stay here and go to school, so it was a lot easier for them to go to school. Our public schools in L.A. were not the greatest at the time. I brought my family back here to live, and bought a house here, tried to get my father's business in order. My brother and I would do that. My mother was still living. We had to take care of some of her things. I stayed here until I guess about '83 or '84, when I did this local film for the Shriners. Then I went back out there. I was separated at the time from my wife in '84, anyway. I went back out to California and started some other projects. I was working for Motion Picture Corporation. *Dangerous Love*—I did that for them, and I stayed there and worked on several others they were producing at the time. After that we did several pictures over there. I'm not sure I did all the editing on them. I don't think I did.

Are any of your children in the industry?

My son Mark is doing some things with video. He tried to do a couple of things, and he's got one I think coming out on video this fall. He's not too into it, not as much as I was [*laughs*]. He likes it, but he says he can't make a lot of money on it. So fine, do your other job. And my twin daughters are out there, and it's very funny. One of them works for the Playboy Channel, in that she is producing for them. It's a radio show she helps put together. The other one— listen to this—works at Disney [*laughs*]! She loves working over there. She wants to be an assistant producer. She wants to produce later on. I give them my best and I help them when I can. I go and visit them when I need to once in awhile. But I'm kind of retired and I like it

---

*"Basketball Bill" Chaffin, a marketing and sales executive, produced this film, which starred Jones, Drew Pearson, Jay Saldi and Thomas "Hollywood" Henderson. On his website, Chaffin alludes to a "mistake" he made in producing this film, but doesn't go into any details. In 1989, he broke a world record by making 190 freethrows in ten minutes.

here, and it's quiet—most of the time. We're about to have another hurricane, I understand, so other than that, it's a good place to live.

Have you seen the letterboxed and restored DVD of *2-Headed Transplant?* The old VHS copies were pretty bad.

I'm sure it was horrible. The same with *The Glory Stompers*. When they first put that on video it was horrible. They took an old print, full of scratches, and this company Trylon Video in New York released it, but it was horrible. I don't know how anybody could watch. So they redid it, and did a beautiful job on the re-do of it, except they printed everything for day—there were no night scenes anymore [*laughs*]! But anyway, you can see it, and it doesn't have the scratches it did before. I wish they had released it widescreen, because it was a widescreen picture. The VHS I have is not widescreen. My kids got to see it. They played it on the Boulevard not too long ago with some other pictures of that period. I said, "Since you've never seen it, go to the theater and look at it, it's widescreen." They were running another bike picture with it that night. They invited the kids to go over and see it free, so they did. And they got to see it for the first time widescreen, because all they'd ever seen was that horrible print on the first try from Trylon. But I haven't seen it on the screen in years, since it was first out I guess.

You know, there are still a lot of prints on *Glory Stompers* that are playing all over the world. I can't believe that I'm still getting residuals off the picture. It's not much, but every year they send me a statement, and I'm getting a few dollars out of it. The real funny thing I find is that when that picture first came out, I think it was one of the trades—either *The Hollywood Reporter* or *Variety*—said that this picture is going to have to be a fast, fast playoff, because it's not gonna last long. And I find that very amusing today.

That was in the *Variety* review.

Yeah, and the fact that it's almost forty years later and it's still playing—that tickles me to death. I'm not much on critics anyway.

Savage Cycles

GARY LITTLEJOHN

No matter how low the budgets were, the biker movies of the 1960s always had two things: impressive stunts and elaborate custom motorcycles. Gary Littlejohn was often responsible for both.

Born in Vermont in 1946, Littlejohn originally headed west to work in the aerospace industry. Already skilled at building hot rods, he turned his attention to motorcycles once he was in the warmer climes of California, and soon found his work gracing magazine covers. Based on this notoriety, American International Pictures hired him to coordinate the motorcycles on Roger Corman's *The Wild Angels* (1966), the film that launched the biker movie craze along with a new career for Littlejohn. For the next decade, he would build and coordinate bikes for almost every motorcycle film that AIP made, and soon was working as an actor and stuntman as well. He worked on or appeared in *Devil's Angels* (1967), *Hells Angels on Wheels* (1967), *The Savage Seven* (1968), *The Cycle Savages* (1969), *Angels Die Hard* (1970), *C.C. and Company* (1970), *Angels Hard as They Come* (1971), and *Bury Me an Angel* (1972), as well as lending a hand on *Easy Rider* (1969).

By the 1970s, he was one of the most prolific stuntmen and stunt coordinators in the business, often working with other biker film veterans like Gary Kent and Chuck Bail. Littlejohn's work is on display in everything from *Caged Heat* (1974), *The Dark* (1979) and *Death Spa* (1988), to *Badlands* (1973, in which he played the sheriff), *Young Guns* (1988) and the recent comedy *The Last Shot* (2004). Littlejohn also made his mark in the BMX world, building and designing a line of bicycles (including the sidecar-mounted Littlejohn sidehack) in the 1970s, and fielding the first uniformed BMX racing team.

Littlejohn has worked on over 300 films in the past 40 years. He spoke to me about his biker film experiences from his home in Vermont.

You were in most of the motorcycle pictures.

GARY LITTLEJOHN: That's because I was so cute [*laughs*].

You went to school in California?

Pierce College. I went out here and was doing a lot of custom work on motorcycles, and American International called me up because they were doing a thing with Peter Fonda and they wanted some motorcycles. A lot of my bikes and stuff were on the covers of magazines, so they called me up and asked me if I'd help them. I went down there and got the motorcycles lined up, and then AIP called me and said they were getting ready to do a thing with John Cassavetes, and I said, "Yeah, if you get my [union] card and let me work on it." And so they got me my card and I worked on it. The rest is history. I just went from show to show. Then I started running them. I was coordinating all the bike stuff, and then I wound up coordinating all the other stuff.

What were you doing at Pierce College?

When I went to work out there in California, I went out to work at Rocketdyne Aerospace. I was a welder out there, and I went to Pierce College. On the side, I was doing the motorcycle stuff. I was taking metallurgical engineering at Pierce.

For the first film, *Wild Angels*, did you just work on the bikes or did you do stunts, too?

I just got the bikes together for them. I didn't even work on it. The first picture I actually did was with Terry-Thomas—*2000 Years Later* (1969) it was called. I had some motorcycles on that. It went from there. The second thing I did was the Peter Fonda thing. Then I did the John Cassavetes film [*Devil's Angels*]. Then I started working as an actor and a stuntman on all the rest of the shows.

What did you do on *Devil's Angels*?

I coordinated all the bikes, got all the bikes together for it. I built a bike for it, and the lead bikes for the principal actors on it. I was one of the actors in it.

Did you have an interest in acting before that?

Like everybody, you kind of dream about it, but you never think it's gonna materialize. Then it did.

Did you get to spend much time with Cassavetes or the director, Daniel Haller?

Danny, I worked two or three pictures with him afterwards. Gosh, what a nice man he was. I really liked him. John Cassavetes was an absolute sweetheart. Every night after work he'd throw a party, and we'd have a party in his room. He was just a nice man.

Could he ride?

Oh, absolutely. Some of the guys on there weren't too good, and they brought them over to me and I worked with them before the show and made sure they could ride okay. I didn't have any trouble with John at all. He was a super guy.

When you built bikes for the movies, what happened to them afterward?

A lot of the bikes, some of them were mine that I rented to studios. I had seven or eight of them. There was another guy, Wild Bill, he had some. There were two or three different guys I used to get bikes from and rent them from them.

There was another guy, I can't think of his name. I had him build the bikes for Peter Fonda and Dennis Hopper for *Easy Rider*. Sonny Barger took the principal bike on that.

The Captain America bike?

Yeah. He was the president of the Hell's Angels.

The Hell's Angels worked on *Wild Angels*, too.

We had them on *Hells Angels on Wheels*. We had the whole California group on that one. Most of them were pretty decent guys. And smart. Sonny was a brilliant man. But they had their own bars, printing companies; they invested well. They had it together. They were doing really well.

Had you encountered a lot of guys in the bike clubs from your custom work, outside of the movies?

A lot of them used to come to me from the Hell's Angels, Satan's Slaves, all those guys. I built bikes for them. I didn't really particularly care about building bikes for a lot of them, because you never knew if they were gonna bust into the shop and steal 'em afterwards.

Did you get any sense of what the bikers thought of the movies?

Most of them thought it was kind of neat. They liked to see themselves in them. We did a picture out there, Dick Compton directed it. I broke my leg first day of shooting on that.

That was *Angels Die Hard*.

Yeah. Bill Smith was in it. I did a whole bunch of pictures with Bill. What a neat man he was. Then he got messed up in drugs and screwed himself all up. We had some Satan's Slaves come up there and try to disrupt it. It was near Bakersfield, around Lake Isabella.

Were the real bikers anything like how they were shown in the films?

It was somewhat close, but you know, the pictures take a lot of liberties. Actually, some of the pictures were pretty mild compared to what some of the Angels and some of the outlaw riders did.

A lot of the bike gangs that sprang up in the Eastern U.S. and overseas actually modeled themselves after what they saw in the films.

The New York group — the Angels from New York — were a bunch of jerks. They really tried to be bad. Actually, as far as the Angels, if you messed with them, you had your hands full. If you left them alone, they left you alone. To me, the New York group were a bunch of jerks.

Where did you encounter them?

They came out and tried to get into some movies and stuff. They tried to impress everybody with how bad they were. If you have to tell somebody you're bad, well, you don't have to worry about those people.

Some of the guys in the California group actually went on to work on quite a few films. Dirty Denny was one.

Dirty Denny was a machinist. He was really wired up. He could hardly walk. He had a three-wheeler, and I used to use him because he was really raunchy looking. But the guy was actually brilliant. He was a good friend of mine. I used him on three or four different pictures, I think.

Dirty actually had a cowboy group, and they used to do live shows up in Bakersfield. He kind of worked with those guys. The motorcycle bad guy stuff, I got him into it.

When did you start doing stunt work?

Right after that. I found out that I could get more work doing stunts than I could acting. When I worked on *Savage Seven* with Dick Clark, the second-unit director was Chuck Bail, and I got to be friends with him. He had been a stuntman, then he got into directing and stuff. Dick Rush, I did two or three pictures with him. He was the one who directed it.

Did you get any training, or just learn on the job?

No, you trained all the time. I used to have a Saturday stunt workout at my house, and I had a trapeze set up. We used to work out three days a week on the trapeze. Then we'd go up and work on the horses. You had to be pretty much all around. If you wanted to be good in your craft, you had to be on your toes all the time and working at it. That's what we did. Some of the guys now think they're stuntmen. They're gymnasts. They go in there and think that's it. Gymnastics is probably a half a percent of what you do.

Was there anybody that you worked with who you learned a lot from?

I learned a lot from everybody. I always kept my eyes open. I was like a sponge. Probably the best stuntman in the business, as far as I was concerned, was Alan Gibbs. I used him on *Savage Seven*, that's where I met him. He impressed me because he was constantly trying to better himself. I had a lot of respect for people that worked at what they were doing.

Did you do *Savage Seven* first, or *Hells Angels on Wheels*?

For Dick? I think *Savage Seven* was the first one, then he did *Hells Angels on Wheels* with Jack Nicholson. To be honest with you, I never thought Jack Nicholson would live as long has he did, because he was into drugs so bad. I thought, "Man, this guy's gonna die." Look at him! He's won Academy Awards all over the place, and he's still one of the most respected actors in Hollywood.

So *Savage Seven* was probably your first stunt work?

I think so.

How was that experience? Did you have any injuries?

Oh gosh, no. That's one thing that I learned. One of the old-time stunt guys told me, "Don't do anything today that you can't do tomorrow." I always prepared myself, checked everything, and made sure everything was safe, and if it wasn't safe I said, "Hey, that's it. This isn't gonna work."

You always found a way to make things work. The picture business is like an illusion. You try to make stuff like it's really very dangerous, and a lot of times it is. A lot of times you get hurt. Jerry Summers was doubling Peter Falk, and just hanging from a tree in the air. He dropped down and busted his foot up so bad, he can hardly walk today. You never know. That's why they have stuntmen. They can replace you in a heartbeat. An actor, they can't.

What was Richard Rush like as a director?

What a blessing to work with him. Such a nice man. Smart, really good. I mean, they used his pictures in colleges for film courses. He was sharp. Last picture I worked on with him was with Bruce Willis, *Color of Night* [1994]. He was trying to go for an Academy Award for directing on that one, but he didn't get it. It was a shame, because it wasn't a bad little picture.

I always thought he should have done more films.

He only worked when he wanted to. He had money. He was financially set, so he didn't have to work. He worked because he loved it. That's the trouble with Hollywood today. It's run by businessmen; it's not run by picture people anymore.

You did an Elvis movie, too: *Speedway* [1968].

Yeah. That was one of the highlights. When we went down there, they said, "If you get caught with a camera, they'd fire you. If you talk to Elvis, they'll fire you." Bill Bixby. Bill Bixby was always complaining that his wardrobe wasn't good enough, his trailer wasn't good enough. I kind of took a dislike to him. But Elvis, I was standing there doing something and he came up and started talking to me. I said, "Hey, you're gonna get me in trouble. I'm not supposed to be talking to you." He said, "Don't worry about it." I said, "Well, autograph my script then." And he autographed my script for me.

Then he invited me to Vegas afterward, and he had a table reserved for me. I wound up working, so I sent my girlfriend up there with her girlfriend. He came out and was walking down the runway to the table he had reserved for me. She was sitting at it. She said she looked up and saw his shoes, and could see the white on his soles where they had polished his shoes. He bent down to kiss her and she said she just froze. She went numb. He took a handkerchief off and gave it to her. But what a giving man. And tough. Red [West] got him into martial arts, and he was tough. Not just pretend-tough; he *was* tough.

The next bike film might have been *Cycle Savages*. Casey Kasem produced it. What did you do on that one? I know you appeared briefly.

They asked me to go in there, and Bruce Dern was supposed to take my hand and squash it in a vice. I only took the job because I wanted to work with Bruce. I was working on something else at the time. I did a little riding in it and got some bikes and riders for it, that was about it.

Did you ever watch that one? It had kind of a weird plot. Bruce was trying to kill a guy because he drew a picture of him. Did you watch many of these films?

I think I've only seen two of 'em. I've done over 300 pictures, and of the 300 hundred I've made, I maybe saw five or six of them! It was basically a paycheck for me. I did another one with Yaphet Kotto, called *The Limit* [1972]. Man, what a neat man he is. That guy had more depth than you could believe. I was called in to do bikes on it. He said, "Hey, how about doing a part?" He had me read something, and he said, "That isn't exactly it. Try this." I did it the way he told me to. He jumped out of his chair—and the guy has hands on him like a couple of hams; he's a big guy. He put his arm around me and said, "That's it, you've got the job."

The film you mentioned before, *Angels Die Hard*—you broke your leg on that?

The day before shooting, yeah. I couldn't put a cast on because I was co-starring in it. They did a fight scene on it, and I was hurting so bad I couldn't get out to coordinate any of it. I saw the fight afterwards and it was terrible!

How did you break your leg?

I went down on a sportster. Just getting ready for the show, getting the bikes ready. I was out screwing around, and just went over. I had to do a fight scene on that and roll down a hill. That's the one we had trouble on with the Slaves. Matter of fact, they scared Dick [Compton] so bad, he wouldn't go out. I had to direct the first unit for three or four days before he'd come out of his room.

William Smith was on that. Was that the first film you did with him?

I did maybe five or six with him. *C.C. and Company* was right after that; Ann-Margret was on that. She was having a party to get acquainted with everybody. She sent the producer over to ask me to dance with her. I could hardly walk. She's a professional dancer, but I went out and danced with her anyway. I fell in love with her. What a wonderful lady she is. One of the nicest people in Hollywood.

Did Smith usually do his own stunts?

No, I doubled him two or three times. I doubled him on a TV series called *The Blue Knight* with George Kennedy. I doubled him on a couple of different things. Pat Swayze, he was on a show, and Cliff McLaughlin usually doubles him. They were on a show and had some riding to do. [Swayze's] a roper and cowboy himself. Really a good hand. He decided to go ahead and do a thing bareback riding through the woods. He hit a couple of trees and broke both of his legs, so they had to shut the film down until after he got better. They don't let actors do their own stunts. That's why they have stunt people. They're insurance.

You played Sitting Bull in *C.C. and Company*.

As a matter of fact, I was on that show up there with Bill Smith and Dick Compton, and they called me up and said that Ann-Margret was getting ready to do a motorcycle show. They wanted me to do the bikes and set things up for her. So I went down there and they had somebody else starting them, and they made a mess of them. They brought everything over to me, Ann-Margret and her husband, Roger [Smith]. They came over to my shop and we got to talking, so I built the bikes.

Ann said, "Why don't you come work on it, and we'll find something for you to do." I went on it and was setting up the bikes and stuff. The director [Seymour Robbie], he had his little boy, and he was supposed to be one of the actors on it, but he couldn't ride. He wrecked the bike, so they took him off it and gave me his part. [Seymour] hated me from the get-go. They were gonna fire him, and I don't know why they didn't. Roger should have directed it, since he was a much better director than this jerk was.

For some reason he hated me. I had nothing to do with it. It wasn't my fault the guy couldn't ride. He wouldn't even give me a screen credit, which didn't make any difference to me since I still got paid.

Could Namath ride?

Not too well. I doubled him on that, too. As a matter of fact, *Life* magazine came up and did an article on it. All the pictures in there aren't him, it's me!

That had one of my favorite casts: Bill Smith, Sid Haig, Bruce Glover.

Bruce has got an acting school now. He broke his arm on that. He went off by himself and he went down. He said a cow ran out. I went and checked it out. There were no cows out there. He just lost the bike and went down out there and broke his arm. That's why he had that thing over his arm the whole time. Sid Haig was a character.

Did he know how to ride a motorcycle?

He wasn't very good. We put him on a three-wheeler so he wouldn't get hurt, and we had Greg Mullavy on a three-wheeler so *he* wouldn't get hurt.

As I understand it, Sid couldn't even drive a car at that point.

That's possible! We had him on a three-wheeler so he wouldn't fall off it. Bruce claimed he could ride, and he seemed to do okay when I checked him out. I think what he was doing was getting a little anxious and lost it.

One of your bigger roles was *Angels Hard as They Come*, where you played Axe.

Yeah! That was Joe Viola. Actually, Jonathan Demme was his partner on it. They were kind of buddies. Jonathan was more of a gopher on that thing, and I did his first picture. I can't even remember the name of it [*Caged Heat*, 1974]. I had to play a cop in it. Then he won an Academy Award. Jonathan's done quite well for himself.

He did a lot of films for Roger Corman at New World.

I guess Joe went back to New York and started doing commercials again. I got him a job with Gene Corman, Roger's brother, on a thing called *Darktown Strutters* [1975]. He started directing that and they fired him because they blamed it on him that things weren't ready. They started shooting before they had wardrobe and everything set up. They didn't have the locations set up, and they blamed Joe for it. It wasn't Joe's fault, it was Gene's fault! They brought another guy in [William Witney] and he finished directing it. But Joe was a good director. It kind of upset me that they got rid of him.

Darktown Strutters **was another crazy movie, with guys dressed up like the KKK on bikes with crosses.**

We did a scene down in Watts, and we were robbing a bank. They came out shooting machine guns, and they didn't have the cops for safety on the street to shut it down. They let people go by. They went nuts. They had a little place down the street where they were selling stuff like a swap meet or yard sale, and one guy lost control of his car, went up over the curb and ran over four or five people. I think two or three of them died.

Do you remember much about the filming of *Angels Hard as They Come*, or your co-stars, Charles Dierkop and Gary Busey?

I coordinated that show and built all the bikes for it. That was Gary Busey's first picture. Joe was trying to get some action out of Gary Busey and couldn't get any action. I said, "I'll get some action." He was carrying a bucket of water coming down the stairs, and I went in and threw a body block on him, knocked him over. Gary's got a vicious temper, and boy, he went off. They got what they wanted [*laughs*]! He almost got me, too!

He was a hippie in that movie, even though he actually rides motorcycles.

He wasn't riding then. He really munched his melon riding a bike a few years ago. He didn't have a helmet on, and he went down and just about killed himself.

It totally changed the way he looked, too.

Yeah. It turned out we've been pretty good friends. Every time he sees me, he grabs me. He says, "You were on my first picture!" Then we did one that Chuck Bail directed. It was kind of a fun picture [*The Gumball Rally*, 1976]. Then right afterward, Gary [got nominated for] an Academy Award for the Buddy Holly movie. So he did okay.

What about Charles Dierkop?

We became friends on that. He's done some nice stuff, too. The only one I didn't see after that was Scott Glenn, but we were friends on the film.

I had to do a fight. [Glenn] was a boxer, a professional boxer. I had to do a fight scene with him, and I had all kinds of trouble. I took him out back and I put two two-by-fours in his hands. Every time we'd start, he'd go into his stance, and I couldn't do anything with him, so I put two two-by-fours in his hands. Then he was okay.

***Bury Me an Angel*, the one with Dixie Peabody, was directed by Barbara Peters.**

They shot a lot of that stuff down at one of the shops I had where I used to build bikes.

You played the shop owner.

I *was* the shop owner [*laughs*]. I never saw that picture, either.

Dan Haggerty was in that.

Dan Haggerty used to work for me. And his brother worked for me.

How did you meet him?

How I met him was that [actor] Ron Starr was a friend of his, and I was doing that thing up there with Dick Compton. He said, "Would you use a friend of mine? He's got a bike and beard and stuff." So I hired him as an extra. Dick liked him and had him in a couple of different fight scenes. Then we got to be friends. I couldn't take him with me on *C.C. and Company*. I had to hire pretty much local people down there. He worked for me for quite a while. Then my dad came out, and I was making gas tanks for motorcycles. I went out to make a delivery and came back, and I said, "Where's Haggerty?" My dad said, "I got rid of him. He's a bum. He's using all your material on his own stuff, and I couldn't handle it anymore."

Right after that he picked up *Grizzly Adams*. My dad moved back to Vermont. I said, "You know who you fired? He's playing Grizzly Adams." He said, "I don't care, he's still a bum!" But what a talent. Haggerty is really a talent. He works well with animals. He had lions, wolves. He could work with leather, do wood carving.

Hadn't he been a body builder?

Yeah, he was quite a body builder. As a matter of fact, Bill Smith was, too. That's where they met.

I didn't know a whole lot about Bill Smith, then found out he had been in the military and spoke something like five languages.

The man was absolutely brilliant. He was so smart. When I first started working with him he was a health nut. He might have a glass of wine and that was it. Then later on down the line, we did a picture and I tried to get him on it, and the director wouldn't hire him. He said, "I can't control him." I said, "Not Bill Smith!" Then I saw him, and his nose was half gone, and he could hardly talk. His voice changed. I said, "Bill, what are you doing?" Right after *Rich Man, Poor Man*, he had a few bucks in his pocket, so I built a bike for him. He'd drive down the street and people used to throw stuff at him, because he played a real bad guy on that. They took it out on him! Here he was, one of the nicest men you'd ever want to meet.

What a shame. What a waste. The guy was absolutely brilliant. And he was just starting to get into some good, heavy-duty roles. I don't know what happened. You get into drugs, and that's the end of you.

Haggerty worked on *Easy Rider*, too, didn't he?

I got him on that. He didn't ride a bike or anything. He was selling vegetables and stuff in that.

How did you get involved with that movie?

I got the bikes together. I got Tex Hall and another guy to do the stunts in the end, where they crashed the bikes. But I was working on, I think, *C.C. and Company* at the same time, so I couldn't go on that show. Paul Lewis was the producer, and we were friends. Anything with bikes, Paul always called me to set things up for him.

James Inglehart prepares to be dragged through the dirt in *Angels, Hard as They Come* (1971), one of the many biker films on which Gary Littlejohn acted as stunt coordinator. He also appeared in the film.

He was on a lot of films as production manager during that period.

He did a thing with Barbra Streisand [*What's Up, Doc?*, 1972], and I had a bike on that. He called me to do that. I met Barbra, and I don't particularly care that much for her.

You said that Sonny Barger took the Captain America bike?

He stole it. After the show was finished, they loaded up the bikes to bring them back, and he robbed the bike. He had it in his front room. There's a guy out here that goes to all the shows and claims he has the Captain America bike. It's a forgery. I didn't even want to go up and tell him that he's full of beans. What's the sense?

For the bike films, were there any particular sequences or stunts you set up that stick out in your memory?

All in a day's work for me. It's what I did. You just try to make things as exciting and as good as you can.

You had a larger role in *Badlands*. How did you wind up with that part?

I spent a year of pre-production on that show with Terry Malick and [production manager] Bill Scott. We went all over the place. That's a true story, the Charles Starkweather case. We traveled to I-don't-know-how-many different states. I built the Mercury for that. I chopped the top on it. I saw Martin Sheen was in some TV series or doing something, and I said, "*Gosh, this guy is really good.*" I told Terry he should get this guy. He brought him in and he got the part. Jack Fisk was the art director on it. I told Terry about him, because I worked with him on a lot of motorcycle things. Fisk was really a hippie. I mean a *real* hippie. His kid didn't wear clothes, animals lived in the house with him, he didn't have a car. I used to have to pick him up. He wound up marrying Sissy Spacek. And then he wound up being a director! He directed a couple of little films that were pretty decent.

I owned three percent of that before they sold it to Warner Brothers. But I built all the cars on that show, and did all the stunts on it. I doubled Martin. I chased myself! I'd have a camera, and I'd run the police car down, then I'd get in another car and run that down. I was going to do a jump with the Cadillacs, but that never materialized.

Not only is Martin a brilliant actor, but he's a nice, nice man. We were coming back and saw a guy that had a flat tire. I told Martin, "I'll drop you off and come back and help this guy." He had one of those bumper jacks and it kept falling off, and I had a floor jack. Martin said no, so we got out and I jacked the car up, and Martin busted the nuts off and changed the tire for him. I did *Young Guns* with Emilio [Estevez] and Charlie [Sheen], so I got to work with the whole family.

On *Badlands* you also worked with Warren Oates.

Boy, what a memory. He came and I had my lady with me, and we had a little party. He came to the party and we talked for probably five minutes. He came back, after he was doing a picture back in the Midwest someplace, *Tom Sawyer* [1973]. He came back off of that, and he said, "Hey Gary, how are you doing? Where's Evelyn?" He was terrific. He remembered that. We got to be friends, and he came and said, "I've got to do a show in some foreign country. I want you to go." He and Bill Holland were really good friends, and Bill died. Warren said, "I'm next." I said, "Don't talk like that, Warren." He said, "Well, I've got to go there, will you go with me?" And then he died. Which was a shame, because he was such a nice guy.

And he was great in everything.

He did *The Wild Bunch* [1969] with Sam Peckinpah, who was my absolute favorite director. Sam Peckinpah was one of the best action directors that was ever in this business.

Another guy I wanted to ask about was Jack Starrett.

Jack Starrett? He was a director. He directed a lot of stuff.

Did you do *Hollywood Man* [1976] with him?

I did two or three films with him. The guy had an imagination that was unreal. He used to park cars down on Sunset Boulevard. He ran a parking lot. I don't know how he got started. He was a good actor, really a good director, and he did a lot of things. But boy, he was like Peter and Jack and Dennis Hopper. They couldn't stay away from the drugs.

I was in El Paso and we were doing a promo. Chuck Bail was gonna direct, and it was called *The Last Ride*. He had Steve McQueen, Jack Nicholson, Peter Fonda, everybody that ever did a motorcycle movie was gonna be in this. They were coming back from the war or something, and they were going on their last ride. He brought me down to coordinate this thing. I built a bike for Jack [Nicholson] and he was working on something else at that time.

That's when I had a lot of magazine articles and stuff like that, so Chuck said, "Get some guys and go down and capture Jack when he gets done off the thing." I went to the motorcycle shop and I said I needed some riders to surround Jack's Cadillac to bring him to the college over there, because I built a motorcycle for him — a brand-spanking new Harley. We brought it in on a helicopter and dropped it down.

The guys got together, and 200 of them showed up. They surrounded the car. Jack thought he was dead. He thought for sure that with all these bad guy motorcycle movies he was involved in, they were finally coming to get him [*laughs*]. Then he got to the college where the football field was, and when he saw me he knew he was okay. They brought the helicopter in and cabled the bike down and gave it to him.

Steve McQueen had cancer at the time and he died. He and Chuck were really good friends. Bud Ekins was good friends with Steve. McQueen got sick and died, and that was the end of that. It was a great script. It was a shame. The preview went off well, because we had Jack down there and captured him. We had Peter Fonda, Jack Starrett, Dennis Hopper. I had to take Dennis Hopper and put him on a bike and get him freshened up. He had straws sticking out of his pocket. Adam Roarke was another one. What are they doing getting straws? I didn't know they were on coke. I wasn't that savvy to it. I didn't know Dennis was loaded and I put him on a bike. I said, "Oh, man, they're gonna kill me if anything happens to him." But he came back okay. Jack got a little anxious and tore up the hotel he was staying in. He got loaded, so they had to send him home.

It could have been a really good movie. They had everybody there. Chuck is really a good director when it comes to action, because he's a good stuntman.

Did anything get filmed?

No, because it was just promoting it and getting all the people together. They didn't really start shooting the picture itself. It was a great script. It had action from beginning to end. What happened was, all these guys went out on their last ride, and they ran into all these gangs and there were fights and crashes and car chases, and everything else in it. They had the money for it, but when they lost Steve, that was it. They decided not to do it.

Chuck Bail is a really good director. I've liked everything of his that I've seen.

He's a nice, nice man. I still talk to him every once in a while. He's out there in Apple Valley. He's got a bunch of horses.

Steve gave him his Steerman airplane, his biplane. He gave a bunch of motorcycles to Bud Ekins, and his son got a bunch of them. Steve had a fantastic toy collection. When you've got a name, everybody's giving you toys. The wife he was with at the time, she wouldn't fly with him, but she kept the toy collection. Chuck got him into flying and that's why he got that Steerman. Had it completely restored like brand new. Really nice. I don't know what Chuck did with it, because he's not flying anymore.

Were you still doing stunt work once you got into the BMX business in the 1970s?

Yeah. That was a farce. What happened was, I had my shop and I could close down and leave any time I wanted to. When I started the BMX company, some kid came in there and he kept breaking his bike. I said, "This is ridiculous. Why don't I just make you a frame?" So I made him a frame, and he couldn't bust that one. Then somebody else came, then another one came, and next thing I knew I was in the BMX business. Then they put me in the [BMX] Hall of Fame, and I'm in the Stuntman's Hall of Fame.

The Littlejohn sidehack still has quite a following. I had no idea what a sidehack was until I saw a photo on the Internet.

That's another thing that I started, too, the sidehacks. I sold my sidehack rights to a couple of brothers, the Barrettes, up in Sacramento. They have them now, and they're continuing. They just bolt onto a 20-inch bicycle frame. They have a rider on it, they start it downhill, and they were doing the regular motocross tracks. Those guys wail.

That was a fun project. I had the first uniformed BMX team. They finally recognized that and put me in the Hall of Fame because of it. Everybody was trying to take credit for being the first, and they finally put it in writing that I was the first.

When did you go back to Vermont?

Five years ago, which was actually a mistake. I thought I'd get a lot of work out here. I didn't even work one day last year. The year before I ran three shows, one in New Hampshire and two here in Vermont. Then I got a call to go to Providence, Rhode Island, and I was supposed to go down there and double a guy, and I wound up playing him. A Mafia guy. *Providence* was the working title. I don't know what ever happened to that. Matthew Broderick was in it.

It came out as *The Last Shot* [2004].

Ah. I played a mafia guy. I went in to wardrobe and they must have spent $500 on suits, shoes and ties, and I blew up four of 'em! I couldn't believe it. So it was a big-budget thing.

Of the films you worked, which are your favorites?

Actually, the one I'm the proudest of is *Badlands*, and *Bat 21* [1988], and *Bird of Prey* [1995]. *Bird of Prey* I'm really proud of because I went to Bulgaria. They wouldn't let me take any stunt guys with me. I did all the special effects, I did everything. I got some gymnasts to do some stuff over there. I did everything on that. Jennifer Tilly and Richard Chamberlain. Jennifer, you'd say hi to her and she wouldn't stop talking for a month! She loved to talk.

That was one that I'm very proud of because, like I said, I did everything. I had to make stuff, because in Bulgaria there's nothing there. I had to fabricate and build to get it done. I did a thing where you had a stair fall in this castle we were working in, and I set up all the cameras and stuff, and the director said, "You're a genius. You'll work with me." As soon as they say that, it's death. Just like Dick Compton when I did that thing up there. I saved his butt because he wouldn't come out of the hotel. I directed first unit for three days until he'd come out. I did all the road stuff. All the running shots. He wrote on the script—I had him put it in writing—and I never worked for him again.

Then I got a call, and they were doing a thing called *Dead Man's Curve* [1978] about Jan and Dean. I got a call to go down there and do some motorcycle stuff, and I didn't know who was doing it. I got a bunch of guys together. The guy was coming around in his Corvette, and I had to come ride my motorcycle down and he'd do a near miss. I thought it was a stunt guy, but they had the actor, who couldn't see, and he was a method actor on top of that. Anyway, I almost ate it on that one. Well, Dick was directing it. I said, "Dick, what are you doing? You said you'd never do another picture without me." Then he got a series and somebody else, Mike Cassidy, was the coordinator on that. So anyway....

Axes to Grind

BART PATTON

Although best known for his performance as the axe-wielding younger brother in *Dementia 13* (1963), actor-producer Bart Patton was actually a key behind-the-scenes player on many of the early films of Francis Coppola and Jack Hill.

Patton, whose family has a long history in show business, began his career as a child actor, playing Scampy the Clown on the early, Chicago-based ABC program *Super Circus*. Moving to the California in the late 1950s, Patton continued working in television (he replaced Burt Reynolds on *Riverboat*) and in films like *Because They're Young* (1960) and *Gidget Goes Hawaiian* (1961) while he attended UCLA. There, he became part of a group of young art, theater and film students who worked on a number of early projects with Hill and Coppola, and included Carroll Ballard, Dennis Jakob, Sid Haig, Eleanor Neil (soon to be Coppola), and Patton's then-wife, actress Mary Mitchel.

When Hill and Coppola went to work for Roger Corman, Patton was often on hand as a production manager or assistant director, helping out on Hill's *Spider Baby* (1964) and traveling cross-country with Coppola on *The Rain People* (1969). Teamed with comedian/director Lennie Weinrib, Patton also produced a series of beach party–spy films notable for their top-notch musical guest stars: *Beach Ball* (1965), *Wild, Wild Winter* (1966) and *Out of Sight* (1966). Later, Patton was part of the first incarnation of Coppola's American Zoetrope in the late 1960s, and even helped film the early screen tests for *The Godfather* (1972).

After his divorce from Mitchel, Patton relocated to Georgia. In 2000, he directed the prison drama *Unshackled*, with Stacy Keach and Burgess Jenkins. He has continued to work in television and commercials, often alongside his wife (makeup artist Judy Ponder-Patton) and their children. His son with Mary Mitchel, Tyler Patton, is a prop master and actor.

Did you grow up in California?

BART PATTON: I was born in Culver City. My dad was a drummer with a couple of the big bands at that time, so I was a road kid. We settled in the Midwest, in Chicago, where I schooled through high school. In 1949 I became Scampy the Clown on a TV show called *Super Circus*, which was a network TV show.

You were credited as "Bardy" Patton on that.

Yeah. Bardy "Scampy" Patton. My name is Philip Bardwell. I quit when I turned 13 because I was taller than the other clowns, and I couldn't play spin the bottle anymore [*laughs*]! I couldn't go to the parties. Boys were kissing girls and I wanted to get in on that action! So I quit in '53, and continued acting all through my high school career.

The cast and crew of Francis Coppola's *The Rain People* (1969) during the cross-country production of the film. Bart Patton is kneeling in front, holding a trumpet. Coppola is perched on a ladder in the background, while the film's stars (Robert Duvall, Shirley Knight and James Caan) flank the motorcycle. Standing on the roof of the van in the background is George Lucas, who was shooting a behind-the-scenes documentary.

Was your mother in the business?

No, she wasn't. She did one 7-Up commercial as a model, which I have a copy of. That's it. My grandmother was an actress, and my grandfather played on Broadway with Lionel Barrymore in a play, which made him sort of an absentee father for my father, who was in Rockford, Illinois. He was on Broadway trying to make it, sending meager checks home.

Where did Bardwell come from?

It came from all the sea captains that are in Bath, Maine. There's actually a Patton museum there. It was originally called Patt*en,* with an e-n. There was a Chauncey, a Hosmer, a Guy, a Bardwell, and a Jarvis [*laughs*]. I guess I lucked out with Bardwell.

My first professional film job was a 4-H film where I met Steve Pendleton, who was Nat Pendleton's younger brother. Nat was huge in the early days. Steve became my dear friend in California. He was an older guy. I came out in the summer to visit UCLA, where I wanted to go. Actually, I think it was in the winter. I auditioned for *Playhouse 90*, and was cast, but I had to get back to school and couldn't do it. So things looked good for a career in L.A. When I graduated high school after some plays and stuff. I did a reading of *The Crucible* and things like that. I went to L.A. and got a *Schlitz Playhouse* immediately with Anne Baxter, and then from that I did *Father Knows Best*. I did five of those. I did two *77 Sunset Strip*s with Ed "Kookie" Byrnes.

Were you at UCLA while you were working?

In fact, I dropped out one semester. I'd been cast in *She Stoops to Conquer*. I got cast in the play for the school, and suddenly I was cast in *Gidget Goes Hawaiian*, so I dropped out of *She Stoops to Conquer* and went to Hawaii instead. It was nice.

In 1959 or 1960 you did *Riverboat*.

I did six episodes. I replaced Burt Reynolds! Burt was not happy with Darren McGavin; the two of them fought tooth and nail. He quit and I was cast, and became a contract player as a result. I did six shows and the show folded. Dan Duryea ended up doing the last few, when Darren had issues with them. So they just suddenly recast the captain. Same name, different guy! It was great; it was the great days of Universal. Cary Grant was in the commissary every day, along with the Munsters in black and white make-up. Very bizarre lunchroom. Cary Grant and the Munsters—jeez!

***Riverboat* had a lot of cast changes to have only lasted a season.**

Oh, Universal. They were the cutthroat motherfuckers. They probably still are. No great love for them. I do have love for Roger Corman, who gave us all our start. *Riverboat*. I forgot about that. As a result of that, I did about six other guest shots on things like *Thriller*.

Do you remember much about your *Thriller* episode?

I had a very small part. It was nothing. I don't remember who was in it except the guy who plays the father in *Sixteen Candles* [Edward Andrews]. The best show I did in those contract obligations after *Riverboat* died was *Tales of Wells Fargo*. I had a great death scene. That was really exciting. I got shot in the first half of the show. I can't get hold of the sucker. I'd love to see it. Then I moved on. I did *Because They're Young*, with Dick Clark and Tuesday Weld. And Mickey Callan and Tuesday were in the dressing room doing things I wished were happening to me [*laughs*].

These wholesome youth films!

Yeah, right. Doug McClure was in that, and we became buddies at that point. Then I went off to do *Gidget Goes Hawaiian*.

Any memories of the *Gidget* film?

I made contact with Deborah [Walley] just before she died. I wrote her a long letter, and she wrote me back. The most wonderful, hopeful thing, and a week later I saw her death announcement in the *Enquirer*. She didn't last long at all when she went to Mexico for alternative therapy. She was swell. We became real good friends afterward. I saw her a couple of times before I left L.A. in 1978.

That was great fun. I got married in 1961, right after *Gidget*. The next fall I got married to Mary Mitchel. Immediately after that, Francis called. Coppola and I made a movie at UCLA called *Aymonn the Terrible*, about an Irish sculptor who did nothing but self portraits that screamed back at him. Really good little film. I produced it, Francis directed it, and Carroll Ballard was the boom operator [*laughs*].

Carroll's latest film totally passed over. This one about the cheetah [*Duma*, 2005]. I saw a piece on TV, on the Sunday morning show. [The film critic] reviewed that movie saying it was one of the best films he'd ever seen, and the son of a bitch isn't even in America! I mean, Carroll can't get arrested in the States. I was going to do a feature from a book by Barbara Kingsolver, who is one of my favorite writers. I got Carroll, he was all hot to try and direct, then Barbara decided she wasn't going to sell the rights to her book. He does a film every fifteen years or so! How long can you last?

Did you first meet Francis, Jack Hill and Mary at UCLA?

Yeah. Jack, Francis, Dennis Jakob, who managed the Doors for a little while. When we were casting our first Universal picture after we did *Beach Ball*, which had a $100,000 budget, $25,000 of which went to Edd Byrnes! Ha! There we were with a ten-day shooting schedule and seventy-five grand. We shot it in Techniscope, which is a half-frame fold out; they get 800 feet out of a 400-foot load in 35mm, then they morphed it into standard dailies. But we had black and white dailies because they were cheaper then. Now they're more expensive. Lennie [Weinrib], my partner, was a comic. Roger called me one day after we'd done — we used to get features that were like a 65-minute film from Russia, some crappy film. Roger would give us the assignment to add 15 minutes to it and weave a subplot and dub it. It was a great learning experience for all of us.

Those were *Battle Beyond the Sun* [1962], *Voyage to the Prehistoric Planet* [1965], etc.

I never knew what titles they got.

The one Coppola did had the penis and vagina monsters.

Um, yeah. I didn't do that one. I mostly did them with Jack and a troupe of actors, some of whom ended up in *Dementia 13*. Jack ended up finishing *Dementia 13*. He did exactly what we were doing to what was Coppola's film. I was the axe murderer. I was an actor, living in Malibu with my new wife, when Francis called and said, "I want you to come over and produce and star in this movie." Roger was doing *The Young Racers* [1963] in Europe, and he said, "Whoever can come up with a script first can go to Ireland. I'll just ship the gear over." They were following the circuit of the Grand Prix race. William Campbell was in it. So he said, "Let's cast him, and you can write anyone else you want."

Francis had a 35-page treatment the next morning. He was a sound mixer on the movie in Europe. He just wanted to go to Europe. Menahem Golan was the grip on the show, and he had about three pages the next morning. Francis won without a doubt, and off he went to Ireland. Francis called me and said he wanted me to produce and star; Mary would star as the fiancée of Bill Campbell, and I'd play his young brother, the axe murderer. Luana Anders was in it. Patrick Magee was in it. Awesome actor.

I acted and Mary acted, and we had a great time. I remember once we were filming in a pub, and pubs closed at 10:00 or 10:30. We were there at the end in a little town called Newtown Mount Kennedy, and everybody was having free Guinness. Oh my God, it was free Guinness! Free Guinness at the pub! They were going nuts. We went back to our carriage house, which I had obtained by telling the guy I was General George Patton's great grandson. An Englishman owns this place in Ireland, and he had a carriage house his daughter was managing. *[In an English accent:]* "Related to George Patton! The savior of the western world! You can have the carriage house. Anybody related to that great man."

"Thank you," I lied.

We had a cook, Mrs. Vines, a cheery, red-faced lady who cooked the greatest meals.

Didn't you pilfer the furniture of the carriage house to dress the sets for the film?

Everything. And I wasn't on the set that day; I was sleeping with Mary upstairs, and all of a sudden, Jane, the daughter of the manor house, came in. "What? What's going on? Where's my carpet? Where are my end tables?" I said, "Don't worry, they're on the set. We're using them as props. They'll be back tomorrow." She was going nuts. Crazy. I calmed her down and everything was returned. By the way, Ellie [Coppola] was introduced to Francis by me and Mary. Eleanor and I and Mary were art students. I was theater arts, Mary was a painter and so was Ellie. Francis wanted me to get Mary, myself, I don't know if Luana was in *The Young Racers*. I don't know how she got involved. She was great. I loved her. What a sad story. She died, and she was awful young.

How did you approach your role as the mad killer?

I was a very instinctive actor. I don't know how I approached it. How do you approach any acting role? They're all different.

What was Magee like?

He was wild. But I want to fill this in. When Francis called me and Mary over to act, another Israeli guy who was producing was on the show, and he asked for an art director. I said, "Ellie's a good artist." They became pregnant with Geo, their first child, in Europe. So that was the beginning of their relationship; it's still a relationship, believe it or not, in this day and age.

We came out of the pub, went back to the house. I lit my own single using Francis and lined it up with the 35mm camera. It's like this close-up of me singing "fishy, fishy in the brook," when I'm in this kind of drunken trance. Lit by Bart Patton, operated by Francis Coppola. We even did the post sync right there because it wasn't a blimped camera. Right in the freakin' din of the manor house! It was fine. Black and white, you can do anything.

Patrick Magee had a scene with Mary just before, and she was supposed to not like him because he was always accusatory in looking for the murderer of Luana. Just before the scene started, he turned to Mary and whispered in her ear, "I'd like to hang you upside down by silk stockings!" Roll please, and action! And Mary went, "Oooooh."

He had that evil voice.

And that strange accent. He had the world record for the most pints of Guinness in one sitting! That's probably what killed him. After that, I thought I'd emerge as a busy actor, but I never got a freakin' call. That's when Roger called for *Beach Ball*.

Before we get to that, Jack had to shoot extra stuff for *Dementia 13*, correct? Did they want more violence, or was it too short?

It wasn't long enough. We pulled out before we finished. That's the famous telegram from Roger. We were sending undeveloped film to L.A. for development in black and white. So Roger was looking at dailies, and he sent us a telegram: "Dailies look great. More sex and violence. Roger." A typical Roger line.

It was short. Francis shot some stuff, and I acted in it, and helped him produce some of the re-shoots. Francis kind of washed his hands of it, and Jack shot a whole bunch of additional scenes. Actually, it was kind of weird. If you look at the scenes with the guy who gets beheaded, Karl Schanzer, that's all Jack's stuff. That whole sequence of the poacher, me and Mary walking in the woods, which happened to be the California scrawny live oaks, not indigenous to Ireland! Like I said, with black and white you can get away with anything.

How did you get involved with *Spider Baby*?

That was the one with the real estate people, [Gil] Lasky and [Paul] Monka. Jack got the deal, but then said, "I want this guy to produce it." I was the line producer, pretty much. And they said okay. I mean, they didn't know from Adam. We had to teach them everything: how to do the budget from scratch, how to break down the shooting schedule, cast it. Standard stuff. We pulled that off in a pretty short period of time.

What did you think when you first saw the script?

[*Laughs*] Jack's perverse, we all know that! I thought it was interesting. My ex-wife starred in it, as a matter of fact. When you get the opportunity to do something, you just make it.

What do you remember about Lon Chaney?

He was great. He had a style, he was the old school, and everybody just kind of fell into it. And then we had Mantan Moreland on that film. [He was] great, just sweet as pie. Very professional. He always made it on the job. No trouble.

Was he happy to get his ear hacked off?

I don't know. I think he just sort of overlooked that part. I think we used a dummy for the cutaway — although it was his last picture [*laughs*]. Another actor was in it that's still in the soaps, Quinn Redeker. And of course Sid Haig — we were all friends at UCLA. Sid and I had done a few things together, and Jack. We'd done quite a few pieces together, now that I think about it. But some of them were, like I said, 20-minute fills.

Bart Patton in an early publicity photograph. (Courtesy Bart Patton)

Spider Baby **has a cult following now. Why do you think people are still interested in it after all this time?**

I don't know. I'm totally amused. I saw a copy of it somewhere. I must have a copy of it. I have no idea. I don't understand the cult film thing very much. I really don't have an opinion. Do you?

It's a unique film for the time. It's very funny, where a lot of films like that had failed at being funny. Also, there's kind of an odd sexual theme that runs through it with Jill Banner, and also between Sid Haig and Carol Ohmart.

Yeah, Carol. She was good, too. Everybody was great. The thing that worked so well was that everybody stuck very closely to the characterizations they created. It was an interaction of mad people, not a sane person among them.

Actually, now that I think about it, the thing that intrigued us all — I was never a horror genre lover at all — but the idea of comedy was what really struck the chord that made us all say, "Hell, let's do it." That really was the bottom line. And I know that's what attracted the old stars, was the challenge of the horror comedy.

There was one other early film I wanted to ask about, *Zotz!* [1962].

Oh yeah. I've got a copy of that. I was the first guy to get zotzed in a classroom. Tom Poston was playing the professor, and we're sitting there. "Does anyone know the history of blah, blah, blah?" And he points at me and I go, "Um, ahhh." That's it. That's the end of the scene. Then my girl, a girl I went to UCLA with, gets zotzed, too. That was about it.

Remember much about William Castle?

He was a force to be reckoned with. Did he direct it, too? He was just, like Roger, no nonsense. Just move on. Not really an actor's director at all. I'm sure the cameramen kept him straight in terms of cutting. A lot of directors don't know what they're doing.

Had you met Roger by the time you did *Dementia 13*?

Yeah. No. I might not have. Let me think about that. I guess not. After that's when I started doing all those add-on movies with Jack. I guess it was always with Jack.

What was Roger's involvement on *Beach Ball*?

Everything. He called me and asked me to have lunch at the Jewish deli on Fairfax, the famous one. And he says *[doing a dead-on impersonation of Corman]*, "Okay Bart, here's the thing, I want you to produce this movie. I have $100,000. $25,000 is going to Edd Byrnes. Here are the following things you'll be responsible for: Camera, wardrobe, makeup, script continuity...." He just named everything in the film! Everything. I said, "Okay, fine, no worries. I can do that." He said, "And I've hired a director, Lennie Weinrib, the comic who has never directed anything except himself." I thought, "Oh my God, this is going to be a disaster." But Lennie was quick to learn and a lot of fun. He took charge and did a good job.

That was done for Paramount?

It was done for Roger. He sold it to Paramount for $350,000.

Why did he pick Lennie Weinrib to direct?

Because he was a comic and it was a comedy. That was Roger's thinking. End of story. That's how Roger thinks. Lennie was friends with David Hammond, who was in charge of merchandising at Universal. Now this guy said, "We're trying to start a youth wing here. Why don't you come on over? Can we see your film? I'll get [chairman] Lew Wasserman in a screening." We said, "Fine, but don't tell Roger. He wouldn't allow it." We were going to show a rough cut in black and white, with eight songs in it. The Supremes, Righteous Brothers, the Hondells. The Righteous Brothers showed up without their drummer, so I played drums in that scene.

So you had a screening with Lew Wasserman.

We were nervous as cats. We had this master scene that was about two and a half or three minutes long, which was long for a master. A lot of walking around, some jokes, a hot little scene. We ordered a color daily of it, and went up into the cutting room with Jack, the editor. He did all of our movies as an editor. Almost won an Academy Award for sound effects. Jack Woods. Wonderful guy. He brought the dailies over, or the rough cut, and started the first reel. This thing came up on reel two, and Lennie and I had reel two up on the rewind thing. How do we fuckin' match this? How are we gonna get this in there? Then we remembered: Edge numbers, edge numbers. Oh yeah, edge numbers!

Wasserman loved it and said, "Sign those boys up to a two-picture deal." The next one we did was *Wild, Wild Winter* with Gary Clarke and Chris Noel, who was in the first one. Our deal at Universal was really exciting. We got $5,000 each or $10,000 each to produce and direct a movie on the lot. It must have been $10,000. We worked on it for months. We shot the interiors first, because the weather was too bad up there, then went up to Lake Tahoe and shot the snow stuff. Don Edmonds went snow blind the first day and had to wear shades the rest of the movie.

So here we are. If we go over budget, it comes out of our ten thousand. What a deal! Christ. The next one was *Out of Sight*, which was written by the little funny guy. Larry Hovis, from *Hogan's Heroes*. It was an over-the-top kind of thing. Besides, *Beach Ball* was the last of the struggling attempts to compete with AIP. After that, nobody gave a crap about beach films or ski films or spy spoofs.

Although people kept on making them, regardless.

I guess they did. A surefire loser. *Out of Sight* happened and everything stopped. Lennie and I were in Universal on a Tuesday, in our office having a meeting with Ned Tanen, the head of everything under Wasserman. On Wednesday I went in. We went alternate days writing a script, and we'd meet together on Thursdays to see where we'd gotten on our newest script.

We were meeting with Ned. I said, "I'll be in tomorrow and we'll pitch you the story." The next morning I came to work on my little Honda 150 motorcycle in my jacket — you had to wear a suit jacket — with my briefcase strapped behind. I got to my parking place in back, and you know how you take a sign off and it's aged around it? No name. I looked for Lennie's spot. No name tag. I went to the office to type a memo. No typewriter. I called Ned on the intercom line and I said, "Ned, what the hell's going on? My name's off my parking place, and our option isn't up until August." It was March. He said, "What do you mean, Bart? I thought you guys were working at home." I said, "Ned, you were in our office yesterday!" [*Laughs*]

He said, "Don't worry, we're going to pick up your option." I said, "Okay, fine." Duh. I went home, and after drinking a few martinis with Doug McClure across the street in the bar across from Universal, I went home and said, "Mary, everything's over. We're dead. We're fired." I was drinking. It was the typical bad day in Black Rock.

We took off for Ireland, where I optioned some books and wrote a couple of screenplays, and never really did anything until we ran out of money. We came back and were sort of getting nowhere fast when Francis— now, what'd he go off to do? Maybe it was *Patton* [1970]. I don't know what that year was. Actually, Francis visited my *Out of Sight* set and drooled the whole time, because I had all these dancers on the stage, scantily dressed. "Bart, this is what I wanna be doing!"

And he got *Finian's Rainbow* [1968].

Yeah, he had *Finian's Rainbow* with a bunch of bad actors, doing bad accents, shot in the Hollywood Hills. What a terrible movie! I was on that set hanging out quite a bit. God, it was awful. I wasn't in the union yet, so I couldn't AD for him, which is what he wanted me to do. So finally I lived at his house for a while because my house was rented when I got back from Europe. I was living in his A-frame up there. He came back and called after *Finian's Rainbow*. He had the ear of the studio head there, who was a really great guy, a young guy who wanted to do some new independent films, and *The Rain People* came along.

Before I ask you about *The Rain People*, I wanted to ask about beach movies. Those three films had a better selection of musical acts than most. How did you get them?

Nick Venet was amazing. He did the first one; he might have done all three. He was a record promoter, and he married an undertaker's daughter and was independently wealthy. As a record producer, he was tied in with Motown, which is how we got the Supremes. I don't know if they were even on the charts yet when we shot them. I don't know; we just had good musical tastes. "Can you get this person? Can you get that person?" And Nick would get them. We got every act in *Beach Ball* for zip. Everyone worked free. The Righteous Brothers, when

Bart Patton on the set of *Wild Wild Winter* (1966), one of three films he made with director Lennie Weinrib (seen in the mirror in the background). That's Gary Clarke in the body cast. (Courtesy Bart Patton)

they showed up in the set, had absolutely no source material, so we ran out and bought a record, and had a record player there for playback. Just a stupid little 33⅓ going around, and me on the drums. I was a drummer, so that was cool. Bob Logan was not a drummer, as you may notice when you look at the picture! We had agents clamoring in our office when Lennie and I moved over to Universal for the third picture. These guys were saying, "You've got to use Jay and the Americans." I'd never even heard of these guys! We ended up using them because the guy was so relentless, and we had an opening.

I read an interview with Chris Noel where she complained about Edd Byrnes trying to stick his tongue in her mouth during their kissing sequences.

You know, I heard about that interview, but she never complained on the set. I'm sure he did! I mean, what the hell is she going to do? Pull away and say "cut"? We don't have enough film for that. I heard that story, but it never surfaced on the set. It's pretty bizarre. I guess she was the only one that knew what was happening!

Did you watch many of the other beach party films?

No. I didn't even care to. We just made our films. I mean, I hardly saw any of them. Mary was in a couple of them. I was on that set all the time because our first born was an infant in that year, it must have been '63. So it might have been '62, or the fall of '63 up at Lake Arrowhead. So of course I saw that one. What's the other one? It was *Ski Party* [1965] with Aron Kincaid. Aron hasn't changed at all. His house is like a museum. You should go do a video of Aron Kincaid at home and take the tour of his house.

So I was a wannabe musician and had a pretty good track record of what was going on in the music scene. Lennie was pretty square. He was the little Jewish boy. I was 27, he was 33, average age 30. That was our ad! He lived at home with his mom and dad, who always pined away for his lost sister who died as an infant, and they had a little memorial to her. Lennie's room was unchanged from the time he was six. He had his trains; it was amazing. And his wonderful Jewish parents who doted on him.

Didn't he move to South America?

He went to Chile. He married a Chilean, his housemaid, *after* he had a baby with her. I never heard from him again. I ran into an old agent friend of ours, a commercial agent. I did a lot of commercials as an actor, too. Most notably, BelAir cigarettes, which paid for my first house.

Lennie had a good sense of timing. In comedy, timing was his strong suit. I never left the set on any of those shows. Actually, I'm in *Wild, Wild Winter*. I'm trying to think where. In *Out of Sight* I'm in a car at the end.

So Coppola contacted you for *The Rain People*?

Around the winter of 1968. He said, "I want you to co-produce with Ron Colby," who was an actor friend of his. We moved into offices at Universal, and then the first thing we did was I shot, Dennis Jakob shot, and Steve Lerner shot footage of Jimmy Caan in flashback sequences of him as a football player. We shot a football game and Jimmy was in it — Jimmy sweeping leaves as sort of a half-baked ex-football star.

We shot that, came back, showed it to the studio, and the studio gave us 900,000 bucks to shoot the road show. At which point we put together the first van. It was a Dodge extended van-grip truck. That was all we had for equipment. We had a dolly on it, a little tiny dolly. A piece of crap. Lights, film, chairs, everything was on this little sucker — and we had George Lucas. George had made his college film, and said he wanted to apprentice on *The Rain People*, so he made a documentary single-handedly of *The Rain People*, with an NPR camera (which is a sizable 16mm camera) and a Nagra recorder with a shotgun mike. One guy. You'd go in to have a meeting and we'd be screaming at the top of our lungs, and under the coffee table was little George [*laughs*]. It's a great film if you ever get a chance to see it, called *Filmmaker* by George Lucas. It might have been better than *The Rain People*!

How did that experience compare to the other stuff you'd done with Coppola up to that point?

We had a Ballard blimp. There's a couple of weird stories that go along with it. Francis went to England to interview Shirley Knight for the role. He pre-ordered an Eclair, a 35mm camera, which we adapted to Nikon lenses. The camera would have been duty-expensive to get back. So Francis and Shirley wrapped every little piece up like Christmas presents and shipped it.

It was one of the noisiest pieces of equipment ever made. Carroll Ballard made a blimp for it called the Ballard blimp, which was a nightmare. It was a big green thing, and when it was blimped, looking through the eyepiece, the camera operator kept moving his head from side to side. I said, "That's really a bizarre way you have of operating. Why are you doing that?" He said, "Because I can't see the sides of the frame!" But it shot the whole film flawlessly.

As far as production, it was the same as Ireland. I pretty much ran the set. We couldn't find an AD anyone liked, so I pretty much wound up running the set. When we finally did find someone that seemed to be okay, then I went and worked the books. Francis was very open, and we were inventive as all get out. We had rain-making machines where you cranked this thing out of a tank. We couldn't get any rain. The whole opening sequence in the Garden

Patton (left) and Lennie Weinrib clown around with Ernest Borgnine (in his *McHale's Navy* uniform), who visited the set of *Out of Sight* (1966). A member of the band Freddy and the Dreamers, who appeared in the film, is seated in the foreground. (Courtesy Bart Patton)

City Hotel was dependent on rain, and it never bloody rained. We had to make our own rain a lot. We had CBs in our nine vehicles. For the whole movie, we drove Jimmy Caan, Shirley Knight, I forget who the third passenger was. It was four people in every car. Ford gave us a couple of automobiles. One, we pre-rigged for side mounts and hood mounts, then the other one was the pass-by car. All of them had CB radios, the worst radio system in history. Basically it was seat-of-the-pants production. We ended up in Nebraska driving from Garden City, Long Island, to Ogallala. I scoured the entire country with Mary, across country to New York. Colby went the northern route and another cameraman went the southern route. I was in the middle. We took picture slides of the whole thing and then had to test the compositions to see where our route would take us.

Then we just sort of headed out. If we saw something, we'd stop and we'd shoot a scene. It was neat in that respect. We'd say, "Now we've got to look for something that will work for this, and then there's a hotel sequence at a Howard Johnson's." Leon Erickson was the art director. He was awesome. He could make butterflies out of garbage. Just an amazing guy. He's in assisted living now. I just ran into his ex-girlfriend, Sharon Compton, who's Roger's right-hand editor now. She went to UCLA with us, too.

Shirley and Francis fell out of harmony very early on, and Francis was going to replace her with Barbra Streisand. It would have cost us too much money. We shot in 16 weeks. They made up. It was all about Shirley being a method actress and Francis being more of a practical director. Anyway, that film we actually finished! But it was a total bomb. It made twenty cents at the box office. Francis won the Palme d'Or for best director, and we all flaked out into commercials because there was nothing going on after that.

You did a voiceover on *THX 1138*.

Oh yeah! What happened after that is I went to San Francisco. Mary and I had separated after *The Rain People*. Francis was starting up Zoetrope, so I went up there, and I ended up screen testing everyone for *The Godfather* when Francis abandoned Zoetrope because he had run out of money.

I prepared like six feature films. There's a Rip Torn story, did you hear that one? He was originally cast in Robert Duvall's part in *The Rain People*. All he wanted was scale. He'd helped Francis with his previous film, the New York movie, *You're a Big Boy Now* [1966]. He was in it and his wife was in it, Geraldine Page. They all worked for scale and were real helpful to Francis. So Francis cast him in this thing, and all he wanted was scale and a brand new Harley Davidson. So Ron Colby, who is probably damned daily by Rip, got him this piece of crap old motorcycle from the Warner Brothers garage in New York City. He parked it in front of his apartment in Greenwich Village, and it was stolen the first night he had it. And he hated it, so he probably had it stolen. Francis got pissed over it and replaced him.

Now, if you look at Duvall's career from *The Rain People* on, it would have been Rip Torn! He would have been the consigliore in *The Godfather* series. It really put a big damper on Rip's career.

You went to San Francisco and started casting these other films.

I was testing for *The Godfather*, that was at the end of the road. Before that, Francis had a six-picture deal with Warner Brothers. We scheduled six movies in a row out of San Francisco, all in the Bay Area. And one by one they got pink-slipped by Warners when the studio head was fired. So Francis was really scrambling. That was a bad day up there when the last script was rejected. Francis heard about the search for a director for *The Godfather*, and literally pulled himself into that project by being Italian! That was really the ultimate reason. I swear to God.

We did a lot of testing. I ran a bunch of screen tests with Al [Pacino] and Diane Keaton and Jimmy [Caan] and all the cast. Francis basically sold the producer based on those tests. Nobody wanted to touch Brando at the time, so Francis and I and Hiro Narita, the cameraman, secretly flew into L.A. and went up to Brando's house to shoot the screen test. I had sound, and a still camera. Francis had a primitive Betamax video set-up. It was two parts, a recorder and a camera. Hiro had a 16mm film camera, and one Haskell Wexler umbrella light. We went to see Brando, and he was not up.

Francis said, "I need some Italian cigars." He was up in Mulholland, so I ran down to the valley and got some Italian cigars and red wine. Brando was [now] awake and sitting in a kimono with his Tahitian wife running around, and babies everywhere. He was sitting in front of his makeup mirror with his makeup man, who was now having his second grapefruit and vodka. He just laid out all the tools in front of Marlon and sat around drinking.

Brando's got false teeth, he's got Kleenex, he's stuffing in his cheeks. He says, "Francis, I want to make him as ugly on the outside as possible, and as beautiful on the inside as possible." Francis says, "Good idea, Marlon. I like that."

We go into the living room to do a screen test. He's got a shirt and tie, and his bottom is a wrap-around from Tahiti, and he's in bare feet. He's sitting on his couch in this ill-fitting shirt with the collar sticking up, a jacket he probably had worn twenty years previous, and a tie. Francis says, "You've read the script. Is there a particular scene you want to do?" He said, "No, I'm ready to go whenever you are." "Do you want sound?" No sound.

We roll cameras. He pantomimes a conversation. Not saying a word, he was having arguments with people in the room that weren't there. It was the most amazing thing I'd ever seen. I shot about ten still shots and just put the camera down. My mouth fell open. I just watched from the floor of the living room.

Finally, right in the middle of it, the phone rings, and he does this gesture like, "Hold it, you motherfuckers" with his hand. He picks up the phone and says hello, but without saying a word [*laughs*]. He shakes his head and goes through this whole conversation and hangs up, then goes back to what he was doing.

Francis always wondered what the person on the other end of the phone must have thought! He was pantomiming to the phone.

Jill Banner dated Brando for a long time.

You're kidding! I loved Jill. What a sweetheart. She died in a car wreck. She was the cutest thing that ever lived. Sexy little number, too. Woo. She knew how to play it. She was only sixteen or something when we started *Spider Baby*. I thought she had a promising career. She had an interesting way of playing a role.

He met her while he was making *Candy* [1968].

Is that the one where he's like in the truck and he lives in a semi [*laughs*]? Made out to look like mountains! That was the funniest movie I think I ever saw, and it was the biggest bomb. I adored that movie.

When did you relocate to Georgia?

Basically, Zoetrope crashed and that's when I moved back to L.A., and back in with Mary to try and recapture our marriage. It never worked. We tried for a couple of years because we had two kids, but we couldn't get back together. So we moved back and the next film to come along while we were plotting a divorce was *The Wilderness Family, Part II* [1978], which I was hired to line produce and AD. By that time I'd hooked up with my present wife, Judy. She was the makeup artist and wardrobe stylist on that movie, which we did with Frank Zuniga. He was a Jack Hill kind of guy from UCLA who'd done a bunch of Disney stuff. I did some Disney stuff, too, and in fact I'd done a couple of Disney TV shows with him in the early 1970s.

Then Judy and I moved to California, and her mother became ill. We went back to Georgia to see her. She died shortly thereafter. It just became easier to deal with the divorce, and cheaper to live in Georgia. We were still traveling. We had a child in 1980 and we continued traveling. We worked in New York, L.A. I worked with Ed Bianchi, who's now doing *Deadwood*. Mainly commercials, traveling all over the country until our kids started school.

Your son in California is in the industry.

He's the prop master on *House*, the TV series.

He got Mary and Roger Corman into the *Looney Tunes* movie.

Oh really? I never saw that movie. He met Hugh [Laurie] on *House* on the mouse movie [*Stuart Little*]. Tyler's doing quite well out there. Judy's children, one is a makeup artist and one is a sound mixer. We work together all the time. Sometimes it will be Judy and Drew and Stephanie and me, all in the same movie. The movie I directed, they were on set the whole time.

That was *Unshackled*?

I was hired. I was called to a meeting with the guy who was supposed to direct it, who was a friend of the co-producer, who was in touch with the guy who wrote the script, whose life it was based on. Harold Morris. We managed to have a very smooth shoot, and turned out a fairly decent film.

Anyway, I went to this budget meeting with the would-be director, and I as the line producer, possibly. I did a budget for the guy for a million bucks, and we finished the budget, and just before Harold came in to go through the budget, he said, "Oh, Bart, put two hundred thousand overhead for commercials I'll lose while I'm doing the movie." By the time we got to that last page, Harold looked at me, and he said, "What's this?" I said, "You explain this" to the director. Harold said, "Bart, can I talk to you outside for a minute?" At which point he said, "That guy's out. $200,000 for nothing? He's out, you're in. You can line produce this. The first thing you need to do is find a director." A few days later I said, "Look, the best director in this town is me." We shot it in 24 days, never went more than 12 hours. It has a great look. I hated the music. It's just not quite as good as it could have been, but what else is new?

What have you been working on lately?

Short films and commercials, mainly. I did that huge commercial where the Marine climbs the mountain. That's my big claim to fame lately. I manage to work enough, and I'm writing a novel now. The names will be changed to protect the guilty [*laughs*].

Will this be based on your Hollywood experiences?

Partly. In flashbacks. The main thrust is more about eminent domain, and how it's turning us into a proletariat society with the corporations. It's all couched in some pretty heavy scenes of the past. I've got about 200 pages to go. I just broke the back of 160. Man, it's slow. I've never done anything that's taken as long as a book. Screenplays I can write in ten days. Maybe that's why they didn't sell!

Brain of Blood

Sam Sherman

When Sam Sherman first began distributing films in the mid–1960s he was something of an anomaly. A decade or more younger than many of his competitors, Sherman entered the business as a fan first, albeit a fan with a significant amount of chutzpah and a knack for concocting outrageous promotional campaigns.

Born in New York in 1940, Sherman grew up watching classic westerns and horror films, and set his sights on becoming a filmmaker. After dabbling with photography and 8mm shorts, he got his first taste of the business at the City College Film Institute (where he raised eyebrows by turning his student film into a horror picture called *The Weird Stranger*), and then through his work for legendary publisher Jim Warren.

Writing and editing for Warren's *Wildest Westerns*, *Screen Thrills Illustrated* and *Famous Monsters of Filmland* brought Sherman into contact with many of his screen idols. In 1962, on assignment for Warren, he met silent movie actor-producer-distributor Denver Dixon (a.k.a. Victor Adamson) and his son, aspiring director Al Adamson, beginning a long personal and professional relationship with both of them. From Denver, Sherman learned the ins and outs of independent film distribution; in Al, he found a close friend and partner whose ambitions matched his own.

Sherman continued his education at Hemisphere Pictures, an exploitation outfit founded by Kane Lynn and Irwin Pizor, where he cut trailers and designed wild advertising campaigns for the company's Philippines-lensed horror films.

Sherman also worked on a number of Adamson's early films, like *Blood of Dracula's Castle* (1969) and *Horror of the Blood Monsters* (1970), but time and again they found themselves out in the cold on the distribution front. At the urging of Dixon, the two men formed Independent-International Pictures, establishing the company with the violent biker film *Satan's Sadists* (1969).

With Adamson as the in-house director, IIP released shocking (and shockingly cheap) exploitation films like *Dracula vs. Frankenstein* (1971), *Angels' Wild Women* (1972), *The Naughty Stewardesses* (1975), and *Girls for Rent* (1974). The company also released a number of foreign horror and exploitation films in the U.S. (including the early films of Paul Naschy), as well as John Russo's *Midnight* (1982) and Sherman's own *Raiders of the Living Dead* (1986).

Sherman is still at the helm of IIP more than 30 years later, and has been busy releasing the company's back catalog on DVD, usually providing informative and amusing commentary tracks for the films.

How did you first get interested in films?

Sam Sherman pauses to visit with J. Carroll Naish during the filming of *Dracula vs. Frankenstein* (1971). (Courtesy Independent-International Pictures Corp.)

SAM SHERMAN: Basically, before there was television, I grew up as a fan of dramatic radio which was a great world of fantasy and things that you had to imagine. It was just incredible. *The Lone Ranger*, *Straight Arrow*, all the things you've heard of. After that, I got involved in comic books and Sunday comics, and movies was an outgrowth of that. When I first went to the movies it was sort of a synthesis of the comics and a lot of the comic characters they were beginning to use in films, plus the radio programs. And I also was interested in photography and making my own films. So that's how I got into that.

You first met Al Adamson through his father, correct?

I was one of the editors of *Screen Thrills Illustrated*, which was a nostalgia magazine published by Jim Warren, who published *Famous Monsters*. I went to Los Angeles in 1962, more or less looking to advance my film career, but I was also interviewing people. One of the people I was interested in was Denver Dixon, a stage name of Al Adamson's father.

Al wished to direct films, and his father decided that both of us should be doing our own distribution if we wanted to produce anything. So we quickly tried to figure out how we would do that, and it became not too quick. It took us about five years to try to raise money to try to start a company, with many false starts, many wrong alleys. Finally, my friend Dan Kennis, who was leaving a company he was with, was interested in what we were doing, was interested in forming a company with us. We decided we'd talk about forming a distribution company. In the meantime, we had had some reversals on projects that didn't go, and we were sort of angry at things that had happened in the industry, and the kind of anger that we had came out in the hostility of the story that Al wrote in *Satan's Sadists*. That's the way they want it, they want it really rough, we'll give 'em something rough.

How involved were you with the actual making of that film, and with the others?

I had various roles on various films. I was more involved in the pre-production and the post-production in *Satan's Sadists*. I was not there during shooting. On other pictures I was involved in everything from the story, the writing, the producing, the hiring, the firing, the post-production, everything. It depends on which picture.

You used a lot of veteran actors in these films, like Scott Brady, Lon Chaney Jr., Kent Taylor, etc. Was that your idea or Al's?

Well, basically it was my idea. Al had an idea that he didn't want to use has-been, old-time actors; that he wanted to discover new, young people and make stars out of them. And I said, "That can be blended with my idea. You can find new young stars and you can build them up. We can also get credibility in the industry by having established people in the films." That's what I needed in marketing. I needed some established people that people had heard of to sell these things, because it gave us more credibility.

Lon Chaney and J. Carrol Naish came as a package from the Jerry Rosen agency. Al was looking to cast the picture, went to various agents, they offered different people. I had certain ideas as to who I wanted. Originally, before it became *Dracula vs. Frankenstein*, I wanted Francis Lederer, who had been in *The Return of Dracula* [1958]. He was also a banker, so he was busy and wasn't available. That was after I wanted Paul Lukas for the role that Naish took. Paul Lukas turned it down as the picture being too gory. Al also wanted Broderick Crawford for the part that Jim Davis later took (Brod wasn't available). But it all has to do with two things: When you're shooting, if they're available; and how much money you're paying. Usually it doesn't have to do with what the thing is about unless it's completely unredeeming.

Isn't there a story about how Angelo Rossitto wound up in that picture?

There was a dwarf written into the picture. I had liked Angelo Rossitto in the early films he did with [Bela] Lugosi, which I used to see on television, and I wanted him. I thought that would be great. Al said, "Where do you get him?" I had no idea. But I knew he had had a newsstand on Hollywood Boulevard, so Al went on several days and walked up and down Hollywood Boulevard looking at every newsstand to try and find Angelo Rossitto. He said, "I can't spend another day doing this. I can't find the guy." And he said that Jerry Rosen, who we got Chaney and Naish from, had his own dwarf, and said, "We'll go with him." So we ended up signing him, and it turns out to be Angelo Rossitto!

What was the response to *Satan's Sadists* once you released it?

It was finished at the end of May of 1969. By that time all the summer play dates for the drive-in theaters were already booked for several months, and I was very concerned that we had lost the playing time because basically most of the business was in the summer. So I took the print under my arm and—literally and figuratively—carried it all over the countryside screening it. The picture screened so well that they took out dates of other pictures that were there and gave us the summer playing time. So the picture screened well for the exhibitors, and it was very successful. It was a big hit. It established a company.

As the 1960s progressed, there was a significant increase in the number of independent producers and distributors in the market. Can you explain what was going on that precipitated all of that activity?

I'll tell you exactly what went on. I had become a distributor, but it was never something I wanted to do. I never wanted any part of it. I wanted to produce and direct films. But it was my meeting with Denver Dixon in Los Angeles in the summer of 1962 that changed my life profoundly.

Denver Dixon was born in New Zealand, and he moved to Australia where he was an itinerant ranch hand. He was discovered in Australia and became a vaudeville star. He eventually made the first western shot in Australia called *Stockman Joe* around 1910, and then he came to the U.S. and worked in early silent films. Through the 1920s he distributed films and produced and directed. He learned about these regional distributors that were called states righters, because they had the rights to certain states. They became later known as sub-distributors because they didn't buy the rights to territories anymore.

Now, as I came into this business, basically you had a certain amount of these sub-distributors around the country, and some of them were an outgrowth of the state righters of the silent era. I had wanted no part of this. In 1963, I bought the rights to the 1934 movie based on the Nathaniel Hawthorne book *The Scarlet Letter*. I had that and I really bought it because I wanted to learn the distribution business, but not to be a distributor — to be a producer. I had that film and I took it around to all kinds of distributors in New York to try and make a contract for them to distribute it. I couldn't ever get anybody who would give me anything near what I considered to be a fair arrangement.

I told Denver I had this, and he said, "We'll distribute it ourselves." He was distributing a picture called *Halfway to Hell* [1961] that he and Al had made. So we got together. His company was Victor Adamson Productions, just as he had been in the 1920s, and I had my company, Signature Films. We worked together on distributing *The Scarlet Letter*.

I tended to work with Denver mainly in the South, but I remember going up to New England to meet a man by the name of Sam Richmond, who at the time was a prominent sub-distributor on Tremont Street in Boston. I figured since it was set in New England, blah, blah, blah — but he had absolutely no interest in that. What he wanted was sex pictures. Not pornos; there was no porno then. These were kind of black and white, European films that had a kind of sexuality to them. The best way to describe them is like the early films that Radley Metzger had at Audubon. Companies like that. Some of them had some horror films sometimes that were imported. There was a bit of business for these sub-distributors that had sex pictures that were softcore, shot in black and white, largely narrated. They didn't have synch sound.

I met Hemisphere Pictures in 1963, because I got *The Scarlet Letter* from Irwin Pizor, who was the president of Hemisphere. His partner was Kane Lynn in New York, and Eddie Romero in Manila. They were doing very poorly in the domestic market. They were lucky to get $35 per rental. Denver was doing about $100 per rental on *Halfway to Hell*, and once we got *The Scarlet Letter* going, we were doing a thousand per rental with an old picture, which Irwin had owned. He was stunned to see that Denver and I had done 30 times per rental what they were doing with *Raiders of Leyte Gulf* [1963], which was a new film that Hemisphere had.

Why were you doing so much better than they were?

Because I tied in with the reissue of the MGM literary classics—*Captains Courageous* [1937] and *A Tale of Two Cities* [1935]. There were eight of those that MGM gave to the independent

Al Adamson (left) and Sam Sherman (right) founded Independent-International Pictures at the urging of Adamson's father, Denver Dixon (center). (Courtesy Independent-International Pictures Corp.)

sub-distributors. They were used with the schools. The schools bused the kids in to see these things. We went the to same sub-distributors that had the MGM ones.

I was officially a distributor. Then I picked up a film from my friend Bill Cannon, which was kind of a black art comedy called *Square Root of Zero* [1963], and I retitled it *This Immoral Age* and played that at the drive-ins. It was the first drive-in kind of movie that I did. I got the idea when I traveled around the country that the sub-distributors were largely interested in easier product to sell: sex product, horror product, and so on. I remember telling them, "I'll be back and we'll have bigger pictures, and I'll have new films! And we'll have films in color!"

Dan Kennis had been involved with one of Irwin's companies, Teladynamics, and he invested in Hemisphere. I remember Kane Lynn, at the time we started Independent, he said to me, "Sherman, why do you knuckleheads think this industry needs another distributor?" I said, "I guess you're right, it doesn't need another distributor, but we've got pictures that Al made, and we made one picture, and we've got to do something with them." Six months later I saw him, and he put his arm around me, because he was kind of paternal to me. He said, "Sammy, I'm proud of you. I heard that *Satan's Sadists* is doing some good business. I'm proud of what you guys are doing."

What a relationship! There's a competitor talking like that. Isn't that incredible? We were close personal friends. Then he and Irwin had a fight and Irwin joined us. So he always asked me, "What's Kane doing?" Or Kane would say, "How is Irwin doing?" They were very fond of each other, but they didn't like the way they each conducted business.

You had a good relationship with Hemisphere. How competitive was the rest of the industry?

Cutthroat! They were cutthroat. There was no friendship there. There were very few companies that I had the relationship with that I had with Hemisphere. We were close to other people because we had that attitude, Danny and myself. Al was very competitive, by the way. He avoided other people. Other independent filmmakers, he thought they were the enemy. "Why are you friendly with him? Why are you friendly with this guy?" He just couldn't see it. He was an athlete, so he was by nature very competitive. He was very nonplussed about these relationships.

A great story that was amazing, when we were going to put out what became *Frankenstein's Bloody Terror* (1972). I needed that because what became *Dracula vs. Frankenstein* was tied up. I got this other picture, trying to substitute it for the play dates we had on the other film. I called it *Horror of Frankenstein's Coffin*, which wasn't as much of a cheat as *Frankenstein's Bloody Terror* because I was playing up the idea that it was a coffin from the Frankenstein family, and out of it came a werewolf, blah, blah, blah.

Well, I get a call from Jerry Pickman at Levitt-Pickman. He said, "Sam, I hear you've got a picture called *Horror of Frankenstein's Coffin*. We've got a picture here called *Horror of Frankenstein*. We can't put out two pictures with such similar titles." I said, "Where are you with yours?" They had trailers made, posters made, and they were ready to book it. I said, "Jerry, we've got nothing made. We're planning this. Based on us having nothing made, that would be stupid to have two similar titles competing. I'll change my title to something different than yours, and it won't come out for six months anyway." He couldn't believe I would do that! When does anybody ever do that? He was surprised.

Conversely, it worked the other way. Bev Miller was a sub-distributor in Kansas City, Mercury Films, and he was a very close friend of Kane's. I liked Bev Miller a lot. He was a fun guy. Bev Miller got involved in making some of the pictures in Manila. He is in *Beast of*

Blood [1971]; he plays the old sea captain. Bev Miller called me up once, and he was very close to Roger Corman, closer than to us because his bread was buttered there. He made a lot of money there. He knew from me that we were putting out a picture called *Women for Sale* [1969/1975], about white slavery. It was a German picture. He said, "Sam, I heard about that picture, and Roger Corman has a picture with the same title, *Women for Sale*." I said, "Where's Roger stand on this?" He said, "Well, he's got the script, he's going to Manila to make the film." I said, "Bev, I've got release prints and posters all done. I'm not going to change it. I can't. I did it for somebody else once, because they were farther ahead, and I think you folks have to defer to us on this. We're gonna release it now." Which we did. It went through the roof.

When Roger put out his movie, he called it *The Woman Hunt* [1975]. Did that do any business? No. Just like Roger had made a stewardess picture, in the middle of all the stewardess movies, trying to be different. He called it *Fly Me* [1973], and it had ugly girls in it. It was an awful picture. It never played. Knowing it was out there, we used to pick it up for a $35 second-feature rate, and play it with *Naughty Stewardesses*. So a lot of this was knowing how to take advantage of situations, knowing how to stand up for yourself.

As I mentioned, the sub-distributors began to grow, and in the 1960s, more of them began to open. More of them began to come out of their little territories and go into multiple territories, and what happened is, they began to be important to people in their own little fiefdoms. In order to play in certain areas, you had to go to certain sub-distributors who were in bed with certain theater circuits.

Sometimes we found some guy who was a little guy no one ever heard of in Baltimore or Minneapolis or Denver. Territories that are hard to do any business in. We got this guy in Minneapolis; we'd never seen a penny out of him. All of a sudden we were getting big bucks. Same up in Denver. We got a guy through a friend, no one ever heard of him and he did big bucks for us.

You had to keep them under a tight rein for getting paid, for reporting, for getting an honest count. There were flaws in that system, but the alternative, having your own salesmen in these areas, was a big mistake. The costs were too great, because if you had your own salesmen, they'd probably find a way to steal from you anyway.

What they did with the majors, the majors had 30 or 40 branches around the country. If a picture played a specific theater and it earned (let's say) $10,000, what the studio would get was their share of the film rental. So the branch manager would be a drinking buddy, and he'd say, "I think we can shave that down to $6,500," because after the picture played, even though you were owed certain money, they'd meet and review the grosses. They'd have what's known as settlements. Why do you have a settlement if you're owed a certain amount of money? All through the film industry, you have a settlement.

Well, "It was raining, it was snowing. You made us pay upfront money on Elizabeth Taylor's picture that died." Whatever. So they'd agree to settle for $6,500. The general sales manager sitting back in L.A. or New York, what did he know? He agreed to do that. Meanwhile, the exhibitor gave this [sales] guy $500 in cash, you follow me? So that's the kind of thing that went on, and I used to say, "Well, if the guys are going to be out in the field stealing from me, I don't want to pay their salary up front on top of it."

How did you keep an eye on the grosses, if there were all these scams going on?

We got a lot of services that got us grosses, we got newspapers that showed where things were playing. It was an imperfect system, but consider there were other factors that were mitigating factors. The key to the whole thing was, we spent as little as possible. We spent the money to make the picture, to acquire it, to make the release prints, to run the campaign. We didn't want to spend more money out in the field on top of it. I felt whatever position we were in, where we didn't have to put up money, and we didn't have to guarantee anything or spend any expenses, we were better off.

I'd say this whole thing began growing around 1967 or 1966. And then it began peaking out around 1978. It started downhill as the drive-ins were closing because the land was too valuable, and the independent circuits were going out of business or being acquired. Sub-distributors were going out of business. By 1982 this was going downhill very fast. I realized I was going to have to get out of it. That's when we got more involved in television distribution and started our own video company, Super Video, and other things that we did.

Why did the drive-in market dry up?

The sub-distributors went first. It's not just that the drive-ins left; all the means of access to the market left. I should also point out, though, that we didn't just service drive-in theaters. We tried with the product we had to play indoor theaters, and to come up with pictures that could also play in indoor theaters. We introduced Paul Naschy into the United States market. We distributed films in 3-D. We were involved in playing all the major circuits, and their indoor theaters. I like to play off people's interests in drive-ins because it's become very quaint. But we would come into New York City with films that we made and play on Broadway. *Dracula vs. Frankenstein* had its first New York run at the Rivoli Theater that had played *The Sound of Music* [1965] for three years, and was a gargantuan hit. We played more than just drive-in theaters. We couldn't have succeeded on just drive-ins alone, but they gave us a core market, and we always tried to expand above it.

What I always thought was interesting was this rise in independent production began at the tail end of an era that had seen a tremendous decline in movie attendance.

I don't think there was a decline. I think there was a decline in the attendance of major pictures. What was happening is, television had made a big inroad by the mid–1960s. People were buying color sets. The beginnings of cable were coming through. The routine pictures declined; things you could see on television because they were commonplace, like westerns and musicals and war films.

The opportunity we as independents had was to have pictures with a little bit of sex, which you couldn't see on TV, pictures with a little bit of horror or gore that you couldn't see on TV, so the majors were getting killed.

They were not quick to respond; maybe it was five to ten years when these guys at the studios were just asleep at the switch. Eventually they woke up to it and they began making the same pictures, but on big budgets. So they began to recognize what they didn't recognize before, that the drive-ins could play first run. They could open some picture first run at an indoor theater and gross $2,000; meanwhile, the drive-in that's running an independent picture first run grossed $12,000. They saw the drive-ins as sub-run in many cases, maybe flat booked the picture for $200, and they didn't realize what they could gross.

It just took them a long time to respond. Once they responded, they acted in concert through the MPAA and, with complete disregard for the anti-trust laws, were able to knock the independents out. At the peak of this, around '74, '75, '76, the independently distributed films were 35 percent of the national box office. Today, independently distributed films are probably one-tenth of one percent.

One of the earlier Adamson pictures you were involved with was *Blood of Dracula's Castle*, which went into foreclosure. You and Al lost your stake in the film.

Al had made *Psycho a Go-Go* [1965], which was originally started as *Echo of Terror*. *Psycho a Go-Go* was then made, and it was kind of an unsuccessful project that went nowhere. And around that time, what became *Horror of the Blood Monsters* was also made, which was called *Creatures of the Red Planet*, and those two pictures basically sat on the shelf.

Al met a man by the name of Rex Carlton, who was a writer and producer. Rex had a script for a play that he wanted to use with Jayne Mansfield. It was supposedly a comedy, with a sexy blond girl as the main lead. We read the script, and I thought it was atrocious. I thought it was not funny, and it was tasteless for that era. So, he had this script called *Feast of the Vampires*. In those years, for a general release picture, it was really tasteless. I remember it had naked girls who were roasted in chafing dishes, and people were supposed to be cannibals. Maybe today they would like it, but at the time I thought it was very gross and very extreme.

Al said, "What would you do with it?" I explained what I would do with it. I would turn it into a real horror picture. I would take out all this comedy, and take out all these tasteless things, and I'd put more suspense in the picture.

I re-wrote it. We both worked on it. I put Dracula in it, and I changed the title to *Blood of Dracula's Castle*. At the time, I explained to Al that I thought there should be some names in the picture, and I suggested John Carradine. Maybe this was before we shot any of the Carradine footage for *Psycho a Go-Go* [a.k.a. *Blood of Ghastly Horror*], so I don't think Al knew John Carradine.

Apparently Rex Carlton was still very active in this thing, and he was still trying to promote his version of it. When you get involved with too many people on a project, it's called too many cooks, too many people, all offering opinions. There's no clear view as to what it was. Al was trying to make a more open picture with some action, rather than a closed-in, interior picture, and he was trying to follow along with what I was explaining to him. But as he always said, he knew nothing about horror pictures. He didn't like them, and he wasn't interested in them. He always got involved in them because of me. He was trying to meet my requirements to make the pictures marketable, but there was nothing I could do to change what they were thinking in this case.

The picture was made and there was a man brought in as one of the producers—he brought in some of the money—called Marty Cohen. Al and I, for our contributions to this, Al was not paid a fee. We were supposed to get the far eastern rights to the movie aside from anything else we could do to sell it, and take a piece of what was sold. It was a very bad deal all around. Al sent the print in to me on the East Coast, and I screened it and I thought it was pretty awful. I sat down and wrote Al a two- or three-page letter tearing the picture apart. I explained my thoughts about it. So he knew how I felt about it. He also knew that he didn't really understand how to make a horror picture.

What was happening was the unraveling of this project through this Marty Cohen and perhaps Rex Carlton, but how that happened is not quite clear. Apparently, somehow they sold a man by the name of Joseph Auerbach an interest in this picture. Somehow he was pulled in to be part of another picture that was being tied in with this film. The other picture was called *Nightmare in Wax* [1969]. Al had nothing to do with it. I had nothing to do with it. But due to the way this set-up was, it stunk to high heaven. They had tied the two pictures in, they called it cross-collateralized, and Al came to New York.

I was here and I was screening the picture around. I screened it for various people that were involved in filmmaking deals, and they had the same criticisms of the picture that I had. They didn't like the script, they didn't like this, they didn't like that. But at the time, Columbia Pictures Screen Gems TV wanted horror pictures for the U.S., and I screened it for them.

I knew they wanted those, and they were willing to buy the U.S. television rights for $65,000, and so I offered this back to Al, and he gave it back to the people there on the coast.

They kept stalling us and stalling us. What they had done was, they cross-collateralized this picture in the lab with *Nightmare in Wax*, unbeknownst to me or Al. Al came back to New York. We were with Bob Crane at Color Service lab, and he was telling us, "Oh you guys are making horror pictures. We can do some work with you." He gave us some credit, blah, blah, blah, and he went on to say they just foreclosed on two horror pictures.

Well, it was a very upsetting thing. We lost out on the Screen Gems sale, we lost out on the money from the far eastern rights that we would have owned for that picture. We could have sold that for some significant money, and there we sat. But we accepted that foreclosure. It's just something that we knew happened, and that was it. Al didn't like the people we were involved with in this. He just wanted to distance himself from that.

And this is what eventually led to Carlton's suicide.

The night of the foreclosure we were screening another film, and Rex Carlton was in New York with us. He came to the screening. I don't know how Al said it to him or why he said it to him, but I guess he blamed Rex Carlton in some way for this whole mess, because he really did put the whole thing together that way. Maybe Al was a little sadistic in the way he said it to him, he said, "Oh, by the way Rex, we were at the lab and found out the two pictures were foreclosed on. The lab took them over, everybody's wiped out. You're out of it." I guess he was annoyed. He'd worked so hard making that stupid picture, and he was wiped out. He might as well bring Rex into the league of fallen men, and let him know he was also wiped out.

That was a Thursday night, we saw him the next day, and he was not saying much about anything. We had some other business with him. Then Saturday he flew back to L.A., and he had an apartment on Sunset Blvd., on the 8000 block. I still know where the building is. I passed it many times. He sat down in the bathtub, put a gun to his head and blew his brains out.

Apparently Rex Carlton had borrowed money for that film or gotten investors who were rather tough people, and he was concerned that they would come after him. It gave Al further impetus for us to realize that we have to try as much as possible to start our own distribution company to produce our own films that the company would own, and we wouldn't get involved with these kind of people. We would own our films, and we wouldn't let labs and con men do this to us. It was a great learning experience.

The funny thing is, after that, in about August or September 1968, I was in London. Sitting there having breakfast was Alex D'Arcy. I'd never met him before. I wasn't there when they shot the film. I said "Alex D'Arcy! I'm Sam Sherman, Al Adamson's partner," and we started talking. *Blood of Dracula's Castle* came up, and he said he never got paid. I don't know how they exhibited that film. It had Screen Actors Guild people in it who were all wiped out and they never got paid. It was unbelievable. So I said, "Welcome to the club! I never got paid either." So as a result, we became friendly and kind of victims of the same crime. Very nice guy. But he wouldn't have been my choice to play Count Dracula.

The whole point of this being, you either understand how horror pictures are made or you don't. Al admitted to me that he never really understood horror pictures. I tried many years with him to make horror pictures, and that's the reason they came out as crazy as they did. He really didn't understand the concept of them, he wasn't a fan of them, and he really wasn't interested in them.

He seemed to like westerns a lot more. His horror films *were* really odd.

Probably the best horror picture that Al directed was *Nurse Sherri* [1978], because it was a very clear story. Even though we went through changes on it, he got the idea of the story. I guess it was more of a murder mystery than a horror picture, but Al was very pleased with the end of the film. He thought the last reel was really exciting. I was just watching the *E! True Hollywood Story* that was done about Al, and they had that interview with him where he talked about the last reel of *Nurse Sherri* being really exciting and really well done. It was the same last reel in all the versions; it never changed. It was really very good. I can take some justifiable pride in writing that with him and coming up with that premise.

So that's the story of *Blood of Dracula's Castle*, which naturally has left a bad taste in my mouth.

Was the other movie, *The Fakers* [a.k.a. *Hell's Bloody Devils*, 1970], finished by the time Carlton killed himself?

There was a complete assembled version of *The Fakers* that we were screening that Thursday night, the night of the day we found about the foreclosure of the two horror pictures. As a matter of fact, we gave him further "good news" that Universal turned down *The Fakers*. He was convinced they would want it.

Did you know much about Rex Carlton?

Footage of bikers Bob Dix, William Bonner and Jerry Mills was added to Al Adamson's espionage film *The Fakers* to create *Hell's Bloody Devils* (1970).

If I can explain Rex Carlton versus Al Adamson and myself, he came from more of a conventional background in the business: that regular writing of regular scipts and regular pictures that were released by United Artists and companies like that. Al Adamson and myself were total mavericks, never worked for major studios, never were involved with them.

I shouldn't say never. Al was involved in two pictures that were kind of bigger. One was *Hammer* [1972] for UA, and the other was *Cry Rape* [1973] for CBS network. But he didn't really belong in those worlds. We were mavericks, totally independent. We didn't get involved in conventional moviemaking, which had so many executives that loaded up these films. People who were participating, a lot of them knew nothing and offered opinions. We did things to suit ourselves.

In the earlier days, because it was hard to record good sound on location, most films were shot in studios. Al wanted to be more like his father and shoot on location. Sound was always a problem until we made *The Naughty Stewardesses*, where we were one of the first companies to shoot an entire film with shotgun mikes. Today that's all they use. We had our offices where Al was at Hollywood Stages, and they had this standing set that you've seen in *Nightmare in Wax*, *Dracula vs. Frankenstein*, it had kind of a brown wood door, and stairs leading down from it. You know that set?

They used that on *Blood of Dracula's Castle* as well.

But in those years, because of the need for conventional sound recording, we were still making studio-type pictures. They were kind of imitation major films, shot in a studio (not a major studio, but a smaller soundstage). Eventually we started to avoid scripts that would force us into studios with mad doctors and labs, and moved outside so we could shoot it all on location, and as such we could record better sound there. We could offer more variety at less cost.

But as I say, the earlier independent people like a Rex Carlton, they were studio thinkers trying to make an imitation major picture on a low budget. They didn't understand, really, much about production. On the other side of the coin, Al and myself were trying to make a totally independent picture devoid of copying what the studios were doing. Other people came up around that time, the George Romeros and John Russos, and Brian De Palmas, Scorseses. All of these people came up from the Roger Corman school and places like that, and they would not be looking to just copy a major picture shot in a studio.

Roger Corman has a similar background to a Rex Carlton. He's basically an imitation major studio kind of guy who's used to having sound stages, used to shooting there. I was there when he was shooting *The Raven* [1963] at Producers Studio, and he was very conventional. But he was also a great innovator and could be very unconventional. He could shoot outside because he had a very flexible mind. Al Adamson had a very flexible mind. They weren't tied to any rigid disciplines of the past that said you couldn't do something. That was, I think, very important.

Before you had IIP and Al had made those first few films, what were some of the avenues that you pursued in trying to get them distributed?

Well, with the first one, which was *Echo of Terror*, Denver told him to come to me in New York, which he did. I screened it and I thought it was pretty good. This was January of 1965, and very few color pictures were made. Technically his picture was head and shoulders above all those Doris Wishman–type pictures made in New York. It was really good, original music, beautiful photography, widescreen. But the film had nothing to market. No exploitation marketing. We ended up changing that to *Psycho a Go-Go*, which was not my idea. I was opposed to it. Then we had a second lousy picture we couldn't give away. But Hemisphere, to humor all of us, decided they would help us do something with this. They failed with it. Then we went through the *Blood of Dracula's Castle* fiasco. Al began to see the folly of this. We needed to have our own distribution company, in which we controlled the rights to the picture. There wouldn't be any people out there who were gonna undo us and take our pictures away and work from within against other people. Typical of independent pictures of that era, the actors never got paid, the director never got paid, everyone winds up foreclosed out, and some clever distributor ends up with the negative and he makes all the money. We learned that lesson fairly early, so as a result it kind of promoted this.

At the time Al was trying to promote pictures. He made several pictures that couldn't be given away out there. We kind of inherited those, around the time we made *Satan's Sadists* as a leader which we could start our company with, and then took those other pictures and put a new coat of paint on them by reshooting them, retitling them, fixing them up in some way as if they were new pictures. They were unseen, but they were not new. Some were three or four years old, but unsaleable. That's why some of these things become so stupid.

Something like *Blood of Ghastly Horror*. Yes, it's got blood, it was ghastly and it's horrible. It was exactly what we promised, but it made money. A lot of fans see something like that, which is unviewable, and they say, "This is a piece of crap." Let's look at the reality. It sold just about everywhere foreign. In the domestic market, while we were beginning to put it on television, that's why we had two titles. *Man with the Synthetic Brain*, that went out through a major studio. Allied Artists played that in all the major markets in television at the same time we were playing it under *Blood of Ghastly Horror* theatrically. It had quite a life, that picture. If you look at it from its content value, you say content value is zero. If you look at it for its salesmanship, the salesmanship value is 90 percent.

We used to have major studios coming to us, to try to take advantage of us in deals. Irwin Yablans, before he made his own pictures like *Halloween* [1978], was a general sales manager for Paramount. He called me up and said, "You've got *Satan's Sadists*, you're about to go into a break in L.A., 50 theaters. I wonder if you'd like to double bill with us?"

Why do I want to do that? He said they had this picture called *The Molly Maguires* [1970]. Major picture, directed by Martin Ritt, starring Sean Connery, all about coal miners in Pennsylvania. They wanted to double bill this with *Satan's Sadists*. I see this is as *Satan's Sadists* on the bottom of the bill, which it really was potentially designed as, so I insisted that it didn't look like that. I just kept raising the limbo bar. I told him that we wanted all paid newspaper advertising, side by side; we don't want this on the bottom regardless of where it will go on the marquee of the theater. We want our own separate campaign. I said, "I'll tell you something else. I want you guys to pay for the whole advertising campaign, no deductions on our end. We split the film rental fifty-fifty, and you pay for the whole campaign."

We got money from the first dollar, and they got advertising bills. That was not to be repeated. I had an idea, a great gimmick if I could make it happen again, but you know how the word spreads. I went to a lot of majors trying to pull that stunt again, but it was not to be repeated. We didn't care.

Al made a few films outside of IIP. One of those was *Jessi's Girls* [1975]. Did you work at all on that feature?

Jessi's Girls was done by Al for Manson International, an independent company. They were our foreign distributor at one time. He wanted to just make a western. I said it was of no commercial value. Al said, "You're kidding!" I said, "I'm in this every day, why would I kid you?" So Michael Goldman gave him the money to do that thing, and he made it for them and they finished the picture. I was out in California with Al to make *Blazing Stewardesses*. They screened it for me and I said, "It's not a bad picture Al, not bad at all."

My thought was, I didn't know if I could figure out a way to market it. I just didn't feel anyone wanted a period western at this time. It made money in foreign theatrical and it kind of died everywhere else. Everything I said was correct. Eventually Manson paid Al a fee and bought him out of it.

What about *The Female Bunch* [1969]?

That was kind of an outgrowth of *Satan's Sadists*. Raphael Nussbaum was gonna put up the money to do it, and we were going to distribute. It quickly turned out that Raphael didn't want to do anything that Al wanted, and he didn't want us to distribute it. So he quickly had Al shoot it, fired Al, re-edited the thing, reshot the picture with Bud Cardos, and he released the picture and it did some business. But it had kind of a sporadic life, and it kind of disappeared.

Were there technological innovations during that period that made it easier or cheaper for the independents to operate?

There were, in a way. In the sixties, there was the possibility of shooting in 16mm and building a better quality blow-up to release a film in 35mm. The best example of that was *Easy Rider* [1969]. Nobody ever knew that was shot in 16mm. That's the same reason *Satan's Sadists* was shot in 16mm. I was personally against it. I was very interested in the technical aspects of the business. I told Al I was opposed to it. Well, he gave me a choice on *Satan's*: "Since you gave me so much money to work with, we can shoot in 35mm with all unknowns, or we can shoot in 16mm and have three or four names in it." Well, what was I gonna say? We needed some names in it. The reason was, when you're making a small, inexpensive film and you put names in it, it makes your film seem more professional. Maybe those [actors] don't bring people into the box office, but it makes it like a Hollywood picture, not like something made in the backwoods of Georgia. There were many of those small pictures made in the South, and they looked like small, cheap films. But it was my policy of putting people who had starred in big films, as much as we could get them in our films, that gave them their life, gave them their longevity and their use. Overseas, it was very important. We had very good money out of overseas distribution, that was a contributing factor, and later when some of these pictures went to television, it was the same thing.

Technically, anything else? You could probably make a film cheaper today on high-def video with a $4,000 camera. Somebody said you could go and blow it up to 35mm for $15,000. That's pretty cheap. You could get the camera for four grand, make the movie for five grand, you've got $10,000 in the movie. With the negative you go up to $26,000. You couldn't do that in those days.

Some of the cheapest pictures made in the South and other places, shot on location, had awful sound, aside from awful actors. We had professional actors, professional sound, and it gave a lot to the film. Now, you couldn't shoot on an actual practical location and get good sound in those years. You had to have blankets up on the wall. It was an impossibility.

We had one of the first pictures in 1973, *Naughty Stewardesses*, to shoot on all practical locations. It gave us the opportunity to shoot direct sound. Well, our regular soundman [Bob Dietz] came along as the photography assistant, and he observed this. He couldn't get good sound on location. Al said, "Bob did some lousy sound for us in the past, but he's promising to buy all new equipment if we use him." I loved Bob. Bob said he could match everything this guy did, and he did it. We stayed with Bob after that.

He had done a bad job on *Angels' Wild Women*. It was terrible. Bad mikes and noisy cables. I was incensed about that, so much so that we post-synched the whole picture, which is something I despised. We were forced to do it because the sound was so terrible. The entire picture

Sherman (right) poses with an unidentified disc jockey and actress Regina Carrol during the promotional tour for *Satan's Sadists* (1969) in Birmingham, Alabama. (Courtesy Independent-International Pictures Corp.)

went to Producers Studio; all the actors had to go there, back the thing up and read the lines. This was horrible. I said, "Well, we can't put out a piece of crap like that." I told Al that you've got to maintain technical standards, or it's gonna be a piece of shit and nobody's gonna play our pictures. They can't look like the worst of the independent films, or nobody will play them. Technically our photography and sound have to be of major studio quality. Try to get the acting as good as possible, too.

Tell me about some of the blaxploitation films that you did.

The black exploitation market came very slowly. It came by adding black leads into mixed-cast movies. With the release of a picture that Roger Corman made called *The Big Doll House* [1971], which featured a mixed cast, we decided to follow that because there was a black component to the audience and they wanted to see black people. They didn't want to see just white people, so we began putting in black players in pictures like *Angels' Wild Women*, and then we made *Dynamite Brothers* [1974]. We had two leads, like in *The Defiant Ones* [1958], handcuffed together. And then we did pictures like *Black Heat* [1976], a.k.a. *Murder Gang*, with Timothy Brown again as the lead. It was more of an action film with some girls' hotel elements thrown in. But we still put him in as the lead. We also used Tracy King in several pictures: in *Mean Mother* [1974], *Naughty Stewardesses*, *Blazing Stewardesses* [1975], and *Nurse Sherri*. So we felt at that time that we weren't truly making all black-cast movies, but we were making casts with a component audience of white and black that could go to several markets. So it could go overseas where black movies didn't necessarily mean anything; it could go to drive-ins where black films only went to black audiences; and it could also play in the black community where we had black leads in the film.

Where did the idea for the stewardess movies come from?

[Kane Lynn] screened *Swinging Stewardesses* [1971] for me. That went through the roof, put them on another level they hadn't been at. Irwin was a little upset because he was out of the company. He asked me, "What's Kane doing with *Swinging Stewardesses*?" I said, "Oh, nothing, Irwin, he's just making millions of dollars." He said, "We need to get a picture like that." I said, "Go out and pick up a picture like that. Do you seriously think nobody else knows the success of the first 3D *Stewardesses* [1970], or the Hemisphere picture? Do you think if anybody has a stewardess movie, they're going to give it to us? You're kidding yourselves! Or they're going to ask for some outrageous advance we can't afford. The only thing we can do is make a picture like that," which I was opposed to anyway, but Danny wanted it. We made *Naughty Stewardesses*, which was a megahit for us.

I didn't want to do it. I thought it was trite, everybody's done that, I want to do something different. I wanted to do *Car Rental Girls*. I said they'll be like stewardesses, but they'll be more like Hertz girls and things like that. "Ridiculous," Dan Kennis said. "Stewardesses have a mystique all their own because they're stewardesses. People don't want an imitation of that." And he was right.

So we just set out to figure out how we would craft such a film ourselves. We went through a very long process of hiring a playwright to write it, to try to give it some quality. He never understood it, so he gave up. And then I decided to write the whole thing, which I did over a period of several months. Then I brought it to my friend Bob Livingston, who was my screen idol as an actor and writer in Hollywood, and he polished it up a little bit, worked with me on characters and dialogue. Then I came out there and produced it with Al. It was shot in L.A., in Palm Springs, in Las Vegas, in San Francisco, up in the snow country in the mountains over Palm Springs. We shot in many picturesque locations, and the film was rather nice. It was a pretty big hit and spawned its own sequel, which again I didn't want to do because I felt that we had done that. But everybody wanted it, so I decided that I would do what I wanted to do— a take-off of what Abbott and Costello had done in *Ride 'em Cowboy* [1942], which was a dude ranch movie with a cowboy hero and action and things, and was a take-off on old westerns. So we did that.

With *Blazing Stewardesses*, the Three Stooges were originally supposed to be in it, but one by one they died. First Larry Fine died, he couldn't be in it. Then Moe Howard was set to be in it. He got ill the first day of shooting. We had to discontinue their being in it, and we ended up with the two surviving Ritz Brothers.

Can you tell me a little bit about Kane Lynn?

He was a distinguished fighter pilot in the Pacific theater in World War II. He had some good rank in the Navy, much honored. After the war he was hanging around the Philippines and he became the production consultant for a CBS network show called *Navy Log*, produced by a man by the name of Sam Gallu, who also did features later on. As a result of being around Manila he got to know Eddie Romero. He made *Terror is a Man* [1959] and *Scavengers* [1959]. Those went out through independent distribution and died. Both good films, but they died and he was wiped out on those. Then he made one for AIP called *Lost Battalion* [1961], and that did a little better. Then he met Irwin Pizor, they started Hemisphere Pictures and they began with their first productions. *Raiders of Leyte Gulf* was the first, and the second was *Walls of Hell* [1964], a great movie with Jock Mahoney, then *The Ravagers* [1965] with John Saxon and Bronwyn FitzSimons, the daughter of Maureen O'Hara. I remember Maureen O'Hara coming to the offices over there, and Dan Kennis taking her to a screening room and screening the 35mm print of *Ravagers* with her. Danny, of course, would like that. He took Maureen O'Hara to a screening [*laughs*].

So Kane Lynn stayed with Hemisphere, and he became very savvy about marketing. He was so smart that nothing was wasted on him. I was all for exploitation and gimmicks for horror pictures, and he picked up on it fast. We were very simpatico on that. Irwin used to think it was crazy!

I'll tell you something about this industry, nothing to do with picture-making or distribution: The most important thing at any level is having friends. The rest of it is meaningless. You can be a brilliant genius. I consider myself to have great ability. I'm hard-working and knowledgeable, good intestinal fortitude, but friends are the best things to have because the whole business is built on relationships. That's what makes you continue. What's the secret of IIP being around? We've got a lot of friends out there, always calling us up and trying to help us. We never expected more from somebody than they could give or produce. We were not unreasonable. A lot of people are unreasonable, and were found to be unpleasant. You wouldn't want to deal with them. I had people say to me, "I like working with you." We tried to have fun, have a few laughs here and there, be on good terms with people.

What are your favorite IIP films?

Well, I would say *Satan's Sadists*, and *Naughty Stewardesses* and *Blazing Stewardesses*.

Why?

Well, first of all, *Satan's Sadists* was a great mix of genres—it had violence, it had sex, it had great music, it had good people in it. It always played well to an audience and it helped start the company, so I have a sentimental attachment to it. The two stewardess movies I had an intimate hand in making. They were really my thoughts on how to craft those things for that market. Al and I worked together on it to figure how to do it. *Naughty Stewardesses* was a very tough picture to make, it had lots of problems, but it ended up being very successful. *Blazing Stewardesses* was a lot of laughs because there were comedians in it and a lot of funny things. It was sort of an object lesson in coming through in both cases.

Looking back, what is your overall opinion of the films that you made?

I think that they were made for a price, for a market. They have their fans, people that like that type of thing. People grew up with them, saw them in drive-in theaters, and they served a purpose. They were niche films created for certain use. No more, no less.

The Girl from Thunder Strip

MEGAN TIMOTHY

Megan Timothy's acting career was relatively brief, but it was certainly interesting. Her résumé not only includes a trio of films for ultra-cheap auteur David L. Hewitt, but shows that she also worked with such disparate figures as Al Adamson, Russ Meyer and even Elvis Presley.

Most fans of schlock cinema will know Timothy from her starring role as April Adams, the big game trapper with the hard-to-place accent in Hewitt's *King Kong* redux, *The Mighty Gorga* (1969). She was also in Hewitt's obscure biker films *Hell's Chosen Few* (1969) and *The Girls from Thunder Strip* (1968). In the latter, she was one of a trio of hillbilly sisters who go toe-to-toe with Hewitt's minimalist biker gang. Timothy did not have the lead in that one, but performed a memorable jailhouse striptease and had what has to be one of the most outlandish death scenes in low-budget cinema: She's blown apart in an outhouse, her passing marked by a roll of toilet paper slowly unfurling down a hillside.

Raised in Rhodesia, Timothy arrived in the U.S. in 1964 with hopes of becoming an actress or a stuntwoman. Her first role was in Russ Meyer's *Good Morning ... and Goodbye!* (1967), followed closely by her Hewitt trilogy and Adamson's Meyeresque *The Female Bunch* (1969). After a small role in the Elvis film *Charro!* (1969), Timothy left acting and, among other things, worked as a musician and a chef, and operated a bed and breakfast in North Hollywood.

In 1999, Timothy embarked on a ten-month, 12,000-mile long solo bicycle trip across Western Europe and parts of Africa — at the age of 59. She faced an even greater challenge four years later, when she suffered an arterial venous malformation that caused massive hemorrhaging in her brain and robbed her of the ability to read, write and speak. After multiple surgeries and intense therapy, Timothy was able to regain about 80 percent of her brain's communications functions, but had to completely relearn the alphabet and how to sound-out words.

Despite these obstacles, Timothy wrote and published a book based on her experiences called *Let Me Die Laughing! Waking Up from the Nightmare of a Brain Explosion*. To publicize the book, Timothy took *another* solo bike tour, this one across the entire United States. I caught up with her in Washington, D.C., where she spoke to me from her hotel room during the annual Book Expo America.

You were originally from Africa?

MEGAN TIMOTHY: Rhodesia, which is now Zimbabwe. A place you don't want to go to.

Why did you come to the U.S.?

A flamboyant Mexican lobby card for David L. Hewitt's *The Mighty Gorga* (1969). Megan Timothy starred in the film along with Anthony Eisley and Scott Brady.

Just always been a traveler, and I decided to come and see what the States were like. I was only to come for a few months, but I'm still here a hundred years later [*laughs*]!

Were you interested in show business when you came here?

At that time I was a professional horsewoman. I used to jump horses and race horses. I always loved the movies, and I thought that maybe I could do stunt work.

So you went to California right off the bat.

Yes. I came on a Greyhound bus from New York, down South and across to California, and I did that for two reasons. One, the Greyhound bus was the only money I had. Secondly, the Greyhound advertising was just terrific. You'd think there was no other way to see America except by the Greyhound bus. It was a little different.

That must have been an interesting introduction to the country, particularly at that time.

It was very interesting. I was still very much in a muddle about America because, being a British colony, the British still didn't want to admit that America existed, being that they behaved so badly 200 and some years ago and threw the British out. I know one *faux pas* I made was going through the South. I was in South Carolina or somewhere. To us, Americans were called Yanks or Yankees. I jumped off the bus and these good old boys were drinking their beers. I went up and said, "Oh, good to meet you, Yankees!" I got an education very fast.

How did you get your first film role?

I arrived in California absolutely flat broke, of course, and stayed on the beach for a couple of days. Then I got organized and got a job as a telephone operator. You're probably too young to remember, but if you had a business, you had somebody who tended to the phones, and there was this great big machine that you put these little numbers into.

The guy thought I was British; he thought I spoke like an English person, and he just thought that would add a lot of class to his office. I didn't tell him I was a colonist. I needed the job, so I wasn't going to argue with him. Half the day through he came rushing down and said, "Can't you learn to speak American? No one can understand you!" [*Laughs*] His little attempt to have this classy British thing didn't work for him. But he was very sweet and they kind of put up with me. He let me hang on there.

They were opening a Playboy Club in Los Angeles at the time, and I thought that was a very wicked thing. In Rhodesia you weren't even allowed a *Playboy* magazine. You went to jail if you were caught with one. I was at the age where you were dying to be wicked, so off I went and I was a Playboy bunny. Which turned out to be a waitress! I though it was going to be so wildly exciting, and all I had was sore feet from wearing high shoes, and those clothes that you wear that you can barely breathe in. A lot of the bunnies were already kind of involved in show business, and show business was involved in Playboy. It was all of that era.

What was your first job in film or TV?

It was *Good Morning ... and Goodbye!*, the Russ Meyer film. I had no idea that Russ Meyer was into softcore, but he was a delightful guy. Everybody told me, "Don't go work for him. He makes those terrible movies." I said, "I need the money, and he thinks I'm too skinny for me to take my clothes off, so that's going to be okay!"

I went there and we were in some place in the middle of California. I arrived there, and my part wasn't that long. The others had been there for awhile. Russ Meyer wanted his actors looking good the next morning, no baggy faces. So there wasn't allowed any liquor, and he used to lock us in our rooms every night. No fooling around! "If you have all that sex all night, you're going to look like hell in the morning. I'm not having any of this!" There was nothing, no fooling around or anything sexual about the things you'd think Russ Meyer would be involved in. It was like a convent [*laughs*]!

He was very nice. I really liked him. I was surprised because of the reputation and the things he did, but it was all just press, I think.

Did you work for him on any other films?

No. I was too skinny. He just wanted one skinny girl, and that was it. He said, "You just don't have it. You don't have big enough boobs," or whatever. He also said, "Don't do this [type of film]. You have talent. Go and do something better." He was a really good guy.

You did three movies for David Hewitt. How did you meet him?

I can't remember. There was one small studio, Hollywood Stages. All of us who were struggling to find some kind of job would hear on the grapevine about something between each other or someone gossiping, and we'd rush over to wherever that was. I probably heard it and went over there and met Dave Hewitt, who was just a real character. He was a funny guy. Everybody was flat broke.

In one of those, *The Girls from Thunder Strip*, you played a hillbilly moonshiner. Did you have any idea what a moonshiner was supposed to be?

No, and of course again he thought my accent sounded like a moonshiner. I wasn't arguing! That was my first one with Hewitt.

Do you remember much about making that one?

It was in a part of California close to the beach. If I had my whole brain I'd be giving you a much better interview! On the way to Malibu there's a place in the mountains where people go and have picnics, like a park. It's on the way to Malibu, almost at the beach, in the Malibu mountains. You're not supposed to go and film there unless you get a license and you pay money. Of course, Dave Hewitt couldn't afford that, so we just used to be driving around that road and this road. We got busted, and then he'd take us somewhere else. There was a guy in that, the disc jockey....

Casey Kasem.

He was playing the federal agent, and was all dressed up. Casey Kasem did not want to get mud on his shoes, or get his hair misplaced. He was a very particular man. We used to give him such a hard time. We used to throw rocks and sand, roll him in the dirt. Poor Casey! He had this big thing on shoes. He used to spend vast amounts on shoes, and you could never get him out of the truck to go walking [*laughs*]. Oh, he was funny. Couldn't mess his shoes.

What was David Hewitt like as a director?

A bit vague. And even more vague after he'd had a little marijuana. But he was awfully nice and a very kind man, and he really wanted to make movies very badly. But Dave wasn't the strongest guy. Some of these half-witted actresses and actors, like myself, they used to give him a hard time. Poor guy; he wasn't really up to putting up with that. He wasn't like Russ Meyer. [Russ] would have given them a quick slap and that would have been it.

You also did *Hell's Chosen Few*.

He was having a hard time with cash. We were also having a hard time with cash, and we really wanted to get paid every week, but it didn't always happen. The crew got together one morning and said, "We're not going to work unless we get paid today." He said, "I'll bring you a check right away." "Dave, checks are no good. We want cash money."

He rushed around and managed to get some cash somehow. I never asked how, because you didn't ask him those sorts of things. You didn't want to know! He said, "You can be at this bank and you can have cash." By then we're all dressed in costume and some of us were on the bikes. There was the wardrobe truck, which is just like a regular truck, and it had a lot of rifles in the back.

At that time the Hell's Angels were in top form, and causing a lot of trouble, the police were really watching them. It was ten o'clock and the bank was opening. We went rushing down there with the truck with all the rifles in the back, and we were looking really sleazy with these Hell's Angels kind of coats on, and we all screamed up in front of the bank. A cop happened to be passing behind, so you can imagine what happened. Suddenly there were about six cops and a plane overhead. We were all lying on the ground with our hands on our heads trying to explain why there were ten rifles in the back and why we screamed up at the bank to get the money.

Luckily Dave came behind, just as they were about to haul us off. We had no ID. He just happened to be passing by, and he said, "Oh my God, there's my cast and my truck!" We waited a little bit, got our money, calmed down the cops and then we went off to work. But that was a typical morning with Dave Hewitt.

Had you ridden on motorcycles?

Just on the back. Do you know that other one? The other movie was done near Las Vegas? A lot of cowboy stuff and horses?

Female Bunch?

The Female Bunch, that's it. That was Al Adamson. He always wore green. Did you ever see him or just talk to him? He always wore green. Green pants, green shirt, green jacket. They had just made a big movie outside of Las Vegas. They needed this set, so they found out that someone had been working on this movie, and there's a set. The set happened to be on the land of Howard Hughes. You're not allowed on there. We had no clue. We thought it was all cool and that he'd gotten permission, which was a silly thing to think knowing the kind of stuff we did. We're there and we had about two days to finish. Just about done. We're doing our thing and up comes this car, with these guys with dark glasses looking like the Tonton Macoute, and these big guns. They were Hughes' henchman or whatever. Security. They were furious. "You get off the land!" So we got everything and got off the land. We're gone and we don't want anything to do with it, because we know Hughes' reputation.

But we had to finish this movie and there was just no way to cheat it. We just had these few things to do, and there was no way to do it anywhere else. [Al] comes to us and says, "We've got to get back." We say, "No way are we going back there." So he gets somebody with a walkie-talkie who sits on the mountain, a big hill above us, and we've got the walkie-talkies

Megan Timothy (in the background on the far left) looks on as Jenifer Bishop displays her equestrian skills in Al Adamson's ***The Female Bunch*** (1969).

below. We can't take the car or anything on this place. We all have to carry equipment, cameras and everything. So we're creeping around in the bushes and there's rattlesnakes and everything. Suddenly, the walkie-talkie would go, "They're coming, they're coming!" We'd all be rushing into these bushes. "They're gone! They're gone!" We got the picture done, but it was a very exciting couple of days.

Did you get to know the other girls like Jenifer Bishop?

She was wonderful. She was the best actress. Lovely girl. Very nice. I had no idea why she was working on a picture like that, because she was a much better actress. Very nice person.

What about Al's wife, Regina?

Eccentric, you could say, but then everyone was eccentric.

Did you go see any of these films when they were released?

Not if I could help it. I went to see my first movie, and I was all excited, and suddenly your nose appears on the screen and it's sixty feet long and high. That scared me to death, and I never went to see another one [*laughs*]. I hated it. Mostly I hated my voice. To watch myself was painful.

The other David Hewitt film was *The Mighty Gorga*. What did you think of Hewitt's version of Africa?

We were supposed to be in the jungle, and that was halfway out of L.A. It had a lot of those weeds that give you itches.

Poison ivy?

Yes. He said, "I've got this wonderful place, but don't push down those bushes, because these are the only bushes we've got. We've got to craft this outside, then when the big shot comes, go running through the jungle." We come running through the jungle, and we were itching for days [*laughs*].

Did you get to know any of the people in that cast like Anthony Eisley or Scott Brady?

I had a huge crush on Anthony Eisley, but that didn't take me anywhere because he was very married — much to my disappointment. He was a lovely, lovely man. I also had no idea what he was doing in that, because he was a good actor. Hard worker, good guy.

Scott Brady was having a hard time because he was kind of doing proper movies and stuff, and then he was getting old and sunk down to this level, and he didn't take that kindly. He was okay to me.

I remember I had a terrible time because I used to stammer enormously. I didn't want anybody to find out, because if they found out I couldn't speak, I was out of a job. Any work in theater was okay, because I could learn the lines, and once I knew them I was okay. But movies were different. I'd get the stuff and learn my lines, then get to work in the morning and it was all changed. They'd give me this whole bunch of new lines, and there was no way I could say this whole speech. So I found a way: I used to run to the toilet, the Porta-Potty. I was sitting there with everyone else trying to get in. I was trying to learn my lines [*laughs*]. After awhile, the director would ask, "Are you all right?" "It's that food that you gave us to eat," I said. The poor guy making the food got in trouble. I felt really bad for that. But the only way I could learn my lines was to go to the Porta-Potty.

Didn't David Hewitt play the gorilla in that film?

Yeah. He had on the gorilla costume, and he was directing. It was really rather peculiar [*laughs*]. He had the whole head and everything on.

Did you do any television during that period?

Just some commercials. That's what got me my SAG card. You're supposed to be this great actress to qualify as a SAG member, and all I had to do was a commercial for a TV within a TV, Motorola I think it was. I wasn't even supposed to be on that. I was trying to find an agent. I went into this agency, and I was sitting there waiting and waiting, and nobody wanted to talk to me. Out of the side of the office came these two people from the agency, and they were talking about this commercial that they were going to have these auditions for that afternoon.

Megan Timothy today. (Courtesy Nancy Layton/Crone House Publishing)

They seemed to be very excited about it. I heard where it was going to be, at one of the studios. I thought, "Well, heck, I'll go," because I heard they were desperate to find some actress who could play a ukulele. I couldn't play a ukulele, but I could play guitar. I figured that was about the same thing. I ran down there and it was hot. I had to take a taxi, and my hair was sticking to my head. I found out where they were having it, and when I got there everyone was Oriental. I found out afterwards that the TV thing was supposed to be someone from Hawaii and they would play the ukulele and sit in the forest under a tree.

I thought, "Oh God, I'm not gonna make this. I don't look Hawaiian." All these girls were going in and out, because none of them could play the ukulele. The guy who was doing the interviews was desperate, and he said, "Does *anybody* in this place play an instrument?" He'd given up on a ukulele. I said, "I do." He said, "You're not Hawaiian." I said, "Who cares? I can play and sing, and no one else can!" So he took me in.

So that's how I got my SAG card. Oh my goodness, you get your SAG card to be this great actress, and all you have to do is play a phony Hawaiian and sit on a rock and play guitar. That's show business for you!

A Thing for Two Heads

JAMES GORDON WHITE

In the 1960s, the biker film became the new western—the picturesque desert vistas of Southern California, Arizona and Utah that had once been patrolled on screen by the likes of John Wayne and Gary Cooper were taken over by leather-clad outlaw bikers on customized motorcycles.

Many of these films were heavily influenced by classic westerns, and nowhere was this more evident than in the films written by James Gordon White. In most of the biker films he penned, White relied heavily on western imagery. *The Glory Stompers* (1968), which featured a pre–*Easy Rider* Dennis Hopper, was originally written as a western, and *Hell's Belles* (1970) was an amalgam of *Winchester '73*, *The Appaloosa*, and *The Scalphunters*.

Born in 1940, the son of a Texas oilman, White had a nomadic upbringing, moving from Houston to Illinois, and even spending part of his childhood in Egypt and Honduras. He originally went to California to study acting at the Pasadena Playhouse, but soon turned to writing. He provided an early outline for *The Hellcats* (1967), a biker film finished by writer-director Robert Slatzer and producer Anthony Cardoza that has since gained new life via an episode of *Mystery Science Theatre 3000*. White also wrote the second Slatzer-Cardoza project, *Bigfoot* (1970), an even more outrageous film that pitted John Carradine and Lindsay Crosby against a family of Sasquatch.

In the late 1960s, White served as a contract writer for American International Pictures, where he collaborated with Maury Dexter on *The Mini-Skirt Mob* (1968), *The Young Animals* (1968), and *Hell's Belles*, and wrote Burt Topper's *The Devil's 8* (1969).

But his most infamous credit remains *The Incredible 2-Headed Transplant* (1971), produced by John Lawrence and directed by Anthony Lanza. The film, which White originally intended as a satire, features an unusually subdued Bruce Dern as a scientist who grafts the head of a homicidal maniac (Albert Cole) onto the shoulder of a slow-witted hulk (John Bloom).

After working on an early draft of the similarly-themed Lee Frost-Wes Bishop production *The Thing with Two Heads* (1972), White left AIP and worked (usually uncredited) on a number of films, including Ted V. Mikels' *10 Violent Women* (1982).

Now back in Texas, White has spent much of the past two decades writing novels. Although he largely sticks to westerns, he and his wife Marie Ardell (since deceased) did write a horror novel in 1994 ... about a monster with two heads.

How old were you when you were living in Cairo and Honduras?

JAMES GORDON WHITE: I was seven and sixteen.

This googly-eyed sasquatch was one of the many stars of *Bigfoot* (1970), which James Gordon White co-wrote with director Robert Slatzer.

Did you go to school there?

Yes, I went to a British school, and I had a British accent, which I've pretty much lost, even though I work for a British company now writing books.

When did you first get interested in acting?

I'd always been interested in acting. I'd done high school plays and college plays and all that. Then when I went to the Pasadena Playhouse, I still had an interest in acting, but writing came to me and I just decided that I might do better that way.

Who was at the Playhouse at that time?

Ahead of me was Christopher Connelly. He acted in some things and then died back in the 1980s. Sid Haig, the character actor, had just finished at the Playhouse when I went in, and he was still hanging around there. Why so many of them would come back, I don't know [*laughs*]. Once I was out, I had no desire to go back! I'm trying to think if there's anybody that really made it. Astrid Warner — Betty Warner — I got Betty her first job in *Glory Stompers*. Jim Reader, I got him in *Glory Stompers*, too. We were all at Pasadena Playhouse together. Al Quick, I think he's teaching now. I'm sure there must be somebody that did make it, but I can't think of anyone that really made it on a large scale.

When did you start writing screenplays?

A friend and relative of mine, Tom Brown, was going to Pasadena Playhouse at the same time. We're both related to Jim Bowie, so that makes us cousins of some sort. He's retiring early next year. He has a metal shop and he's done *Star Trek* and *Star Wars* and *Rocky*, you name it, he's made the jewelry and metal work for them. He and I were at Pasadena Playhouse, that's where we met, and he told me about writing classes. So I went and sat in on one of the writing classes, and then he and I came up with an idea for a Nancy Drew–type thing, and we thought we'd try for a TV series. So we sat down and wrote a few, and Arthur Lubin, who did *Francis the Talking Mule* and *Mr. Ed*— we knew him from Pasadena Playhouse — we went and talked to him about it. He said there was not any demand at the moment for that.

How were you making a living?

I was just doing whatever I could. Parking cars at the Brown Derby — mostly parking cars! I desk clerked for awhile at the Hollywood Ardmore. Edgar Buchanan was staying there, so I met him. He was encouraging about sticking to it. He didn't get into acting until he was 40; he was a dentist.

So what was your first actual paying job in the movies?

This indie producer came to me. He was looking for a writer, and he had an idea for a two-headed monster. So that wound up being *The Incredible 2-Headed Transplant*. He was paying me and I was still parking cars at the Brown Derby, doing that on the side.

That was John Lawrence?

Yeah. Then by the time the script was finished, he went to [American International Pictures] and AIP wasn't interested in horror at the time. Motorcycles were in. So he came back to me and said we'd have to put the *Transplant* script aside, and see what can be done with motorcycles. Well, I had an unsold outline that was a western outline [*The Glory Stompers*]. I changed the Indians to the Black Souls, I changed the Cavalry to the Glory Stompers, I changed the old gunfighter to Jock Mahoney, an older member of the gang.

That was started independently on $10,000. We went up to Corona and stayed there. We shot in Panamint, and the other side of Panamint is Death Valley. We stayed up there for a whole week. MGM had tried back in the 1940s to shoot in Panamint. It's a ghost town now, but they couldn't last but one day in the heat.

You were on the set for the whole production?

I got a production job on it, which helped me out because I didn't get that much for the screenplay. God, if I had had points. I don't care what the critics say. Critics don't take into account that number one, you're making something on a very low budget. You're doing the best you can with what you've got to work with. You're not MGM doing *Gone With the Wind*. And you can't judge a picture that's a B picture the same way you would judge an A picture. These idiots don't grasp that. I don't think any of them ever saw *Glory Stompers*. All they do is knock it without even seeing it. It's not a great work of art, but it made a hell of a lot of money, and it got me an exclusive contract with AIP. To my knowledge I'm the only one that was under contract with American International as a writer.

I talked to Anthony Lanza, and he said the same thing. It sill plays periodically, and he still gets checks.

So it made money! I wish I had had some of it! See, they ran out of money and they shopped it. AIP was doing motorcycles, and they said if you have a motorcycle thing, to show it to 'em.

So they looked at it, and liked the western idea. AIP started doing westerns back when they first changed over from American Releasing Corporation to AIP, and they did one with Lloyd Bridges [*Apache Woman*, 1955], and it bombed [*laughs*]. They [AIP's 1950s Westerns] are not that bad. I saw some of 'em. I guess television must have been killing the western at the time. So AIP said they'd never do a western, and to my knowledge the only western they did was back in the 1970s. That's the only western they did after the early 1950s when they did the Lloyd Bridges one, and *Five Guns West* [1955] with Dorothy Malone.

So they didn't really make money with those, and they decided not to do them. What they liked about *Glory Stompers* was the western feel. Well, it came from a western to begin with!

Any memories of the cast?

Lindsay [Crosby] and I were buddies. He said I reminded him of one of his brothers. He killed himself. We were out of touch by the time that had happened. He was a cheerful guy and all that. I don't know why he did it. Then Casey [Kasem] had the radio shows, and he was still doing those at the time of *Glory Stompers*. Casey was also in *Free Grass* [a.k.a. *Scream Free!*, 1969] and he was also in *Incredible 2-Headed Transplant*. I lost touch with about everybody.

Tony Lanza told me he had some trouble keeping Dennis Hopper reined in on that film.

I called him Grass Hopper, because he was always running off between takes into the bushes and smoking pot [*laughs*]. He and I didn't get along very well. He didn't like the script. Well, it wasn't my fault. We had to change it for budget. I had a much fuller script, so we had to tone it down for budget.

Then he started ad libbing. I'd tell Tony, it's fine if he wants to ad lib, but don't do it on key lines, don't throw those away. And the asshole — I'm not fond of him after all these years. That's the thing, pardon my French, but the shits of the business seem to last forever. Like Ross MacDonald said in *Moving Target*, which was made into *Harper*: The bottom's filled with good people; only cream and bastards rise. That's how it is in the movie business!

Around that same time, you worked on Hellcats.

Yeah. In fact, I had done the outline on *Hellcats*, and I'd started about ten pages of the screenplay, and then *Glory Stompers* came through. There was more money offered, and it was a definite thing, where [Anthony] Cardoza was still looking for money.

How did you meet Cardoza?

Through Don somebody, an actor and independent director. He was the one who Cardoza knew, and he in turn introduced me to John Lawrence. I'm trying to remember who I met Cardoza through. I'm sure a few hours from now I'll recall. He wasn't anybody big in the business or anything like that.

Didn't he live near you?

Yeah, I was at the time living with Tom Brown, and then Tom got married. He and I were sharing a place across from Columbia Pictures at the time. I happened to run into Fess Parker there, who was a fraternity brother of my father's, different years, and he guided me in to watch him shoot one time.

Then Cardoza did eventually find the money.

They began shooting when we were on break for *Glory Stompers*, and they were shopping it around for a distributor. So I didn't have anything outside of just the original story, which they made a lot of changes on. That's the problem. Screenwriting is, as they say, a collaborative art. A writer might not like that, which is why I'm much happier with books. People read the book and say, "Gee, that was great." And it's all me! If they say they didn't like it, then that's still me. With screenplays you get blamed. Like Elvira, Cassandra Peterson, told me talking about *Incredible 2-Headed Transplant*. I said, "I didn't write that part."

That's how Slatzer's name wound up on the script.

Yeah, and Tony Huston.

You weren't involved in filming?

I came to the set one day during that break in between *Glory Stompers*, and outside of that, that was my only involvement.

Did you know Slatzer?

Yeah, he and I were big buddies. He died last year of cancer. We were in touch from that time until he died.

Did he and Cardoza get along?

I don't believe so. Cardoza is one of those guys where you've got to count your fingers after you shake hands. So is Lawrence. So I don't think they got along too well. I know we all got screwed financially. I don't think they were that great. There were two that he did for Cardoza, *Bigfoot* and *Hellcats*. Slatzer called me in when he was working on *Bigfoot*. I was under contract at AIP at the time. They said I could do anything on my own, just as long as it didn't interfere with what I was doing for them. So he called me, and I went over and read what he had done. He showed me all the stuff on Bigfoot, which we now know was all B.S. The guy made it up, and it was his wife running around in a monkey suit.

So Slatzer got that idea from the famous Roger Patterson Bigfoot film.

That's where he got the idea. So we sat down and started working on it. What's funny, the reason I really remember that is because he was over at General Service Studios, which now is called Zoetrope or whatever. I don't know if it's still Zoetrope. He had offices there, and at the old Jaguar company, which was Alan Ladd's company that Bob Hope and his brother George had bought and put Slatzer in charge of it. They told him not to make any movies under Jaguar because it was a tax write-off company. So when he did something, he couldn't do it under Jaguar!

We were there one night and Slatzer got a call from a girl that he'd been seeing. He said, "Why don't you come and bring a friend?" I said, "Look Bob, I came over here to work. I've been busy all day at AIP." He said, "No, meet the girls, we'll have some drinks." Well, it turned out that was my [future] wife!

No kidding!

He told them to meet us at the studio gate as we were leaving. I had a sports car, a two-seater Triumph, and she rode with me and his girl rode with him. It turned out we hit it off that night and began dating, and a year later we were married. We were married for 34 years. She died two years ago in January. Lung cancer. So if you smoke, don't.

What exactly did Slatzer do for a living? I know he did some publicity work.

Well, to my knowledge he started doing publicity for 20th. I don't know if 20th was his first job or not, but that's how he met Marilyn Monroe, doing publicity for *Niagara* [1953], the movie with Joseph Cotten. So he worked at Columbia and knew Harry Cohn, and I believe that he was also doing publicity there, too, besides writing.

He wrote for TV.

He wrote the old *Joe Palooka* TV series back in the early 1950s, and a lot of western shows, too. When I met him, he wasn't really doing any TV, and the only movies I know that he did were the two that I was involved with.

***Bigfoot* had a pretty crazy cast. Did you work on that film during production?**

Bob called me in to do set re-writes. I worked on that most of the shooting. Joi Lansing was in it. They got Joi Lansing because I insisted the girl that they had wasn't right. Cardoza, you could give him a million dollars to do a movie and he'd screw it up! That's being truthful; that's not sour grapes. He had a terrible leading lady, so she got bumped down to the second lead. They got Joi Lansing, which was an improvement, and name value. She wasn't a huge name, but for a little B movie it was okay. James Craig went to Rice University in Houston, so he and I were buddies. He was much older than me. And then Chris Mitchum was in it. I became friendly with him for a little while. Then after he started doing the movie and playing the lead, he started getting big-headed. He was not his dad! I don't think he really made it. [John] Wayne tried to help him out and put him in a couple of his movies. Last I heard he had worked for Henry Park, a Korean producer who I did a script re-write for some years ago.

***Bigfoot* was shot in Griffith Park?**

It was shot over in Bronson Canyon. In fact, some of *Glory Stompers* was shot there, too. Everyone and his dog has shot there. In the 1930s, old Gene Autry movies like *Phantom Empire* [1935] were shot up there. Bronson Caves is up there, a man-made thing. I don't know what they were drilling for. That's always used any time you see 'em going into a cave. When John Wayne chased Natalie Wood in *The Searchers* [1956], that was in Bronson!

Do you remember much about the "Bigfeet"? One of them was Jerry Marin, from *The Wizard of Oz* [1939].

One guy claimed to be a relative of Errol Flynn's, and he was one of the creatures [*laughs*]. I don't know if he really was or not. So many people would claim that they're this or that. It's just a bid for attention. Then a girl was one of the creatures. I really didn't get to know them. Mainly I was re-writing, cutting down to fit budget and all that.

Another one of your motorcycle films that had a western influence was *The Mini-Skirt Mob*.

That was after Norman T. Herman and AIP took *Glory Stompers*. *Glory Stompers* was started without an IA signatory. AIP was IA, so to get around that they set up Norman T. Herman Productions, and we went through NABET, which we'd already been with. So Norman T. Herman was watchdogging the thing for AIP, and that is no bull that AIP would pull pages if you were behind. It was done judiciously—it wasn't just, "Let's open the script and yank 'em out." But that's what happened! If you got behind, suddenly you weren't behind any more! That's the thing about screenwriting. You don't have any control; once you sell that script, that's it.

On *Glory Stompers*, Norman T. Herman took a liking to me. He went to Arkoff and Nicholson, told them about me, and they set up a meeting. I went in there and met with them, and they said, "We liked the western feel of *Glory Stompers*." They said they had another motorcycle movie, but I hadn't joined the union at that time. We'd just finished *Glory Stompers* and they were still doing pick-up shots. They said, "We'll pay you for the weekend's work. Here's a two-page outline. We want you to develop it into a 10- or so page outline. If you do a good job, we'll give you a contract to do the screenplay. If we don't like it, you'll be paid for the weekend."

Maury Dexter was there, and Maury and I became good buddies. That was our first meeting. We left and went to Maury's office, which was over at Crossroads of the World, not far from AIP. Maury and I talked about it. I went home, and because this was the first real legitimate deal, nerves and anxiety set in, and I really didn't get down to hard work until Sunday night. I did the whole thing Sunday night.

I went in there without sleep. Maury read it and loved it. He sent it over to AIP. Nicholson had gone to Paris, so they air messengered it to him in Paris, and we sat around the office shooting the bull, waiting to hear. Nicholson got back to Maury, and I had the contract. From there, I then got *Born Wild*. Again, with the movie business, if you haven't done something, they don't think you can do it. I'd already done *Glory Stompers*, *Hellcats*, and *Scream Free*, and so this was a youth picture, *Born Wild*.

That was released as *The Young Animals*.

Yes. It was originally *Implosion*, and they changed it to *Young Animals*, and then they changed it to *Born Wild*. I had to audition for that, too. I had to do an outline, and I of course got the job because Maury Dexter was rooting for me, and I did a good job on it. So they gave me the screenplay assignment on that. About two weeks into it, they offered me an exclusive contract as staff writer for AIP.

***Born Wild* was an existing idea?**

AIP loved titles, so they'd build a movie around a title. Like *Mini-Skirt Mob* was from when mini-skirts were in. It was originally called *The Mini Skirts*, then they added *Mob*. With *Born Wild*, at the time there was a Mexican group of high school kids, I think they were called the Brown Shirts or something like that, and so that's what AIP wanted to capitalize on. We did that in Tucson. Maury Dexter shot all three of the ones I did for him in Tucson.*

When you were on set doing re-writes, did they just stick you in a room with a typewriter?

I'd be on the set ready to do something. Sometimes I'd be doing it right there on the set, changing dialogue as they were getting ready to shoot the next scene.

One of the next ones would have been *The Devil's 8*, the Burt Topper film. That had several writers listed.

What happened on that, Lawrence Gordon was the story editor at AIP. He had a story assistant, a young guy named Willard Huyck. Huyck was put there by his agent to get experience. By the way, I might be living in Beverly Hills if I'd done it, but I did everything on my own without an agent.

Huyck was put there, and they needed another assistant, and they said, "Do you know anyone?" I told them I could talk to my friend Tom Brown and see if he'd be interested. Then they brought in someone who was just out of USC, but who also had an agent and was put there to get some experience, and that was John Milius. So the two of them were Larry Gordon's story assistants. I knew them, but not real well. I did the first draft on *Devil's 8*, then I was given

---

*This film was based on the 1968 Chicano-rights student walk-outs and the contemporary "Brown Beret" movement.

something else to work on. They were put on it to get their experience and screen credit. So the two of them re-worked and did the second draft.

I didn't come into the studio all the time. I set my own hours unless something was going on. I was brought in one day and spent from early morning until late in the evening with Dick Clark doing the action scenes that Arkoff wanted me to punch up on *Killers Three* [1968]. So I went back in there, and the next thing I knew—I didn't even know they'd been put on *Devil's 8*—they were gone! They got their credit, so they left for bigger and better things. So that's B.S. that Milius was a beach boy and starving to death. It's all nonsense. His agent put him in there. He was not a starving kiddie.

What did you think of the film?

I didn't like it. They took the southern flavor out of it, and I'm from the South, so I know from whereof I talk!

Were you on the set?

No. [Burt Topper] didn't get along with me.

But he'd be around AIP.

Yeah. He got in with Arkoff and Nicholson. In fact, they bailed him out on the motorcycle movie he did, *The Hard Ride* [1971] or something. He did it and couldn't find anyone [to distribute it]. They decided to take it just to save his ass. That happened with *Easy Rider* [1969]. There's so much about that that's all B.S. On *Easy Rider*, the investor had the money in it, and it looked like AIP turned it down, and when AIP turns down a motorcycle picture you're pretty much out of luck. Crown International turned it down. The guy was really in a bind, so again—the old saying about who you know—he went to his relative at Columbia and got a deal at Columbia because his relative bailed him out. Then Columbia put their people on it and their editors. Hopper sat there throwing darts. Bob Tessier told me about that. Tessier and I were working on a script that didn't get produced, and he was telling me about what was going on. Bob's another one that died from cancer from smoking. I quit smoking about 10 years ago, so I don't know if it's going to catch up with me or not.

***Scream Free!* was another John Lawrence film.**

Scream Free! was done right after. I didn't like working on the script. The guys that had the original story credit were given that for putting up the money. That's another thing: Screenplay writing also isn't like book writing. Say we're going to write a book together. We sit down and we do it. With a screenplay, you do a draft, and someone else does a draft. I never met R.G. McMullen on *Hell's Belles*. So when you see these names on screenplays, it doesn't mean that they said, "Let's sit down and write a story." It means somebody did a draft, and then somebody else did a draft, then some producer or director came in with their pet writer. I was Maury Dexter's pet writer. They have them in to rework a script, and that's how it goes. That's why I'm happier doing books! Money's not as great, but you've got the creative freedom.

Were you around Hollywood Stages much?

That's where that was shot. That was Ray Dorn's place. *Incredible 2-Headed Transplant* was shot there. All kinds of things were done there.

What kind of place was it?

It's right on Santa Monica, across from the unemployment office [*laughs*].

That's convenient.

Behind it is General Service Studios, which is now Zoetrope. Zoetrope is a bigger lot. They're just a building. That's where *Ozzie & Harriet* was shot, *Mr. Ed*. I used to go over and visit the *Mr. Ed* set because I knew Arthur Lubin real well.

Hell's Belles was the other biker film you did right around that same time.

Again, AIP loved titles and they stuck that on it. It was originally called *Riley's Run*. They said, "Oh, this is the one that we're going to put *Hell's Belles* on!"

That was an update of Winchester '73 [1950].

Here's what really happened on that. Of course, you think of *Winchester '73*, but going back to *Glory Stompers*, that was a much fuller script. In *Glory Stompers* they went to Mexico to get the girl out. The whole thing of getting back across the border and shooting down a helicopter and all that. Since none of that was used, I said to myself, "I think I should try to do something with it." So I came up with an outline where the guy — which was like *The Appaloosa* if you saw that movie [1966] or read the book — well, the guy's motorcycle instead of the appaloosa is swiped by this Mexican gang. He has to go into Mexico to get it. I showed it to Maury Dexter and he said, "That's nice, but I don't have the money for it at the moment. See if AIP might be interested."

So I went to Larry Gordon, and he said, "Oh, you hit me at just the right time, because I have an idea for *The Scalphunters*." So he set up a screening, and I saw *The Scalphunters* [1968], that Burt Lancaster western, Lancaster's furs are taken and he's given a slave. Then he wants to get the furs back, so he goes after the Indians, but the Indians have been done in by Telly Savalas's scalphunters, and Telly Savalas has the furs. Lancaster goes after them to get his furs back. So between my thing and Larry's thing, we came up with *Hell's Belles*. I started it, and I did the outline, and then I started on the screenplay. I went to the office and Larry said, "You have been promoted. We're giving you a Sammy Fuller project." So I said, "Fine, what about *Hell's Belles*?" He said, "Someone else will do that, and you'll do this."

Old two-gun Sammy Fuller was given this project. I was supposed to write and he was going to direct it and possibly co-write. It was a black sheriff in the South, and they got me because I was the only southerner around there! Larry's from Louisiana. But anyway, we got beat to the punch with that by MGM with ... *tick* ... *tick* ... *tick* ... [1970], so AIP scrapped it. Fuller was paid off, and by the time that happened, the first draft had been finished on what was *Hell's Belles*. Maury Dexter said, "Now that you're free, I want you back!" So I came in and re-wrote and finished *Hell's Belles*.

Oh, I forgot to say, on *Devil's 8* I was brought back in. They sent me to see the screening of it. Then I had to go the next day and write scenes to plug up the continuity that old Burt Topper hadn't filled in. So I started *Devil's 8*, then I wound up dong the final thing on *Devil's 8*! Milius and Huyck had been long gone by then.

You also did a film for David L. Hewitt, The Tormentors [1971].

Oh, yeah. Another one where you count your fingers! I stupidly got involved because of my buddy Al Quick. Al was in that playing the religious nut, and so on that one I came in with some money people on it, too, and did the script. Then we wound up taking the picture away and finishing it because Hewitt was not tending to business. We finished the thing, put on USC sweatshirts, and we went out there shooting without a permit. "Student film! Student film!"

A student film with Nazi bikers.

Yeah! We shopped it around and I don't remember who wound up taking it.

Then at that point, *2-Headed Transplant* got made.

John Lawrence came to me and was saying," Let's do this or that." I said, "Look, you've already got a script, *The Incredible 2-Headed Transplant*. Do it!" He went back and read it and said, "Yeah, I think we'll do that!" My big chance at acting came, and I turned it down. They wanted me to do the other head, because I'm slender [*laughs*]. I said *nooooooo*. They shot the motorcycle sequence to raise money. That's why it goes on so long. That was done independently at first, and then AIP came in.

What did you think of it?

Oh, it was okay. Nothing great. When I was working on it back years before, I was seeing it as a tongue-in-cheek Frankenstein kind of thing, yet the critics seem to think it's a serious thing and it stinks! I was seeing Vincent Price as the lead, and Shirley Eaton, the *Goldfinger* girl, as the leading lady. And what did we get? Pat Priest, who was a little overweight at the time, and of all people, Bruce Dern! Him playing the scientist? I was disappointed.

Berry Kroeger (left) and Bruce Dern prepare for surgery in *The Incredible 2-Headed Transplant* (1971). James Gordon White also had a writer's credit on *The Thing with Two Heads* (1972), and later wrote a book called *The Beast* about a two-headed monster.

It didn't come off nearly as wacky as it should have been

No. And so again, that's the problem with screenwriting. You see one thing when you're working on it, and you get something different in the finished product. Arkoff had me in his office one time talking, and he said, "You know, your scripts are much better than the movies!"

The two-headed monster idea was so good they did it again a couple of years later in *The Thing with Two Heads*.

What happened there were the two guys, Wes Bishop and Lee Frost, went to AIP and they said they had a two-headed thing they wanted to do. Now it had no relation to the original one, and Lawrence and I had worked up a first draft on a follow-up to the first one. So AIP bought that script and shelved it, and then did Frost and Bishop's movie. Lawrence, as part of the payoff, was given the executive producer credit. He had nothing to do with the movie. I was given the first draft on it. So I did the first draft, and Frost and Bishop did the rest of the draft.

Frost and Bishop were pretty interesting characters from what I've heard.

Yeah, I kind of liked them. I didn't really get to know 'em too well, but they had nice personalities. Frost had started directing old X-rated movies, and so that's where he got his experience to then move on to bigger and better things. They had done something before then. I think it was a motorcycle movie. So then they got in to do that for AIP, and then they did something at 20th.

What did you think of their film?

I liked the other one better [*laughs*].

The only other screenwriting credit I had for you after *2-Headed Transplant* is the Ted Mikels film *10 Violent Women*.

There was another one after that, a U.S.–Yugoslav movie, *The Last Nazi*. It was first called *Ransom*, and then they came out with the Mel Gibson movie *Ransom*, which was a remake of the Glen Ford *Ransom* movie [1956]. This was an American-Yugoslav production — Noble Productions, Ika Panajotovic. I did a lot of rewrites for him, putting the American touch to things. I did that for quite a few companies on things. I don't know if they ever made 'em or not. *Julie Darling* [1983, directed by Maurice Smith and Luz Schaarwachter] I did un-credited.

When did you stop working at AIP?

Nineteen seventy-two was my last thing with AIP, *The Thing with Two Heads*. Then from there I was doing re-writes for various companies. Korean, Spanish, Italian, all over the place. So I was doing these re-writes, but they just slap on their friends' names over there! Then through Ted Mikels, I met Ika. They're both from Yugoslavian backgrounds.

How did you meet Ted Mikels?

Back when *Glory Stompers* was finished, a bunch of us were over at Ted's office for something. I forget what. Then a few years later this girl had had an interview with Ted, and I was trying to get something going on my own, and came close to it. I had Phil Feldman, [producer] of *The Wild Bunch* [1969], and he had to invest quickly. I tried Corman, because he said if I had something I thought he might be interested in, to let him know. Unfortunately, he was doing *Von Richtofen and Brown* [1971] at the time. I sent the script to him in Ireland, and he said, "I like it, but I'm doing this right now." Phil Feldman's money people needed to dump

(From left) Elaine Gefner, Eddie Hice, William Lucking, Jocelyn Lane, Astrid Warner and Kristin Van Buren in *Hell's Belles* (1970). The film borrowed plot elements from the westerns *Winchester '73*, *The Appaloosa*, and *The Scalphunters*.

it for investment purposes, a tax write-off or whatever, and he couldn't wait, so I lost the deal. I've tried that several different times, and missed by as good as a mile.

Anyway, this girl told me about Ted, and I said, "Oh yeah, I was in his office years ago." There was a party, so she had Marie and me come with her to meet Ted. Ted and I hit it off and have been buddies ever since.

Of the films that you wrote, which are your favorites?

The three from Maury Dexter.

Why?

He followed the script, number one, and he's a nice guy [*laughs*]. But he did follow them; he wouldn't let the actors start getting off on tangents or anything. He'd say, "It's written here, follow it." [*Laughs*] Those are the closest to my scripts. With *Hell's Belles*, I would have liked to have seen more energy from the guys. If you've ever been to the South, the people — particularly the ridge-runner–type characters— have an energy to them. Adam Roarke, he was so laid back, and I didn't write the character like that. I wrote him as a laughing and scratching type.

And the big guy was supposed to be a Slim Pickens type. Even in *Mini-Skirt Mob*, Jeremy Slate, when he comes up there the first time they have the fight that leads Diane McBain to say, "He knocked you on your ass and we've got to get back at him." When he comes up saying, "Sir, we are a grievance committee," that was supposed to be like an old southern evangelist, that type of thing, Elmer Gantry. But the energy wasn't there, either. I guess people just don't know the southern flavor of things.

Devil's 8 is just junk. It was shot in California, and they might as well have set it in California. There was no southern flavor at all. It was originally supposed to be with Jack Palance, and have older guys. But Palance got a big part in *Che!* [1969], which was 20th Century–Fox, so he pulled out. Then AIP said, "Well, we'll have to do it with younger folk." That's when I was put on something else and Huyck and Milius got it. I'm not that much older than them!

You wrote a novel that had a monster with two heads, correct?

The Beast. My wife and I wrote that. That was Leisure Books. I had done three westerns for Leisure, and the head of the story department there said, "I'm a big fan of *The Thing with Two Heads*." Well, that's one of my least favorite movies, but I bit my tongue. He said, "I'd like to do a horror book with you." I'm not much of a horror fan. I like the old Universal things, back in the 1940s, but I don't really like the horror they do today. The closest I came to that was the psychological things. I liked *The Innocents* [1961], the Deborah Kerr movie. That and *The Uninvited* [1944] and *The Haunting* [1963] are, I think, the three greatest horror movies.

So the publisher wanted another two-headed monster?

He wanted to work with me on a horror book, little knowing that horror is one of my least favorite subjects. My wife and I had a story that we were working on and we thought it might work for that. We made a few minor changes and pitched him on it.

It's funny, because in the blurb on the book they said nothing about there being a two-headed creature. I don't know why thy picked the title of *The Beast*, because there's about three or four books with that title.

When did you start writing novels?

Back in 1988 I sold my first one, but it wasn't published until 1993. It was *The Nomad Queen*.

Are you still writing books?

I've got one coming out in May. It's called *Hanging Party*, a western. I just sold another one; I sent the contract to London last week. Another western, *Barbary Coast Gun Down*, will be out either the end of this year or early next year. I've been doing mostly westerns.

The last movie was that *Last Nazi*, and that starred Cheri Caffaro and George Montgomery, the old cowboy actor. He died a few years ago. And Cassandra Gava. She was the witch in *Conan the Barbarian* [1982], and she was in *High Road to China* [1983]. That was the last thing, early 1990s.

I went out with a winner because even though it's not a great movie, *Last Nazi* won the China Golden Butterfly for best foreign picture of the year.

INDEX

Numbers in ***bold italics*** refer to pages with photographs.

Act of Piracy 30
Action U.S.A. 73
Adamson, Al 1–3, 5, *9*, 14, 17–22, 27, *18*, 30–31, 34, 47, 52–53, 57, 65, 70, 72, 116, 119, 122, 126, 128–129, 134, 141, 145, 156, 185, 186–190, 193–198, 200–201, *189*, 202, 206–207
Alderman, John 126
Alien Terror 102
Alienator 70
Allen, Bambi 53, 127
Anders, Luana 137, 174
Andrews, Tige 34
Angel 69
Angels Die Hard 159, 161, 163
Angels Hard as They Come 159, 164–165, *167*
Angels' Wild Women 5, *9*, *60*, 65, 123, 185, 198–199
Ann-Margret 81, 163–164
Apocalypse Now 77, 102
Arkoff, Samuel Z. 95, 214, 216
Armed Response 70
Arzner, Dorothy 77, 104
Ashton, Tara 56
Auerbach, Joseph 193
Ayres, Maray *117*

B.O.R.N. 70
Back Door to Hell 87, 89–90, 92–23, 99
Bad Charleston Charlie 59, 66
Badlands 159, 167–168, 170
Badlands of Dakota 50
Bail, Chuck 116, 123, 125, 130, 159, 161, 165, 168–169
Ballard, Carroll 171, 173, 180
Ballis, Socrates 27
Band, Charles 30, 42
Banner, Jill *75*, *103*, 106, 113, 176, 183
Banyon 23
Barger, Sonny 160, 167
Barrett, Tomi 116, *131*
Bat 21 170
Batman (TV) 79–80

Battle Beyond the Sun 174
Battle Flame 119
Beach Ball 74, 85, 171, 174, 177
Beams, Dovie *49*
Beast from Haunted Cave 87, 89–90, 93
Beast of Blood 191
Because They're Young 171
The Bees 102
Benson, Joey 18
Berman, Harvey 91
Berry, Don 10
Beyond the Valley of the Dolls 110
The Big Bird Cage 85, 102
The Big Doll House 82, 102, 110, *112*, 199
Bigfoot 14, 26, 148, 155, 209, *210*, 213–214
Billy Black 42
Bird of Prey 170
The Birds 32
Bishop, Jenifer 14, *15*, *18*, *20*, *25*, 34, *206*
Bishop, Larry 125
Bishop, Wes 209, 219
Biskind, Peter 2
Black Heat 5, 199
The Black Klansman 116, 124, 140
Black Samurai 5, 11
Blanchard, Mari 138
Blazing Stewardesses 10, 197, 200–201
Blood Bath 74, 77, 107
Blood Mania 129
Blood of Dracula's Castle 1, *2*, 5, 8, 10, 14, 18, *20*, 29, 32–33, 37, 51–52, 140–141, 185, 193–194
Blood of Ghastly Horror 1–3, 6, 10, 193, 197
Bloom, John 38, *150*, 153–154, 209
Bogdanovich, Peter 116, 118, 124, 134, 141
Bolling, Tiffany 43
Bonner, Bill *11*, 22, 24, 26, 123, *195*
Bonnie and Clyde 2
Boorman, John 74, 79
Borgnine, Ernest 45, *181*
Brady, Scott 8, 34–35, 47, 51, 56–57, 119, 126, 128, 187

Brain of Blood 5, 11
The Brain That Wouldn't Die 8
Brando, Marlon 77, 106, 118, 183
Breaking Point 45
Browing, Ewing "Lucky" 53
Brown, Timothy 11, 199
Bubba Ho-Tep 116, 130–131, 133
Burstyn, Ellen 79, **80**, 113
Bury Me an Angel 159, 165–166
Busey, Gary 45, 165
Byrnes, Edd 172, 174, 177, 179

C.C. and Company 81, **82**, 159, 163–164, 166
Caan, James 180, 183
Caffaro, Cheri 221
Caged Heat 159, 165
Cain's Cutthroats 51
Campbell, William 174
Campo, Wally 61
Campos, Rafael 25–26
Candy 183
Candy, John 45
Candy Stripe Nurses 45
Canutt, Yakima 32
Cardos, John "Bud" 5, 10, 22, 28, 30, **31**, **36**, **40**, **43**, 47, 50–51, 54, 55, 121, 123, **132**, 146
Cardoza, Anthony 1, 14, 24–26, 62, 148, 155, 209, 212–214
Carey, Timothy 148–149
Carlton, Rex 8, 34, 52, 193–196
Carnival Magic 6, 12
Carpenter, John 121
Carradine, John 8, 19, 20, 32, 51, 56, 141, 193, 209
Carrol, Regina 5–6, 14, 21, 27, 66, **199**
Cassavetes, John 27, 118, 159–160
Castle, William 177
Chaffin, Bill 157
Chamberlain, Richard 170
Chaney, Lon, Jr. 9, 22, 33, 34, **75**, 77, 78, 107, 113, 176, 187
Charro! 202
Che! 221
China 9, Liberty 37, 87, 98–100
The Choppers 150
Christian Licorice Store 95
City on Fire 102
Clark, Bob 30, 45
Clark, Dick 30, 39–40, 43–44, 161, 173, 216
Clark, Greydon 1, 5, 22, 30, 54, 126
Clarke, Gary 177, **179**
Cockfighter 87, **88**, 97–98
Code of Vengeance 69
Codename: Silencer 148
Coffy 102, 110
Cohen, Martin B. 33–34, 142, 193
Cole, Albert **11**, 38, 150, **153**, 209
Collins, Roberta **112**
Color of Night 162

Commando Squad 70
Compton, Richard 161, 163, 166, 170
Coppola, Eleanor 171, 174–175
Coppola, Francis 1, 77, 87, 91–92, 102, 104–105, 171, **172**, 173, 174–175, 178, 180–183
Corman, Gene 165
Corman, Roger 1, 45, 58, 84, 87, 89–95, 102, 104, 110, 124, 133, 138, 159, 165, 171, 173–175, 177, 184, 191, 196, 199, 219
Coscarelli, Don 116, 133
Crawford, Broderick 8, 33, 187
Creature from the Haunted Sea 89
Crechales, Tony 27–28
Cresse, Bob 128
Crosby, Cathy Lee 44
Crosby, Lindsay 25, 152, 209, 212
Cry Rape 196
Cult of the Dead 102
Cunha, Richard 47
Curb, Mike 153
Currie, Sondra 26
Cycle Savages 148, 159, 163

Daktari (TV) 59
Dance of Death 102
Dangerous Love 148
Dannaldson, James 32
D'Arcy, Alex **2**, 8, 14, 32, 194
The Dark 30, 44, 159
Darktown Strutters 165
Davis, Altovise 42
Davis, Jim 34–36, **36**, 41, 43, 46, 187
The Day the Lord Got Busted 136
The Day Time Ended 30, 35, 43–44
Dead Man's Curve 170
Dead of Night 30
Deadwood '76 30, 47, 50, 148, 150
Death Dimension 11, 13
Death Ship 102
Death Spa 159
DeCarlo, Yvonne 10
Dementia 13 171, 174–175
Demme, Jonathan 164–165
De Palma, Brian 116, 119, 196
DePriest, Ed 126
Dern, Bruce 38, 58, 64, 126, 140, **142**, 153, 163, 209, **218**
Desert Gems 148, 156–157
Devane, William 44
Devil Wolf of Shadow Mountain 35, 119, 121
Devil's Angels 159–160
The Devil's 8 59, 65–66, **67**, 209, 215–217
The Devil's Rejects 74
Devine, Andy 41, 56
Dexter, Maury 64, 76, 209, 215–217, 220–221
Diary of a High School Bride 136
Diary of a Mad Housewife 95
Diaz, Vic **78**, 92

Dierkop, Charles 165
Dietz, Bob 35–36, 50, 198
Dietz, Hedy 36
Dime with a Halo 14, 16
Dinah East 155
Dix, Richard 8, 47
Dix, Robert 8, 10, 19, 30, 37, 41, 47, **49**, **54**, **56**, 128, 139–140, **195**
Dixon, Denver 5, 185, 186, 188, **189**, 196
Doctor Dracula 12
Donlevy, Brian **111**, 113
Doomsday Voyage 156
DoQui, Robert 30, 42
Dorn, Ray 148, 155, 216
Dracula vs. Frankenstein **6**, 8, 37, 185, **186**, 187, 190, 192, 196
The Drag Racer 30, 42
Drake, Oliver 41, 57
Drury, James 48
Duffy, Dee **63**
Duvall, Robert 182
The Dynamite Brothers 11, 199

Eastman, Carole 94
Easy Rider 134, 143, **145**, 159–160, 166, 198, 209, 216
Echo of Terror 193, 196
Eegah! 150
Eisley, Anthony 9, 126
Ekins, Bud 169
Emperor of the North 79
The Epitaph 92
Estrada, Joe 92

Fargas, Antonio 113
The Female Bunch 9–10, **11**, 14, 21–22, 27, 34, 37–38, 123, 198, 202, 206–207, **206**
Find the Lady 45
Fineberg, Jay 126, 128
Finian's Rainbow 178
Firebrand 76
Fisk, Jack 168
Five Bloody Graves 5, 8, 35–36, **36**, 39, 52
Flight to Fury 87, 89, 92
Fly Me 191
Flynn, Juan 38
Fonda, Peter 143, **145**, 146, 159, 168
The Forbidden Dance 74, 85
Forbidden Planet 47, 48, **49**
The Forest 129–130
Forte, Fabian 136
Forty Guns 47–49, 50
Foxy Brown 102, 113
Francis, Coleman 148
Frankenstein's Bloody Terror 190
Frankenstein's Daughter 50
Freebie and the Bean 116
Freedom Riders 148, 156–157

Frost, Lee 145, 209, 219
Fuller, Samuel 47–49, 217
Futz! 138

Galaxy of Terror 84
Gannaway, Albert 41, 139
Gava, Cassandra 221
Gefner, Elaine **220**
Genuine Risk 74, 85
George, Christopher 59, 66, **67**
Gibbs, Alan 125, 162
Gidget Goes Hawaiian 171, 173
Girard, Bernard 24
Girls for Rent 10, 13, 185
The Girls from Thunder Strip 116, **117**, 122–123, 202, 204–205
Glenn, Scott 165
The Glory Stompers 148, 151–153, **154**, 158, 209–215, 217, 219
The Glove 59, 68–69
Glover, Bruce 164
The Godfather 171, 182–183
The Godmothers 14
Golan, Menahem 74, 85, 174
Goncharoff, Sergei 28
Good Morning ... and Goodbye! 202, 294
Graver, Gary 5, 37, 53, 65, 69, 127
Grease 134
Grefé, William 14, 26–28
Grier, Pam 74, 83, 102, 110, **112**, 113
Grier, Rosey 59
Growing Pains (TV) 85
The Gumball Rally 165

Hagen, Ross 59, **60**, **63**, **67**
Haggerty, Dan 166
Haig, Sid 74, **75**, **78**, **80**, **82**, 104, 107, **111**, 164, 171, 176, 210
Halfway to Hell 5, 7, 9, 188
Hall, Arch, Jr. 150–151
Hall, Arch, Sr. 30, 47, 148–150, 152, 155
Hall, Jon 62
Hall, Tex 166
Haller, Daniel 1, 160
Hammer 11, 196
The Hard Ride 216
The Hard Road 116, 127
Harrington, Curtis 137
Hartford, Ken 69
Hee Haw (TV) 14, 23–24
Hell Squad 134
The Hellcats 59, 62, 63, 209, 212–213
Hellman, Monte 1, 87, 116, 121–122, 124, 133, 134, 138
Hells Angels on Wheels 30, 32, 116, 125, 141, 159, 160, 162
Hell's Belles 209, 216–217, 220
Hell's Bloody Devils 6, 47, 52–53, 128, 195, **195**

Hell's Chosen Few 116, 126, 202, 205
Helmond, Katherine 118
Hemisphere Pictures 11, 185, 188–190, 196, 201
Herlihy, Leo 66
Herman, Norman T 152, 214
Hewitt, David L. 1, 109, 116, 122–123, 126, 202, 204–208
Hice, Eddie **220**
Hill, Jack 1, 74, 76–77, 86, 87, 91–92, 102, 171
The Hired Hand 95
Hitchcock, Alfred 30, 32
Holliman, Earl 48
Hollywood Man 168
Hollywood Stages 122, 141, 148, 155, 156, 196, 204, 216
Hooper, Tobe 44
Hope, Harry 11
Hopper, Dennis 134, 137–138, 143, **145**, 148, 152, 154, 160, 168–169, 209, 212
Horror of the Blood Monsters 1, 14, 17, 47, 141, 185, 193
Horvath, Louis 127
The Host 75, 76, 77, 102, 104
Hot Rod Action 148
House of 1,000 Corpses 74
House of Terror 28
The House on Haunted Hill 110
Hovis, Larry 178
Howell, Hoke 59, 72
Huyck, Willard 215, 217

I Pass for Human 103
If a Man Answers 30
Iguana 87, 99
Impulse 14, 27
The Incredible 2-Headed Transplant 3, 30, 38, 129, 148, **150**, 153–154, 158, 209, 211–212, 218–219, **218**
Inglehart, James **167**
The Irv Carlson Show 148, 155
Is This Trip Really Necessary? 148
It Seemed Like a Good Idea at The Time 45
It's a Bikini World 74

Jackie Brown 74
Jackson, Larry 40–41, 47, 56–57, 139–140
Jacobs, Newton P. "Red" 62
Jaeckel, Richard 26, 28, 44
Jakob, Dennis 171, 180
Jane 69
Jason of Star Command (TV) 83
Jennie: Wife/Child 148, 151, 156
Jessi's Girls 5, 13, 26, 197–198
Jones, Donald M. 116, 123, 124, 127, 129–130
Jordan, Judy 25
Jud 41
Julie Darling 219
Julien, Max 125
Just the Ten of Us (TV) 85

Kama Sutra '71 144
Kantor, Igo 41, 44
Karloff, Boris 92, 105, 141
Kasem, Casey 55, 122, 152, 163, 212
Kastner, Elliot 98–99
Kelly, Jack 48
Kelly, Jim 11
Kemp, Bruce 126
Kennedy, George 164
Kennis, Dan 5, 8, 186, 190, 200–201
Kent, Gary 1, 30, 35, 116, **117**, **120**, **132**, 159
Killers Three 34, 39–40, 216
Kilpatrick, Lincoln **31**, 42
Kincaid, Aron 180
King, Joyce 3, 134
Kingdom of the Spiders 28, 30, 42–43
Kirk, Tommy 10
Kitt, Eartha 134–135, 137, 143
Knight, Shirley 180–182
Konow, David 3, 5
Kotto, Yaphet 163
Kovacs, Laszlo 5, 33, 36–37, 61, 127, 140, 149, 151
Kroeger, Berry **218**
Kurtz, Gary 93
Kwan, Nancy 59, 66

Ladd, Diane 142
Landis, James 156
Lane, Jocelyn 220
Lansing, Joi 214
Lanza, Anthony 148, 209, 211–212
Larson, Glen 86
Las Vegas Hillbillies 139
Las Vegas Strangler 41, 47, 57
Lash of Lust 5, 123
The Last Movie 95, 134, 143
Last Nazi 219, 221
Last of the Comancheros 8
The Last Ride 168–169
The Last Shot 159, 170
Lawrence, John 38, 151–153, 209, 211–213, 218–219
Lazenby, George 11
Lease, Maria 127
Lee, Alesha 25–26
Legends of the West 45
Lewis, Paul 93, 127, 143–144, 166
Lidberg, Eric 59, 62
The Limit 163
Lippert, Robert 50, 89, 92
Lipton, Peggy 106
Littlejohn, Gary 159
Live and Let Die 47, 52, 57
Livingston, Bob 10, 200
Lost 6, 12
The Lost Battalion 201
Lucas, George 74, 81, **172**, 180
Lucking, William **220**

INDEX

Lugosi, Bela 42
Lynn, Kane 185, 188, 190, 200–201

The Mad Room 14, 24, **25**
Magee, Patrick 174–175
The Magic Spectacles 152
Mahoney, Jock 152, 201
Majors, Lee 84
Mako: The Jaws of Death 14, 26, 28
Malick, Terrence 97, 167
The Maltese Bippy 14, 23
A Man Called Dagger 116, 124
The Man of Kingwood 148, 156
Manson, Charles 30, 38, 65, 123, 144
Mark of the Gun 61
Martin, Dick 23
Mary Hartman, Mary Hartman (TV) 79, 83
Maslansky Paul 146
McBain, Diane 62
McCambridge, Mercedes 35, **120**
McCrea, Jody 152, **154**
McFarland, Mike 127, 130
McKinney, Bill **40**
McNamara's Band (TV) 84
McQueen, Steve 59, 168–169
Mean Mother 200
Merritt, Jerry 63
Meyer, Russ 1, 110, 202, 204–205
Midnight 185
The Mighty Gorga 2, 162, 202, **203**, 207–208
Mikels, Ted V. 116, 124, 134, 209, 219
Milius, John 65, 215–217
Miller, Bev 190–191
Mills, Jerry **195**
The Mini-Skirt Mob 59, 62, 64, 209, 214–215, 221
Minor, Bob 11, 112
Miranda, Vince 126–128
Mitchel, Mary 171, 174, 178, 184
Mitchell, Cameron 34, 122, 138, 142
Mitchell, Edgar 130
Mitchum, Christopher 43, 214
The Molly Maguires 197
Mondo Keyhole 105
Montoro, Ed 30, 44
Moore, Roger 47, 52
Moreland, Mantan 108, 176
Morris, Barboura 89
Moss, Thelma 130
Murder on the Yellow Brick Road 59, 71–72
Mutant 30, 44

Nagy, Ivan 66
Naish, J. Carrol 10, **186**
Namath, Joe 81, **82**, 164
Nash, Gene 155
Nashville 134, 146
The Nasty Rabbit 148

The Naughty Stewardesses 5, 10, 185, 191, 198, 200–201
Nelson, Connie 127
Nicholson, Jack 11, 30, 36, 58, 87, 91–94, 122, 138, 162, 168–169
Nicholson, James H. 214–215
Nielsen, Leslie 48, **49**
Night Creature 59
Night Tide 137–138, 143
Nightmare in Wax 30, 33–35, 193–194, 196
No Place to Land 138–139
Noel, Chris 152, 177, 179
Nurse Sherri 194, 200
Nussbaum, Raphael 21, 37, 198

Oates, Warren 87, **88**, 91, 98, 168–169
Ohmart, Carol 78–79, 107, 110, 176
One Million AC/DC 116, 126
One Shocking Moment 116, 124, 126
O'Neill, Robert V. 67, 69, 129
Osborne, Ken (Kent) 55
Out of Sight 171, 178, 180, **181**
Outlaw of Gor 30
Outlaw Riders 14, 24

Palance, Jack 45, 221
Patterson, Roger 63
Patton, Bart 74, 171, **172**, **176**, **179**, **181**
Peabody, Dixie 165
Peckinpah, Sam 1, 30, 41
Perkins, Millie **93**
Peters, Barbara 165
Pit Stop 79, **80**, 102, 110, **111**
Pizor, Irwin 185, 188–190, 200
The Playgirls and the Bellboy 105
Pock, Bernie 70
Point Blank 79
Polan, Claire 59
Pollard, Michael J. 45
Pollock, Gene 119
Poston, Tom 176
Powers, Bruce 14, 18
Presley, Elvis 25, 64, 162–163, 202
Price, Vincent 218
Priest, Pat 218
Psycho Lover 129
Psych-Out 30, 34, 39, 116, 126, 140
Pulp Fiction 114
Pushing Up Daisies 59, 66
The Pyramid 116, 130, **131**

Race with the Devil 134, 145–146
Raiders of Leyte Gulf 188, 201
Raiders of the Living Dead 185
The Rain People 171, **172**, 178, 180–182
Rainy Day Friends 130
Raney, Sue **56**
The Ravagers 201

The Raven 91, 196
The Raw Ones 105
Ray, Aldo 11
Ray, Fred Olen 59, 69–70, 74, 84
Raymond, Paula *2*, 8, 32
The Rebel Rousers 33, 47, 58, **135**, 142–143, ***142***, 145
Rebellious 70
The Red, White and Black 30, ***31***, 38, 41–42, 47, 55
Redeker, Quinn 107, 176
Renay, Liz 50–51
Reservoir Dogs 87
Reynolds, Burt 173
Ride in the Whirlwind 87, 93–94, 116, 121–122, 133, 138
The Ritz Brothers 10, 200
Riverboat (TV) 173
The Road Hustlers 40–41, **40**, 55, 57, **56**, 139
Roarke, Adam 168, 220
Robbie, Seymour 164
Roman, Ruth 28
Romero, Cesar 30, 42
Romero, Eddie 83, 200
Rooney, Mickey 14
Rossitto, Angelo 187
Rothman, Stephanie 74, 77
Route 66 (TV) 59
Rowan, Dan 23
Run Home Slow 30, 35, 116, 119–120, **120**
Rush, Richard 1, 116, 118, 124–126, 130, 134, 140–141, 161–162
Russell, Kurt 24
Rustam, Mardi 21

The Sadist 2, 148–149
The St. Valentine's Day Massacre 95
Sakata, Harold 11
Saletri, Frank 42
Sandor, Greg 94
Sanford, Isabel 42
Satan's Sadists 3, 5, **7**, 8, 12, 13, 27, 35, 37, ***43***, 47, 53–54, ***54***, 116, 119, 124, 128, 185, 187, 190, 197–198, ***199***, 201
The Savage Seven 34, 39, 116, 123, 125, 140–141, 159, 161
Savage Sisters **78**
Saxon, John 59
The Scarlet Letter 188
Scavengers 200
Schanzer, Karl 106, 114, 175
Schary, Dore 48
Schoolgirls in Chains 129
Scott, Linda **120**
Scream Free! 148, 212
Secret Places, Secret Things 127
Sergeant Preston of the Yukon (TV) 30, 32
Shadows 118
Shane, Gene O. 19, **20**

Shatner, William 27–28, 42, 43
Shatter 97
Sheen, Martin 167–168
Sherman, Sam 1, 5, **6**, 7, 10, 19, 52, 66, 128, 185, ***186***, ***189***, ***199***
Shields, Brooke 45
The Shooting 87, 93–94, ***93***, 97, 116, 121–122, 133, 138
The Sidehackers 59, 62, 64
Silent Night, Deadly Night 3: Better Watch Out! 87, 100
Sinthia, the Devil's Doll 116
Skeleton Coast 30
Ski Party 180
Ski Troop Attack 87
The Skydivers 148
Slade, Mark 42
Slate, Jeremy 30, 42, 59, 64, 221
Slatzer, Robert 59, 62, 64, 155–156, 209, 213–214
Smith, Glen R. ***142***
Smith, Roger 164
Smith, William **82**, 161, 163–164, 166
Solomon, Joe 1, 42, 125
Sorceress 102
Sorel, Peter 61
Spahn, George 38
Spahn Ranch 3, 10, 22, 38, 65, 123, 144
Speedway 64, 162
Spelvin, Georgina 5, 10
Spider Baby 74, **75**, 77–79, ***103***, 106–110, 171, 174–176
Square Root of Zero 190
Squezze Play 148, 156–157
Stanley 28
Stanton, Harry Dean 64, 96, 138
Stanwyck, Barbara 48–49, 61
Starrett, Jack 123, 126, 168
Steckler, Ray Dennis 3, 116, 119, 122, 149–149, 155
Stein, Ronald 107
Stevens, Stella 24
Stevens, Warren **49**
Strasberg, Lee 14, 16
Streisand, Barbra 167, 182
Strode, Woody 42
Suburban Confidential 116
Sugar Boxx 103
Sullivan, Barry 50
Sullivan, Tim 35, 119–120
Supercock 59, 62, 68
Sweet Sweetback's Baadasssss Song 111
The Swinging Cheerleaders 114
Swinging Stewardesses 200
Switchblade Sisters 102–103

Taking Off 95
Tales of a Salesman 151
Tamblyn, Amber 70
Tamblyn, Russ **7**, 8, 14, 21–22, 34, 37, 53–54, 70

Tanen, Ned 95, 178
Tank Commandos 134, 136
Tarantino, Quentin 74, 86, 87, 102–103, 109, 123
Targets 124, 141
Taurog, Norman 64
Taylor, James 87, 96
Taylor, Kent **9**, 12, 37, 54, 128, 187
10 Violent Women 209, 219
Tenser, Marilyn Jacobs 63
Tenser, Mark 63
The Terror 87, 91–92, 100, 105
Terror Is a Man 200
The Texas Chain Saw Massacre 43
The Thing with Two Heads 209, 219
Thompson, Ben 52
Three in the Attic 39
Thriller (TV) 173
The Thrill Killers 116, 119
THX 1138 81
Tilly, Jennifer 170
Timothy, Megan 202, ***206***, ***208***
Tonight for Sure 105
Topper, Burt 64, 134, 136, 138–139, 209, 215–217
The Tormentors 217
Torn, Rip 182
The Torture Zone 102
Towne, Robert 90
Trapped Ashes 87, 100
Trikonis, Gus 59, 64, 68
Tucker, Forrest 19
Two-Lane Blacktop 87, 94–96, ***96***
2000 Years Later 160

Uncle Tom's Cabin 12
Unshackled 171, 184
The Untouchables (TV) 76

Van Buren, Kristin ***220***
Venet, Nick 178
Vengeance Is Mine 45
Victor One 148
Viola, Joe 165
The Virginian (TV) 24
Volante, Vicki 11, 19, 53
Von Richtofen and Brown 219
Vorkov, Zandor **6**, 12
Voyage to the Planet of Prehistoric Women 124
Voyage to the Prehistoric Planet 174

Walker, Robert, Jr. 140

Walley, Deborah 42, 173
Walls of Hell 201
Walston, Ray 84
Warlords 84
Warner, Astrid 210, ***220***
Warren, James 185, 186
Washburn, Beverly **75**, ***103***
Wasserman, Lew 95, 177–178
Weinrib, Lennie 85, 171, 174, 177, ***179***, 180, ***181***
Weld, Tuesday 173
The Werewolf of Woodstock 34
Werewolves on Wheels 144
West, Sonny 25, 64
A Whale of a Tale 43
What's Up Front! 148, 151
White, James Gordon 209
The Wild Angels 95
The Wild Bunch 30, 41, 168
Wild Guitar 148
The Wild Ride 87, 91
Wild Wheels **49**, 55
Wild, Wild Winter 171, ***179***, 180
The Wilderness Family, Part II 183
Wiles, Buster 32
Wilkerson, Joy 26
Williamson, Fred 11
Wilson, Dennis 87, 96
Winchester '73 209, 217
Winters, Shelley 24
The Woman Hunt 191
Women for Sale 191
Wonder Women 59, 66
Wood, Ed 126
Woolman, Harry 51, 123–124
The World's Greatest Sinner 148–149
Wynn, Keenan 44

Yarnell, Bruce 56
Young, Ray **20**
The Young Animals 209, 215
Young Guns 159, 168
Young Jesse James 50
The Young Racers 174
You're a Big Boy Now 182

Zappa, Frank 121
Zombie, Rob 74
Zotz! 176
Zsigmond, Vilmos 9, 33, 36, 50, 52, 61, 127, 149, 151, 156

www.ingramcontent.com/pod-product-compliance
Ingram Content Group UK Ltd.
Pitfield, Milton Keynes, MK11 3LW, UK
UKHW050532150426
5217IPUK00026B/1896